THE ALTERNATIVE HOLIDAY GUIDE TO

Exploring Nature in the Wilds of Europe

by

Julian Cremona and Robert Chote

Ashford Press Publishing
Southampton
1988

Published by   Ashford Press Publishing 1988
              1 Church Road
              Shedfield
              Hampshire SO3 2HW

British Library Cataloguing in Publication Data

Cremona, J.
   The alternative holiday guide to exploring
   nature in the wilds of Europe.
   1. Nature study—Europe—Handbooks,
   manuals, etc.
   I. Title   II. Chote, R.
   508.4   QH53

   ISBN 1-85253-059-6

Designed and typeset by Jordan and Jordan, Fareham, Hampshire

Printed by Robert Hartnoll (1985) Ltd., Bodmin, Cornwall

Acknowledgements

This book is based on the experiences of twenty-two St. Mary's College expeditions, over the last twelve years. Hence, all those hundreds of people who took part in, or helped with these ventures must share part of the credit.

Each expeditionary team has included one person whose responsibility it has been to write a day-by-day account of the journey. These reports have provided invaluable background material. In particular, we must thank Dave Webb, Paul Baldwin and Paul Etherington, for their work on Iceland and Spain. Peter Kemp has made useful comments on both the reports and the early drafts of this book.

We would like to thank Dr. John Elliot for helping with all the expedition health problems, and for producing the breakdown of medical matters in the Introduction. Similarly, Merry Oak Spares and Brooklyn Engineering, both in the Southampton area, have given their expertise in preparing our vehicles. They have also helped produce the check-list of vehicle spares.

Several biologists have helped with the discovery and identification of species. Paul Stanley and Paul Etherington demonstrated their botanical skills in Norway and Spain. John Buckley has contributed his knowledge of both plants and animals, in Iceland, Ireland and the Uists.

Since the first expedition set off in 1975, Brenda Cremona has provided crucial support as Deputy Leader. She has also produced the maps for this volume.

Contents

The Hebrides

Ireland

Norway

Iceland

Iceland, continued

Spain

List of Maps

List of Photographs

Introduction

This book is written for everyone who appreciates the natural world. In an era of package deals and "all-inclusion", more and more people are choosing to travel independently. They feel limited by the constraints of tourist resorts, or hassled by the rush of an organised tour. Such feelings are understandable. Nowadays, the wonders of "wilderness Europe" are within the reach of the backpacker, the adventurous family, the youth group – any nature lovers with a couple of weeks to spare.

Despite this growing interest, many of these areas are still unspoilt by the interference of man. But for how long, is anyone's guess. This freedom from development is also a major problem for many people who would like to explore them. Where do we go? Is a given route passable? Will there be anywhere to stay? What can we see?

It is for people asking these questions that we have written *Exploring Nature in the Wilds of Europe*. The main part of the book is a series of routes – covering western Ireland, the Hebrides, Norway, Iceland, Spain and areas of France. These do not pretend to be exhaustive guides. Instead, we offer a single journey through each country, which we have found to encompass much of the variety and flavour which that country offers. We have travelled along every kilometre of the routes which we describe. As a result, the details can be specific. However, where a number of interesting alternatives exist, we describe them in full. Thus, you cannot expect to easily visit all the places which we describe in the course of a single tour. We have also tried to avoid a collection of bare facts, and instead attempted to give a lively impression of the places through which our routes pass.

The book is unashamedly biased towards the natural sights of Europe. We originally chose to visit most of the places because of their special botanical, zoological or geographical interest. Once again, we have attempted to provide more than bland lists of species. Hopefully, the description and/or the photograph will permit identification in the field. We also try to explain why a particular plant or animal is of special interest to the naturalist. In addition, we hope to discuss the relationship between some species, and the habitats in which they are found. Without being too technical, we hope that this information will be of use to groups undertaking a more rigorous biological study of the areas concerned.

Brief descriptions of towns and places of architectural or archaeological interest have been included. These are aimed principally at outlining one or two major sights which will be of interest to someone passing through, or staying for a couple of hours.

The descriptive chapters will be useful at two stages of planning. Firstly, by reading them all, you can decide which country suits you best, both in terms of what it offers, and what resources you have available. Secondly, having selected your country, the detailed route will provide an excellent basis around which to plan your itinerary. You will have to accept some inaccuracy as the book dates with time – attempting to revisit a town in northern Spain one year, we arrived to discover that it had been razed to the ground, and rebuilt elsewhere. The valley in which it had originally been situated had been flooded to produce a massive lake!

To complement the country-by-country chapters, we have included a section on Planning and Preparation, which draws on our own experiences. It includes the practical information required to set about travelling to the locations we describe. For example, we discuss which vehicles are most suited to the journeys, and whether a vehicle is even necessary. Types of accommodation and equipment are considered, as well as medical matters and money. A check-list of points to remember is provided at the end. We try to cover the problems facing everyone from the lone backpacker to the leader of a twenty-person youth group.

Similarly, each of the main chapters begins with an introductory section. As well as providing an overall view of the geography and plant and animal life of each country, practical details are also included. Road conditions are discussed, together with the availability of diesel and petrol. Do the laws of the country permit camping on open land? Can you pay for fuel with a Barclaycard? Which are the best maps, and where can they be obtained? We describe the climate you will face, the best foods to buy locally and the medical problems that can crop up.

Ultimately, our hope in writing this book is to inspire you to discover the beauty and fascination of the wildernesses of Europe and the British Isles for yourself. After climbing across a glacier in Norway, circling a volcano rim in Iceland, discovering a field of orchids in the Pyrenees, or unearthing a scorpion in a Spanish desert, you may never be satisfied by lazing on a beach again!

Typical road conditions, interior of Iceland.

Planning and Preparation

Naturally, you will have to begin the planning and preparation for an independently organised journey, much earlier than you would for a package deal. School or youth group leaders will need a rough itinerary and costing as much as twelve months in advance, in order to give time for individuals to pay. Similarly, you will need a rough plan if you are approaching companies and other organisations for financial support. This should be done well in advance.

Even if you intend to follow the recommended route precisely, you should be sure to get hold of the necessary maps well before departure, in order to plan an accurate route. In some cases (especially Iceland) these will have to be ordered, and can take some time to be delivered.

Camping and Accommodation

To best appreciate the more isolated areas in Europe, there is really no substitute for taking your own tents and rough camping. The major disadvantage is the frustration of having to set aside time at the end of the day to find somewhere to spend the night. Official camp-sites also usually offer toilets and washing facilities. However, you have to put up with fellow campers, and pay for the privilege. Note that it is usually cheaper to stay in an official site if you have a few large tents rather than several small ones.

Although it is nice to stay in an area with toilet facilities, the standard varies enormously. Taking a chemical (Elsan) lavatory not only gives you greater independence, it can also be more pleasant and hygienic for the user. The same applies to showers. The independent traveller can have a very satisfactory portable shower unit, in the form of a Killaspray plant spray!

If you stay near large towns, then there may be a shortage of rough sites – an official camp-site may be unavoidable. If you are a member of the IYHF (International Youth Hostel Federation), then you can stay in youth hostels (non-members can use the Icelandic hostels). Unfortunately, these can be scarce in remote areas.

For larger groups, it may be possible to obtain accommodation in schools, if you travel out of term time. Enquiries must be made well before departure.

Your choice of tent should be influenced by the climate in your destination. In hot areas, it can be unbearable inside some tents. Manufacturers such as Trigano give their fly-sheets a silvered finish, to help reflect the heat. You can improvise by fixing a thin foil emergency blanket over your fly-sheet. For rough camping, a separate fly-sheet is essential together with a LARGE quantity of spare tent pegs. The grooved plastic pegs are especially strong. A good supply should be bought in the UK, as they are expensive on the continent.

When camping on rocky ground, it is sensible to place a spare ground sheet underneath the main one, to prevent tears. An old pair of curtains or a blanket would serve just as well. If you stay on sandy ground, then tent pegs should be reinforced with rocks or heavy objects.

There are a number of ways to provide lighting for tents. The best is to use a fluorescent light powered by a vehicle battery. These can last for hours, without running the battery down. Coleman also produce lights that are powered with petrol.

The choice of sleeping bag is even more determined by climate, than the choice of tent. For northern countries, a "Four Seasons" sleeping bag is vital, even during high summer. However, bear in mind that high altitudes tend to be just as cold, wherever you are. Thus, you need a decent bag if you plan to spend much time in the high Sierra Nevada of southern Spain, for example.

We recommend a Holofil sleeping bag in preference to the down-filled version. Although Holofil tends to flatten with time, it is far easier to dry than down, which becomes lumpy. You may also never have realised that you had an allergy until you spend a couple of weeks in a down-filled sleeping bag!

It is always wise to take inner linings for sleeping bags. These can be washed regularly, and also used on their own on hot nights. Rather than buying one, you can easily make it yourself from a doubled-over cotton sheet.

As well as the sleeping bag, you will need something to go underneath – for insulation and protection against lumps. A camp bed is more comfortable, but is also bulkier than a foam Karrimat. Air-beds are pleasant to sleep on. However, they are a pain to inflate, and you may also need a mat to go underneath, to prevent punctures.

Some camp-sites, especially in Spain, have "bungalow" facilities for hire. These are simply blocks of rooms, with spartan bunks.

Vehicles

There are both advantages and disadvantages to taking a vehicle on an exploration of Europe. The most obvious plus factor is the degree of independence which it offers. Public transport often misses out on the most interesting areas, and travel is limited to given times. On the other hand, a vehicle is sometimes costly to transport to the country concerned. It can also be expensive to maintain. If possible you should obtain a set of spares on a "sale or return" basis. (There is a list of suggested items at the end of this chapter.)

In several parts of the journeys which we describe, a four-wheel drive vehicle is a considerable advantage. In some cases it is a necessity, although alternative routes can usually be taken for these stretches.

When it comes to choosing a four-wheel drive vehicle, the international reputation of LandRover is well deserved. LandRover has a wide range of dealers, and mechanical problems can usually be fixed without a great deal of difficulty. In Spain, LandRovers are built under licence by LandRover Santana, and hence they are well supported across the country. For travelling over especially rugged ground, a short-wheel-based vehicle presents less danger of grounding.

An important question to be considered when choosing a vehicle is whether to opt for diesel or petrol. Diesel vehicles are more common in Iceland and Spain, but diesel fuel is often less widely available than petrol. Diesel is also better value for money, as it costs less and is more slowly consumed. However, if you cook with petrol, then it may well be easier to deal with only one fuel.

Having said all this, a LandRover is not essential. In all but the most rugged of landscapes, you should not be surprised to see a Citroen 2-CV or Renault 5 appear on the horizon.

Clothing

In hot climates, you will find that loose cotton clothing is best for keeping you cool. A sun-hat is essential to avoid the unpleasant effects of sunstroke. In cold climates, it is preferable to wear a large number of thin layers, rather than a couple of thick ones. Wool is particularly warm. Good waterproofs are also vital. Hypothermia is a real danger if you are exposed to a cold wind in wet clothes.

Food and Cooking

The dilemma of whether to take food from the UK, or to buy it in situ, is academic for the backpacker. However, it is an important problem for larger groups. In the more isolated areas, it may be difficult to find a source of food. If you do find one, then they will often be unwilling to disappoint regular customers by having their stocks bought out by tourists. Even if you intend to buy all your food on-site, you should still take a small reserve supply.

Your decision may be influenced by the price of food in your chosen country. In Spain, purchases are relatively cheap, while prices in Iceland, and especially Norway, vary from high to astronomic. Health considerations are also important – taking your own food reduces the risk of "Spanish tummy" and its international variants.

The major difficulty with bringing food from the UK is the sheer bulk. The best way to keep this to a minimum is to use dehydrated products. McDougalls produce an excellent range which will cater for most of your needs. Their Refresh Fruit Juices are very good, as is the selection of main courses – Chicken Supreme, Curries, Stews etc. For a large group, these should be bought from a Cash and Carry if possible. For the sake of convenience, it is a good idea to divide food up into daily units. Remember to clearly label and firmly seal all the daily portions. Make sure that you keep a safe copy of the cooking instructions.

Camping Gaz is the most popular cooking fuel for independent travellers. However, the price of Gaz varies enormously from country to country. In France, it is particularly expensive. The tanks are also very bulky, and the flame is almost useless in cold and windy conditions.

Cooking with petrol works out very much cheaper in the long run, as well as generating considerably more heat in a given time. Two companies produce excellent petrol stoves. Optimus burners are ideal for the lone backpacker and the small group. Coleman burners can cope with up to three pans at a time. The petrol is forced from a hand-pumped pressurised chamber. It emerges as a vapour, and thus the cooking technique is the same as with gas, only quicker. These burners are designed for lead-free petrol. If leaded petrol is used, then you will have to periodically clean the burner. In addition, you should take spare generators and pumps.

Other spirit stoves can be used, but these are generally less convenient than the petrol-fuelled variety.

You should not automatically assume that camp fires are permitted. They are generally banned in Spain and Iceland, while they are restricted to certain areas elsewhere.

Health

As we noted above, many health problems experienced abroad can stem from food. Fruit is often grown with the help of pesticides, and thus you should always wash it before eating. This is best done with a solution of potassium permanganate crystals, or sodium isocyanurate. The latter is the principal ingredient of Puritabs. However, it is far cheaper to buy the raw material direct from the chemist. Remember – be careful with the concentration.

A large group will generate considerable quantities of washing-up. It can be very difficult to try to keep a large eating/cooking area hygenic when rough camping. Take a large bucket, fill it with sodium isocyanurate solution and use this to store crockery and cutlery from meal-time to meal-time. This works on the same principle as sterilising with Milton fluid, but it is cheaper. In addition, a tub of disinfectant Savlon solution is ideal for people to wash their hands in. This must be changed on a daily basis.

However thorough your precautions, stomach upsets are always possible. Before leaving the UK, ask your doctor for suitable prescriptions. Imodium is a powerful anti-diarrhoea tablet, while Lomotil is especially good for combinations of diarrhoea and vomiting. The inoculations required vary from country to country. However, you should always be sure to have a tetanus injection/booster a few days before departure.

Interfering insects are a common problem when camping. As well as trying to camp some distance from marshland and bogs, it is sensible to take other precautions. Midge Spray (available from camping shops) is a good aerosol repellant, while Jungle Formula comes in a lotion for the skin. People especially sensitive to insect bites would be well advised to take a course of anti-histamine tablets throughout their journey. You should also have a supply of antiseptic cream, in case a bite becomes infected.

The problems of exposure to the sun may be obvious in the semi-deserts of Almeria, but problems also occur further north. At high altitudes in Norway and Iceland, the effects of powerful ultra-violet light can be very painful, especially in windswept conditions. A sun-barrier cream is almost essential – UVistat is very good. An anti-chapping preparation for the lips is also useful – Melrose is excellent.

In the event of more serious medical problems, you may need treatment. Insurance packages can cover the cost of returning you to the UK, if this is necessary. However, there is a system by which the citizens of EEC countries can receive health care abroad – free or at very low cost. You will need to obtain an E111 form. These can be applied for at DHSS offices, but do so well in advance. A pre-departure dental check is a good idea if you will be spending some time away from civilisation.

If you are taking a large group abroad, it is well worth cultivating the help of your local GP. He/she will usually be eager to assist with advice and prescriptions.

If you are in any doubt over what to do while you are abroad, then it is always best to seek local help. In Spain, the pharmacists are particularly knowledgeable.

Money

The traveller has a number of ways of taking money abroad. The most obvious point to make is that you should not set off with a huge wad of £20 notes! Most currency should be taken in Travellers' Cheques. Those issued by American Express, Thomas Cook and major banks are widely accepted. We find it most convenient to take Travellers' Cheques denominated in sterling – especially if you will be travelling through more than one country. The advantage of using foreign denominations is that you know what you can afford to buy when you get there, whatever the exchange rate at the time. However, you will lose out when converting any surplus back into sterling on your return.

You should, however, take a small sum in the currency of each country to be visited, as you may arrive during a holiday period when banks are closed.

Eurocheques are useful. You pay your bank about £3 for a Eurocheque guarantee card, and then receive the cheques for free. These cheques are written in the currency of the country in question. Cashing a cheque costs about 28p, as well as a 1.6% handling charge.

Visa and Access cards are cheaper to use than Eurocheques, and also cheaper than American Express and Diners' Club. They can also be used to obtain cash from a wide range of banks.

You should also keep a list of the numbers of all passports carried by a group. This will be very helpful to the consulate in the event of theft.

Insurance

Insurance will be needed to cover health (see above), personal belongings and vehicles. These are covered at reasonable cost by the 5-star package, which is available from the AA. This covers vehicle recovery throughout Europe. Group leaders may also want insurance against being sued by members of their parties. Royal Insurance offer a suitable policy.

Photography

Film is generally cheaper when bought in Britain. It should be kept cool, although there is no need to become paranoid over this point. While camping, dust and sand is a persistent problem. A good supply of resealable polythene bags is more effective than most camera cases. Equipment can be cleaned with lens tissues. These are preferable to a cloth, which simply passes grit from place to place.

An ultra-violet filter helps reduce the intensity of blue at high altitudes. It will also prevent the lens from scratching.

Sources of Information

The AA will be able to give you up-to-date information on fuel prices.

Maps are best purchased before you leave home. Those for the Hebrides and Ireland can be purchased through the Ordnance Survey, Maybush, Southampton or through a local book shop. The most comprehensive stock of worldwide maps is held by E. Stanford's Map Centre at 12 Long Acre, London WC2 (Tel. 01 836 1321). Orders can be made over the telephone and Stamfords will send details of maps covering every country in Europe.

For further details of the country you intend to visit, start by getting information from your travel agent. General literature can be obtained by writing to the country's tourist office – the addresses are given at the end of each chapter. The Royal Geographical Society is helpful in providing very detailed information about remote locations. You do not have to be a member, but this can be useful if you become very involved in world travel. Their library is most comprehensive. They also run an Expedition Advisory Centre. The EAC produces a compilation of brief details of the different expeditions that travel each year – the Expedition Yearbook. They also have a large collection of full expedition reports which you can read. The Young Explorers' Trust (based at the RGS) produces regular reports on travel to places in Europe.

LandRover produce a number of useful publications on driving techniques, vehicle preparation etc. Most of these are free from their publicity department in Solihull. Overlander Ltd. specialise in four-wheel drive vehicle publications. They also run excellent day courses in off-road driving techniques. Further details from David Bowyer, East Foldhay, Zeal Monachorum, Crediton, Devon, EX17 6DH.

Important sources of information for the relevant countries are given at the end of each chapter.

Equipment Checklists

1. Vehicle Spares – with particular reference to petrol-driven LandRovers. Your local vehicle distributor, Unipart dealer or motor accessory shop will be able to modify this list to suit your particular vehicle.

This is the list of items we would carry for a five-week trip. You will find that many guidebooks include a list four times its length. Other things may go wrong but we have found these spares to be suitable for our needs. They will also pack into one large box. You have to strike a balance. The shorter your trip, and the greater the availability of spares in your destination, the fewer items you need to take. Hence, you would need nothing like the list below for a fortnight in the Hebrides. Always prepare your vehicle well in advance of departure. Normally this will just involve a service, but modifications may be necessary for Iceland.

Fuel pump repair kit
Exhaust valve
Decoke set

Spark plugs
Distributor cap
Coil
Contact set
Condenser
Rotor arm
Reconditioned water pump
Carburettor kit
Brake hoses for front and rear
Front and rear axle kits
Slave cylinder kit
Clutch master cylinder kit
Bushes and Shackle pin
Universal joint
Brake master cylinder kit
S/H Rear half shaft
Set of light bulbs
Fuel pump
Fan belt
Set of radiator hoses and heater hoses
Radiator cap
Hose clips
Clutch plate and cover
Release bearing
2 litres of brake/clutch fluid
1 litre of Gear Oil EP90
Exhaust bandages and silencer repair paste
Instant gasket
3 metres length of petrol pipe
Rad seal
Petrol patches
Hose bandage
Epoxy resin
WD 40 or equivalent
Engine oil – calculate amount and then double it. LandRovers tend to be thirsty for oil, especially if the terrain is hard going.
2 short-handled shovels
Range of spanners, sockets etc.
Hammer, screwdrivers, hacksaw
Insulating tape
Emery cloth, assorted nuts and bolts, screws.

2. Medical Supplies – The following is a list of most common ailments found in a group of approximately eighteen persons staying away for four to six weeks and remaining in remote areas. Ailments will vary according to the country you are visiting, but the list is biased towards hot climates. Suggested treatment is also given, although names of drugs are largely avoided. It is recommended that you should consult your GP for details of these as some are prescription drugs. These are the problems that we have come across, and the remedies that we have found effective, so bear in mind that these are only our suggestions. Professional advice must be sought before departure.

Ears, nose and throat:
Congestion, catarrh and rhinitis – long acting decongestant eg. Dimotapp.
Painful and sore throat – antiseptic painkilling oral rinse, throat lozenges.

Intestinal:
Diarrhoea and sickness – Imodium for diarrhoea, Lomotil for both. The latter is suitable for children. Persistent diarrhoea causes loss of salts. Rehydrate helps to restore the balance, as do Electrosol tablets.
Vomiting – antiemetic eg. Stemitil.
Indigestion – antacids.
Colic – Antispasmodics eg. Buscopan (suitable for children).
Travel sickness – eg. Stugeron.

Dressings for cuts, etc.:
Crepe bandages.
Antiseptic swabs.
Plasters/Butterfly sutures.
Non-allergenic plaster eg. Micropore.

Other pains and problems:
Headache and general pain – painkiller eg. paracetamol.
Hay fever and other allergies – antihistamine tablets.
Chafing and sore skin – an antifungal cream with hydrocortsone and an anti-inflammatory eg. Econacort.
Insect bites – antihistamine eg. Anthisan cream.
Muscular pain – eg. Algesal cream.
Eye infection – eg. Murine eye drops.

THE
HEBRIDES

THE HEBRIDES

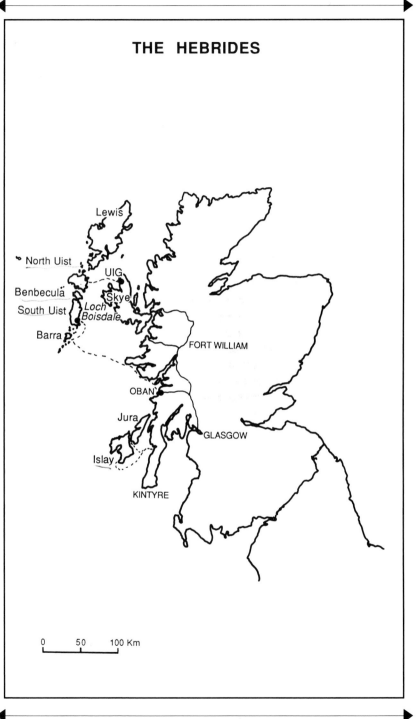

Lewis

North Uist

UIG

Benbecula

Skye

South Uist

Loch
Boisdale

Barra

FORT WILLIAM

OBAN

Jura

GLASGOW

Islay

KINTYRE

0   50   100 Km

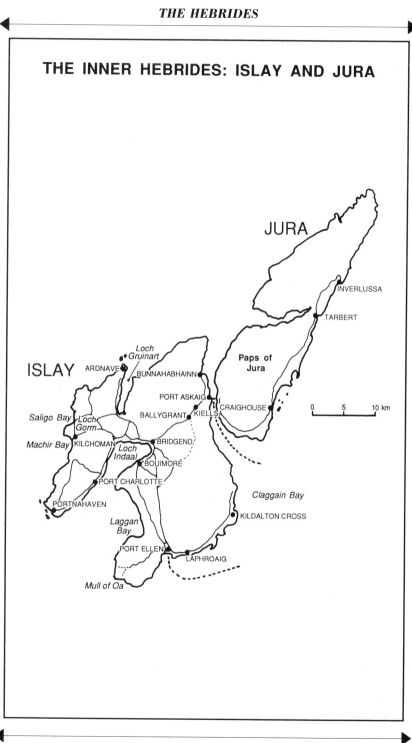

THE INNER HEBRIDES: ISLAY AND JURA

JURA

INVERLUSSA

TARBERT

Paps of
Jura

Loch
Gruinart

ISLAY

ARDNAVE

BUNNAHABHAINN

PORT ASKAIG

BALLYGRANT

KIELLS

CRAIGHOUSE

Saligo Bay

Loch
Gorm

Machir Bay

KILCHOMAN

Loch
Indaal

BRIDGEND

BOUIMORE

PORT CHARLOTTE

PORTNAHAVEN

Claggain Bay

KILDALTON CROSS

Laggan
Bay

PORT ELLEN

LAPHROAIG

Mull of Oa

0   5   10 km

THE INNER HEBRIDES: SKYE

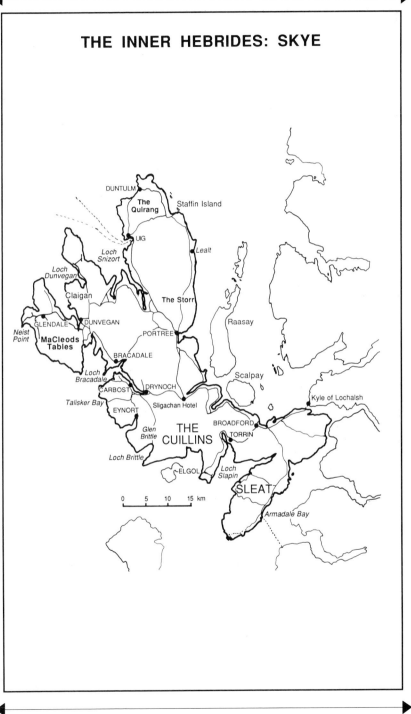

DUNTULM

The Quirang

Staffin Island

UIG

Loch Snizort

Lealt

Loch Dunvegan

Claigan

The Storr

GLENDALE

DUNVEGAN

PORTREE

Raasay

Neist Point

MaCleods Tables

BRACADALE

Scalpay

Loch Bracadale

CARBOST

DRYNOCH

Kyle of Lochalsh

Talisker Bay

EYNORT

Sligachan Hotel

Glen Brittle

THE CUILLINS

BROADFORD

TORRIN

Loch Brittle

ELGOL

Loch Slapin

SLEAT

0   5   10   15 km

Armadale Bay

THE OUTER HEBRIDES

To Tarbert

To Uig

Machair Leathann
Griminish Point
Newtonferry
Beinn Mhor

BALRANALD

Loch Maddy

CLACHAN

Eaval

Ceann Iar

NORTH UIST

Baleshare

**MONARCH
ISLANDS**

Ceann Ear

Loch Eport

BALIVANICH

Grimsay

CREAGORRY

BENBECULA

Wiay

Loch Skipport

STILLIGARRY

HOWMORE

Hecla

**SOUTH
UIST**

Rubha Ardvule

ORMICLATE

MILTON

Loch Eynort

THE MINCH

DALIBURGH

Loch Boisdale

POLLACHAR

Eriskay

EOLIGARRY

Greian Head

BARRA

BORVE
Loch Obe

CASTLEBAY

Vatersay

MINGULAY

Barra Head

To Oban

0   5   10   15   km

Introduction

The name "Hebrides" is derived from a Norse word meaning "the isles on the edge of the sea". The peripheral position of the islands gives a real sense of isolation and remoteness to the visitor. Although the people may initially appear reserved, they are hospitable and friendly. The rugged landscape is dotted with small crofting settlements and surrounded by a varied coastline. Away from the sea, the land rises to form mountains. These are flanked by desolate moors, which undergo dramatic variations in colour with the changing seasons. The area is a hill walker's paradise. A sensation of true wilderness is enhanced by the eerie call of the eagles which soar overhead – one of the islands' greatest attributes is their bird life. A lack of intensive farming has ensured that many plants and animals have their last stronghold here. The spectacular coastal scenery affords such a wide variety of habitats that there are few better places in Europe for seashore studies. In addition, the Gulf Stream deposits an interesting selection of tropical flotsam from the Caribbean.

Geography

The Hebrides are a flooded landscape with deep fjords and skerries. These skerries form thousands of tiny islets lining the coast. They give refuge to seals and nesting seabirds. The rocks of the Outer Hebrides consist of Lewisian gneiss. This diamond-hard material is named after the island of Lewis.

Skye is famous for the volcanic rocks from which the high Cuillin mountains are formed. Limestone can also be found in the extreme south. Islay is geologically varied with both hard and soft rocks. This accounts for its u-shape, because the soft rocks across the centre are more susceptible to erosion.

It is the hard rocks of the Hebrides which yield the poor soils and vast moors. The high humidity helps to promote the wet heaths and blanket peat bogs. Generally, the western coasts are exposed to the Atlantic swell. Rocky inlets with high cliffs are typical. The west coasts of the outer isles form sweeping bays which are carpeted with sand dunes. Closer to the mainland, all the islands are mountainous. Some reach 1000m in height. The rocky eastern coast is sheltered and silted up in parts. Deep sea-lochs cut inland. South Uist has almost been divided into two halves by Loch Eynort.

The tidal range around Islay and Jura is one of the shortest in Britain.

Climate

The climate is typically warm and wet – especially in the outer isles. This encourages a profuse growth of Sphagnum, or Bog Moss, which is the moss that ultimately becomes peat. The inner isles have more snow and frosts than the outer ones. Nonetheless, they are warmer than the Highlands. Biting mosquitoes plague the mainland. They are also common on Skye. These are absent from the outer islands, perhaps because of the unrelenting wind! Storms and gale force winds are a fairly regular feature in the Hebrides, but this should never deter the traveller.

Flora and Fauna

Machair is the name given to the vegetation which develops behind the coastal dunes. It is unique to the north and west of Scotland. The sand is made up of crushed shells. Hence, calcium produces an alkaline soil, and there are few other minerals present. The machair is a blaze of colour in summer and is used by the crofters for grazing their cattle. The dunes can drift up to 100m in height, spreading in from the coast to cover areas of moorland.

The Hebrides form a chain of islands stretching several hundred miles into the Atlantic. Many such arrangements of isolated communities have been shown to yield subspecies and variants by natural selection. A number of animals have managed to reach some or all of the islands, leaving behind their competitors on the mainland. A greater quantity and variety of food is then available to them. Adaptation to the new circumstances has lead to variations. For example, the wren found on the St. Kilda group has become a different species and has taken the islands' name as its own. All the islands have a different variety of Field Mouse and this is reflected in the subspecies name *Apodemus sylvatica hebridensis*. Most of the adaptations to life on these windswept isles have taken the form of an increase in size, but a reduction in the extremities – the animals have small ears and shorter tails.

The mountains and hills are dominated by heathlands. The rocky crags play host to many alpine flowers. The Dwarf Juniper is also abundant in the almost treeless landscape. Islay has several primeval-looking woodlands of hazel and birch, whose branches are covered by moss.

Travelling to the Hebrides

All the main islands are well served by the shipping company Caledonian MacBrayne. The timetables can be obtained from most travel agents or the head office in Gourock. The car ferries are relatively small and on occasions the driver may have to manoeuvre onto a lift which descends into the hold. Prices are reasonable and an island "hopscotch" is available – a cheap way of moving from one island to another.

All the islands discussed in this chapter are linked by air to Paisley airport, at Glasgow. Flying in the small Islander aircraft is an expensive option. However, on a clear day the journey over the Highlands and the Inner and Outer Hebrides is an experience never to be forgotten.

Motoring in the Hebrides

Once you have landed it will become clear that the islands' roads are affected by the elements. Thus potholes are not at all rare. With the exception of the main route on Skye, the tarmac roads are a single track with passing places that are signposted at intervals. The roads are slow and bumpy but quite adequate.

Petrol stations are few and far between. Outside Skye they are little more than a pump located next to the village store. Hence, it is often necessary for the driver to ask in the shop for an assistant. Petrol prices are always higher on the isles, often by as much as 15 or 20 pence a gallon.

Camping and Accommodation

There are few official camp-sites in the Hebrides. Luckily, there is little need for them as it is very easy to find a place in which to pitch a tent. Areas of sand dunes are often the most simple. In addition, there are numerous small hotels and guest houses, as well as a large number of self-catering cottages.

Fishing

The Highlands are renowned for salmon and trout fishing, and the isles are no exception. Suitable rivers can be found on all the main islands.

Food and Shopping

Locally caught fish and shellfish are the main speciality advertised in the restaurants and cafes. Fresh fish can be purchased easily in the fishing villages. Other foods are expensive to buy and not always available. Virtually all food has to come via the ferry from the mainland. As a consequence, it is not always fresh. There is a chain of VG Stores on the islands. Bread may have to be ordered several days in advance.

Most of the food shops remain open on every day of the week. However, times of opening vary considerably according to local whim. You should also beware of sudden Bank Holidays! If there is a local event (such as a Highland Games) all the shops will shut.

Medical

There are no problems with the medical facilities on the islands. A doctor is usually available. Treatment requiring a hospital simply necessitates a flight to Glasgow. The pharmacies are usually located near the surgeries.

Local Industry

For centuries the islands have been self-sufficient and isolated from the mainland. In recent years a flood of young people has left for the big cities. This emigration has depleted the population. Empty and delapidated crofts are a common sight. Many island industries have gone into decline, partly because of the cost of transport to and from the mainland. The alginate industry, which removes chemicals from seaweed, has also dwindled.

However, the lack of jobs on the mainland has driven many back to the islands. Some smaller businesses are now beginning to thrive. Harris Tweed is now made throughout the isles and local knitwear shops are very common. There is jewellery production in South Uist, a perfumery on Barra and cheese is made on Islay. However, one cannot deny the importance of whisky distillation. Skye has one distillery at Talisker, while Islay has eight, although the number is dropping as one after another closes. The malt whisky is no cheaper here but on a chilly day a distillery is a fascinating place to visit. This is particularly so because Scottish hospitality affords an opportunity to sample the product after the tour is completed!

Routes

In most cases, it is possible to hop from one island to the next. You could start with Islay and Jura in the Inner Hebrides. Then drive north to Oban and catch the ferry to Barra, the most southerly of the inhabited outer isles. Travel through these isles until North Uist and then cross back to the inner isles by taking the ferry to Skye.

In the text below the Inner Hebridean islands of Islay, Jura and Skye will be considered first, followed by the Outer Hebrides.

The Inner Hebrides

Islay

Getting there:

Our route begins from Glasgow. Follow the urban motorway past Paisley and over the Irskine Bridge towards Dunbarton. Here you join the A82 to start the 190km journey to Lochgilphead and Kennacraig, where the Islay ferry departs. Whichever route you choose to take, it will cross the beautiful highlands of Argyllshire.

Initially, the road follows close to the western banks of Loch Lomond, twisting its way to Tarbet which lies approximately halfway along the lakeside. Take the A83 and cross the highlands to the far west coast. To begin with, it winds along the upper reaches of Loch Long. After a few kilometres it veers inland, entering Glen Croe. The gradual slope from sea level soon starts to climb very steeply. The mountain to the right is Ben Arthur. Just behind is Beinn Ime, which is 1000m high. The road levels out at a junction called "Rest and be thankful". It is worth stopping here to admire the views across this glaciated landscape. At Easter time there can be a blizzard blowing in this spot, even though the weather at sea level may be quite mild!

The road descends through Glen Kinglas to the upper reaches of a sea-loch called Loch Fynne. The A83 continues along its northern edge to Lochgilphead. The road is flanked by beautiful mixed deciduous woodland. In the spring the area is studded with primroses and violets and later Bluebells and Wild Ramson. This route takes you via Inveraray, which is well worth stopping in. A brisk but excellent walk can be made to an obelisk, above the woodland, from where there is a superb view down to Inveraray and across the loch. The walk begins just before the bridge and the castle, as you enter the town.

The ferry leaves from Kennacraig – 27km on from Lochgilphead. However, if you have plenty of time, take the right-hand turning out of the town on to the A816, and then on to the B841, a mile or so later. This road follows the west bank of the delightful Crinan Canal. The left turn on to the B8025 is a dead end, but it leads to delightful views and interesting wildlife. Firstly, the road passes through the Knapdale Forest, where there is an Information Centre and a number of walks. It is a good area for birdwatching. There is a left fork off the B8025 in the forest. This narrow road follows closely to the edge of Loch Sween. At the end there is an excellent view across the Sound of Jura to the island itself. The two peaks – the Paps of Jura – are invariably capped in cloud. The Sound has the smallest tidal movement in Britain. As a consequence, the water of Loch Sween hardly seems to move, and the seaweeds are not always uncovered. At the most sheltered end, the seashore habitat is described as a backwater community. It contains a mass of coloured seaweeds and gently moving jellyfish. Starfish, sea urchins and brittle-stars are also common. The road is on a peninsula of land. Near its tip is a twelfth-century ruined castle and at Kilmory, a chapel. Both are worth visiting.

On most days, the car ferry from Kennacraig leaves twice daily at around 0730 and 1400 hours. (On Fridays and Sundays there is only one sailing per day.) The crossing takes less than 2 hours. Caledonian MacBrayne ferries tend to be fairly spartan, as are their terminals. A small cafeteria is the only entertainment on board! However, the passing scenery is entertainment enough, as you try island spotting in the mist. Black Guillemots are a common sight – dodging the swash of the boat. The landing on Islay takes place in one of two locations – Port Ellen (one of the largest towns) or Port Askaig (one of the smallest).

Where to stay:

Islay has numerous self-catering cottages and Bed and Breakfast establishments. Details of these are available from the tourist board. Two comfortable places with very pleasant landlords are the Dower House Guest House near Kildalton Castle (7km east of Port Ellen), and the Port Charlotte Hotel in the village of that name. Both have excellent views over the sea. The former is surrounded by daffodils in spring – a feature typical of Islay. The latter hotel has a "bunk house" for groups, such as divers, and also a self-catering chalet. There are a number of such cottages at Port Charlotte and details can be obtained from the Croft Kitchen Restaurant.

An alternative is to stay at the Islay Field Centre in Port Charlotte. You can take one room or rent the entire house. It is

The exposed coastline near Portnahaven.

self-catering and has a well equipped kitchen. In addition to a number of bedrooms, there is a lounge, dining room and a small lab with a library. The Centre was established by a charity called the Islay Natural History Trust in memory of Rodney Dawson, a well-known local naturalist.

There are no official camp-sites on Islay but farmers will often give permission for the use of their fields. The dunes near Ardnave, in the north of the Rhinns, are very suitable. However, you should remember that all the land is owned by someone, and that you should always ask permission first. One of the few signposted camping areas is on the dunes to the east of Loch Gruinart, the nature reserve run by the Royal Society for the Protection of Birds. Turn off the B8017 to Craigens and speak to the farmer. Several of the villages have small fields which are used by campers – check with the local hotelier or cafe owner. The main land owner is the Islay Estates. It pays to call in to the office with your map and point out the areas where you hope to camp. Many of the lakes (such as Loch Tallant) and woods also belong to them. You should ask permission to gain access. Islay Estates also issues fishing permits. The office is at Bridgend – as you leave to go to Bowmore the building is on the left.

Port Charlotte:

Port Charlotte is a good base. It has a small supermarket with petrol pumps. There are delightful views across Loch Inadaal, which splits Islay in two. As you enter the village from Bowmore there is a road to the right. This takes you to a creamery with a small shop from where cheese can be purchased. It is also possible (usually in the morning) to see the cheese being made. Very near the creamery is the Museum of Islay Life. Here there are interesting exhibits such as illicit whisky stills and artefacts of prehistoric life on Islay.

Port Charlotte is on the western part of Islay, which is known as the Rhinns. In fact, Islay is more like two islands – joined by the marshy, alluvial soils at Gruinart.

The Rhinns:

This region of Islay, being the most exposed part of the island, has a wild and rocky coast line with occasional narrow sandy bays. From Port Charlotte the main road follows alongside Loch Inadaal in both directions. Travelling in a clockwise direction around the Rhinns, the first village is Portnahaven, at the very westerly tip of Islay. The rocky shores here are typical of areas exposed to wave action. The rocks are barnacle dominated. At the low-water mark the usual kelps have been replaced by a very resilient species – the Dabberlocks. This seaweed is found along the lochside, merging in with the kelp near Port Charlotte. Grey Seals can often be seen basking on the rocks in the harbour at Portnahaven, while herons and Oystercatchers are a common sight fishing amongst the seaweeds.

The minor road which goes to Kilchiaran passes over some desolate moorland. As the road descends towards the bay you can stop and walk down to the wave-swept beach below. Kilchiaran is famous for its round farmhouse, which is clearly visible from the road. There is also an ancient chapel on the cliff. Just beyond it, a track to the left leads one kilometre up the hill. Leave your vehicle here and follow the track around the contours for a bracing walk to Machir Bay and Kilchoman.

About a mile on from the farmhouse there is a lake to the left of the road – Loch Conailbhe. There are similar lakes further on. Red-throated Divers have been spotted in the area but it is the frog population that is most noteworthy. In spring, hundreds spawn here. The road back to Port Charlotte cuts across a moorland of heathers and sedge. To see the northern part of the Rhinns it is necessary to drive back onto the main road via Bruichladdich. The black and white buildings which front this village are a malt whisky distillery. This can be visited by prior appointment.

A few miles on from Bruichladdich there is a junction with the B8018 which will take you to the north of the Rhinns. The road cuts through a cliff and climbs northwards. This cliff runs in an arc around the upper reaches of Loch Inadaal. It is an excellent example of a raised beach. Thousands of years ago the sea would have crashed against it, but movements of the land have lifted it upwards and a new cliff has been formed further down the shore. There are many raised beaches along the north eastern coast of Islay. After several miles the B8018 forks to the right whilst a minor road continues to Machir Bay. Although there are some sand dunes here, it is not true machair as the name would seem to suggest. The bay is a long, sweeping sandy one with a wreck clearly visible at low tide, partly buried in the sand. There are numerous wrecks around Islay's coast and divers travel great distances to search for them. A good collection of artefacts and photographs are on display in the bars of the Port Charlotte Hotel. Large numbers of rabbits feed on the dune grasses. There is little control of rabbits and hares on the island.

The most interesting species here is the rare Chough, a member of the crow family with red legs and beak. Choughs can be seen feeding on the wetter grassland. Almost a mile back from the beach the land rises steeply to the church of Kilchoman. The cliffs behind the church are home to the choughs and at times as many as a hundred can be seen in noisy flocks. In the churchyard there is a Celtic cross below which a smooth, rounded pebble lies. Legends suggest that the stone possesses fertility powers. For centuries women have come to rub the stone in their hands in hope of conceiving.

From the church there is good view of Loch Gorm. A minor road circles the lake and the track to the south-east brings you close to the marshy shores. A small island offshore has a pile of stones which was once a broch – an ancient castle in the form of a tower. Wading birds come to feed here and Oystercatchers and Curlews nest in the heather. From Kilchoman you should follow the road along the coast. This will bring you to Saligo (simply a small bridge over a rushing stream) and then to

Saligo Bay. Go through the gate on the other side of the stream and walk across the machair grassland toward the sea. Even on an apparently calm day the waves crash onto the rocks and sand. It is an amazing sight with eroded rocks and colourful seaweeds.

By comparison, the shores of Loch Gruinart are very tranquil. This is the loch that helps divide Islay into two parts. Tidal silting has meant that it is relatively shallow. The loch empties at low tide, uncovering a vast expanse of sand and mud which is home for a rich variety of burrowing invertebrates. Consequently, numerous birds come to feed here and it is now a nature reserve run by the Royal Society for the Protection of Birds. The birds for which Islay is famous are especially common here in the winter and spring: the Barnacle and Greenland White-fronted Geese. Islay is their main overwintering site, and their numbers can reach several thousands. The Barnacle Geese are black and white. They can be seen feeding in the fields around Loch Gruinart and also on the mudflats near Bridgend. Also feeding in the fields with the geese are very large populations of hares, a common sight all over Islay.

The easiest way to leave Port Charlotte is to take the main road to the other end of the raised beach, and then turn onto the B8017. The road straightens as it crosses the marshland of the Gruinart Flats. As the road climbs the hill, there is a minor road on the right. This is opposite the reserve warden's house and leads down to the western edge of the loch. In 1598 a battle over land rights took place on the upper marshland – between the MacDonalds and the MacLeans. The MacDonalds won. The bodies were burnt and buried near the chapel at Kilnave on the banks of the loch. An eighth-century cross also stands nearby.

Driving to the end of the minor road brings you to Ardnave Loch and Ardnave House. This is now just a ruin and the land is used for grazing. Follow the track (on foot) and this will take you across a stable dune system and dune cliffs. Below is a wild expanse of sand protected by a rocky shore beyond. The man-made pools are for rearing lobsters. It is a beautiful and wild area. In early summer the dunes are in flower and dotted with hares. Walking to Ardnave Point, you pass numerous little bays and there is a clear view to Ardnave Island. Eider Duck, plovers, sanderling and Oystercatchers are abundant. The splash zones of the rocky outcrops have an amazing variety of colourful lichens.

Bridgend to Port Askaig:

The shore at Bridgend marks the most sheltered part of Loch Inadaal. At low tide a vast expanse of sand and mud is uncovered. It is in this bay that the geese are particularly abundant. The richness of most of the burrowing animal life is difficult to see. However, the Sand Mason worm is easy to spot along the low-water line. It secretes a mucus which binds sand grains together to produce an intricate tube, just the top part of which protrudes above the surface of the sand. It feeds on the debris washed in by the tide. Other species include the Tellin shells. Their beautiful white and pink shells are like butterflies when they lie open on the sand. Lugworm and a strange-looking burrowing brittle-star can also be found. There is plenty here for the wading birds to feed on.

At the main road junction in Bridgend the area around the river is wooded. In spring the woods are carpeted with daffodils, primroses and celandines. Butterflies and longhorn beetles are abundant in summer, while deer can be seen at most times of the year. The road to Port Askaig passes through a wild area of moorland. Note that the region north of the road has little vehicular access. It is dominated by heather and Deer Sedge. Grouse are common, together with nesting curlews and buzzards. Several tracks go a short way into this moorland. Most stop near lochs such as Loch Finlaggan, the largest body of water in the region. At the northern end is a small island with a ruined castle from which the Lord of Islay once ruled.

Loch Skerrols, near Bridgend, is a favourite fishing lake and is thickly wooded around its perimeter. Just beyond the loch there is a turning left from the main road to Scarrabus and Balole. The track en route to the latter passes through a copse of birch and hazel, all stunted. The floor of the wood is covered with flowers. Roe Deer are common.

In the village of Ballygrant there is a right turning on to a minor road. This takes you upwards into the high moorland to the south where the River Laggan rises. Near the beginning of the road, as it climbs through woodland up onto the moor, you pass through an area which is used for deer stalking. This is commonplace on these isles. Between August and February you must phone Port Askaig 232 or Bowmore 204 before venturing northwards onto the moor. The narrow road passes several sets of standing stones and a number of mountain lochs. The ground is very wet and bogs dominate. The unfenced road gradually bears to the west as it crosses numerous tributaries of the River Laggan. There are some delightful ravines here. They are steep sided and have a stream at the bottom. The high humidity encourages the growth of mosses and lichens. Sphagnum mosses have other plants growing in them. These include marsh orchids and insectivorous species such as sundews and bladderworts. Mammal trapping has revealed Bank Voles as well as Field Mice. These small valleys show a good transition from heathland at the top to a willow marsh at the bottom.

A mile on from Ballygrant a small road to the left goes past some ruined buildings at Mulresh. To the left of the road are some deserted lead mines. These are the best surviving relics of the lead mining industry which was operating here in the nineteenth century. The last ore was removed in 1880 and the ruined buildings here are the remains of miners' cottages and the wheel house. The shafts are fenced off but there are plenty of pieces of rock which have been brought up from below. There are good views from here.

Bunnahabhain can be reached by road from Kiells (another lead mining village), about a mile before Port Askaig. The road is very narrow at times but offers breathtaking views as it winds

A wreck near Bunnahabain.

above the cliff tops. On a clear day, the view across to Jura shows the raised beaches very well. The remote northern tip of Islay is also composed of raised beaches. The sheltered rocks around Bunnahabhain Bay are rich in marine life and one of the better places for starfish. The outcrop of rocks to the right of the bay have good kelp beds as well as the rusting wreck of a ship which has run aground here. It too has been colonised by seaweeds and barnacles. The lagoon area to the north is good at low tide and the Dabberlocks seaweed grows exceptionally long and broad.

The distillery here is well worth a visit. An appointment can be made by telephoning beforehand (Tel. 049 684 646). This is the first of many possible visits to Islay's distilleries. Each has unique features that are worth seeing – and tasting! Bunnahabhain has the least peaty flavour of the Islay whiskies. The grain is malted in Ireland and delivered here by ship. A few kilometres away at Caol Ila (which means "Straits of Islay"), a brand new distillery has replaced the old one which was established in 1846.

Port Askaig is the place from where to catch the boat to Jura. In the harbour and along the Sound of Islay, Black Guillemots can often be seen and heard.

Bowmore and the South of Islay:

Bowmore is the capital of Islay, and it is here that the oldest distillery thrives. In season, a tour usually takes place at 1030 and 1430 hours, Monday to Friday. A phone-call will confirm. The main street runs away from the sea. It leads up the hill from where the church commands a view across the loch. Like several buildings on Islay, the church is round – supposedly to prevent the devil from being able to hide! There is an excellent bakery here. On your way into Bowmore you pass the Islay Farmers Cooperative on the left. There is a large shop here and it is probably the cheapest store on the island.

The left turning directly behind the church is a minor road which joins up with the B8016 at Laggan Bridge. This road from Bridgend by-passes Bowmore on the way to Port Ellen. The bridge is a good place to stop. You can walk across the wet moorland and follow the meandering River Laggan. The river cuts deep into the banks here and there is little vegetation. However, the waters are rich in trout, mayflies and stoneflies. The moorland is very lumpy to the north of the bridge. These tussocks are formed by the accumulation of a succession of Sphagnum mosses which grow out of the bog pools. As conditions become drier, Purple Moor Grass and heathers begin to grow. As height increases, so the sweet smelling Bog Myrtle (and eventually willows) can grow. If the hummock is narrow, the presence of bushes will cause it to topple and the entire structure breaks up to start again. It is possible to see different stages in the growth of hummocks in this area. The process of ecological succession, as it is called, can also be investigated at Loch Tallant.

Loch Tallant lies a kilometre away, to the north of the Bowmore road. The western end is quite shallow, largely because of the accumulation of dead plant material from the reeds and mosses. As these grasses grow, so the material they produce each year is laid down, making the loch shallower still. These grasses then move further out and Bog Myrtle begins to establish itself. The yellow-flowered Bog Asphodel is abundant in the marshy ground. By walking westwards from the water's edge, you will pass a succession of communities. These include Bog Bean, Reed Bed, Bog Myrtle, willow and (on dry land) birch. The conclusion of a succession is a stable community called the climax – in this case the birch. (This process of succession from water to dry land is called a hydrosere.) Loch Tallant is a rich site for both flora and fauna. It makes an interesting comparison with Loch Conailbhe. The latter is based on acid rocks whilst Loch Tallant collects water from across alkaline limestone.

The River Laggan can be followed seaward by a path on its northern bank. Just before the main road it deviates onto a minor road. Opposite the junction with the main road is another road (very potholey and muddy) which goes down to a viewpoint at Laggan Point. As you start on the track, the wood to the left will almost guarantee the sighting of Roe Deer. They can often be spotted on the track or just in the bushes. The land on either side of the track is a good place for watching geese and hares. The meandering river is clearly seen and reached from the road. The pressure of the river water is enough to keep the sea at bay.

The long sandy beach of Laggan Bay (good beach combing) is fringed by sand dunes and machair. The best examples are in the northern part, near the Laggan River. The stable dune zone merges with the moorland behind. Geese and other birds feed and roost in the area from the beach to Muice Duibhe, the extensive bog behind the main road. To the south, the dunes are occupied by the aerodrome and golf course. Flowing under the road here is the

River Glenegedale. By following its course up to the high land above, you will pass through narrow gorges and ravines. These provide good, humid shelter for small mammals and flowers.

Port Ellen is the major town on the south coast. It is a harbour for the ferries from Kennacraig as well as being a base for fishing boats. The distillery here carries out the malting of the grain for other distilleries on the island, such as Lagavulin.

The southernmost point of Islay is the Qa penninsula. Accessible by a single, narrow road, it is a wild and remote area with little habitation. The road ends a mile short of the cliffs at the Mull of Oa. There is no clear path, but with care, it is fairly easy to cross the fields to the monument on top of the cliffs. This is the American Memorial. It is dedicated to the Americans who were killed when the Tuscania was torpedoed and the Otranto wrecked in 1918.

The high cliffs here are home to many seabirds. Between May and July, Kittiwakes, gulls, Fulmars, guillemots and Razorbills can all be seen. Choughs also breed here. There are many caves along the cliffs nearby that were used in the days of smuggling.

The road east from Port Ellen is delightful, with tiny rocky and sandy inlets. The first three of these each has its own distillery. Laphroig and Lagavulin are perhaps the most famous of Islay whiskies, both heavy with the smell of peat. The first is fairly automated, with stainless steel fermenting tanks. Visitors can see the malting of the grain. This is allowed to germinate, causing the starch to change within. After several days it is then placed in kilns which are heated with burning peat. Lagavulin still uses wooden fermenting vats. Both can be visited by prior appointment (Lagavulin: Tel. Port Ellen 2250. Laphroig: Tel. 0496 2418). Ardbeg is the third distillery. However, it no longer produces whisky – its buildings are simply used for storing casks.

The bays and inlets are a haven for seashore organisms. Seals can regularly be seen basking on the rocks offshore. The inlet immediately before Kildalton Castle is a sheltered rocky shore with spider crabs, sea slugs, hydroids, sponges, sea squirts, tidal fish and squat lobsters. On the rocks is the Tortoiseshell Limpet. The woods behind the road are rich in a ground flora of Wood Sorrel, primroses and bluebells.

The Dower House guest house stands above a small sandy cove in which scallops are plentiful. The road climbs steeply upwards passing through narrow woodland strips. The bark of the trees is cloaked in mosses and lichens. A few miles on there is a turn to the right, up to the remains of Kildalton Chapel. The eighth-century Celtic cross is worth seeing. This is a good centre for some tremendous walks. You can make your way inland through the sparsely wooded hillsides, or set out for the remote cliffs and inlets of Ardmore Point.

Jura

Staying on Jura is difficult, as this is only permitted in official accommodation and camping is not allowed. The island is accessible only from Port Askaig on Islay. The ferry is an old red landing craft which plies regularly across the fast flowing water of the sound. A day trip from Jura is possible but the island is deceptively long and the road's quality worsens with distance. A useful little book, entitled *The Long Road – a driver's guide to Jura* can be purchased on Islay.

Jura is a wilderness. There is little traffic and only one road running the length of the island, which is on the south coast. The Paps of Jura are four high mountains (785m) at the Islay end. Like the rest of the island, they are covered by a blanket bog.

Red Deer on the hills of eastern Jura.

There is little variety in the plant life, with the exception of the heathers and moor grasses which are able to cope with the acidity. Most of Jura is dominated by the Red Deer, who greatly outnumber the human population. In Craighouse (where there is a distillery) you can even buy venison burgers! The deer are very easy to spot and their herds regularly feed near sea level. In spring the heather is burnt to encourage new growth for them to eat.

Walking on Jura requires more planning than Islay as it is not only the wilderness that you have to cope with, but also the hunter. Before setting off for a day's hike into the remote north, it is important to check at the Isle of Jura Hotel that no hunting parties are in your area. Signs will be found on gates telling you if walking is restricted. The Paps of Jura are spectacular peaks to climb. Not only do they present a splendid view of Islay and Jura, they also have many alpine plants on their slopes. There are several routes, none of which are well marked. Beinn a Chaolais is the lowest peak (at 734m) and is accessible from Inver Cottage. There is a track to the left as you leave the Feollin Ferry. A heronry can be found amongst the trees here. To reach the other Paps, the best route is to follow the Corran River which crosses the main road at the other end of Craighouse Bay. From the top you will be able to see the raised beaches along the coast.

The moorland supports grouse but the bird to look out for is the Arctic Skua. This feathered pirate nests on the open ground, and attacks terns to make them regurgitate food. It exists in two forms: a dark and a light phase. The latter is the most abundant here whilst the darker form increases in frequency as you progress north to Iceland.

Jura is almost cut in two by Loch Tarbert. Its sheltered backwater is near to the road. A path from Tarbert goes down to the lochside. At Tarbert there is a small sheltered bay. The seashore communities are interesting because of the extremely short tidal range which bunches up the zones of seaweeds. A walk around the right side of the inlet brings you onto a small outcrop of rock. At low tide the seaweed changes from Dabberlocks and Thongweed (typical of extreme wave action) to Bladderwrack and Knotted Wrack (typical of shelter), within a distance of only 20m around this tiny headland. Red Deer are very common in this region, and they can often be seen feeding down on the seashore. All the way along here are delightful inlets with steep woodlands behind them.

The road beyond Ardlussa is of very poor quality. It may be wise to give up by the time you reach Lealt, unless you have a

LandRover. The main attraction lies 8km further on. Barnhill was George Orwell's home at the time he wrote *1984*. The remoteness may have helped his inspiration, but the damp atmosphere did little for his health. He died later from tuberculosis. Walking from Barnhill will take you to several good viewpoints overlooking the Gulf of Corryvreckan. The gulf is infamous for the whirlpools which form offshore, and in which Orwell once almost drowned.

In conclusion, Jura is a place in which to get away from civilisation. However, its geology and ruggedness reduce the variety of natural history considerably. By contrast, Islay has a wide diversity of species but not the high mountains or remoteness. It is fortunate indeed that they are so close together.

The Isle of Skye

Getting there:

Every day, the ferry plies across the notorious Minch, from Lochmaddy to Skye. The two-hour journey brings you to the pier at Uig, in the north of the isle. Alternatively, there is a half-hourly ferry service across the Kyles of Lochalsh. This concludes a long route from Fort William. The journey to Mallaig is a slightly smaller distance, but the crossing takes half an hour longer and may require advance booking in the summer. The short Kyleakin crossing is a third ferry service, which only operates during the summer. Loganair run daily flights from Glasgow, landing near Broadford.

Where to stay:

Skye is the most visited of the Hebridean islands. As a result, tourists are well catered for, and there are a large number of Bed and Breakfast establishments. Up-to-date details of self-catering cottages are available from the tourist offices at Portree or Broadford. Several of the island's church halls (Portree, for instance) are suitable for large groups in search of self-catering accommodation. At Torrin there is a small field centre recently renovated from the village school house. It is let at reasonable rates, and is in an ideal setting, just south of the Cuillins.

There are youth hostels at Broadford and Uig. There are several camp-sites on the island. One of the most scenic is in

Glen Brittle near the Cuillins. There are sites at Sligachan and on the Storr road from Portree. Rough camping is possible, but any suitable land will belong to one of the Skye estates and permission will be needed. Midges can be a problem in the summer months – especially if you camp near Sligachan.

The island scenery:

The island is surprisingly large – 77km by 38km. It may take almost an hour to reach Portree from the Kyleakin Ferry. Sheep farming took over after the croft clearances of the nineteenth century. Hence habitation is less scattered than in the crofting communities of Barra and South Uist. Most of Skye is dominated by extensive tracts of peat moorland, over 8000 acres of which is now owned by the Forestry Commission for pine tree plantations.

The highland in the centre of the island is famous for the Cuillin Hills. There are two types of hill. Some Cuillins are made of hard gabbro rock – a volcanic material that has been etched by glaciers to yield a series of jagged, craggy peaks. The highest is Sgurr Alasdair, at 1000m. The second type are the Red Cuillins, made from a pink tinged granite. This slightly softer rock produces a rounder peak than the gabbro. There are twenty different peaks. Fifteen of these are over 900m and are known as the Munros.

Skye is divided up into several regions, each with its own character. Trotternish is the northernmost area and one of the most spectacular, with the Storr Ridge rising over 600m. Waternish and Duirinish are to the west. In the south west is Sleat, pronounced "slate", which is the greenest part of the island. The rock is mainly gneiss, the oldest in Skye, with some outcrops of limestone. This area includes the largest woodlands, which are home to herds of Red Deer. With its lochans and rivers, the scenery is reminiscent of the Uists.

Broadford and the Cuillins:

Broadford is the main settlement area in the south. It is a sprawling town with no defined centre. There are all the usual amenities including a tourist information office. Broadford Bay, and especially the stretch to Ardnish, has a wealth of marine life. For the birdwatcher, it is a good place to spot sea ducks. Seals can be seen basking on the rock outcrops opposite Pabay Island.

Broadford is a good base from which to tackle the eastern peaks of the Cuillins. Beinn na Caillich (732m) is an enjoyable walk from the town and not too demanding as an introduction to the peaks. It should be remembered that these mountains are dangerous and that specialist equipment is necessary for most of the high peaks. In Broadford and Portree it is possible to purchase guidebooks and detailed maps which have been specially prepared for climbers. Behind the town of Broadford there is an outcrop of limestone. This fertile ground has been well utilised by crofters. A road goes past this area towards the sheltered bay of Heast. A mile beyond Broadford, this bends round to the left. The steep valley to the right is Glen Suardal. In the valley floor is a superb birch woodland with a rich ground flora. Among the rarities to be found here are the Mountain Avens *(Dryas octapetala)* and Red Helleborines.

The A881 leaves the A850 at Broadford and is of much poorer quality. After several kilometres it runs alongside Loch Cill Chriosd. Unlike most other lochs on the island, this one collects and drains water across limestone outcrops. The resulting nutrients make the loch very productive. There are examples of hydrosere succession around the edges. Common Reed and Bog Bean extend outwards into the open water. Near Torrin, a few miles on, the limestone manifests itself as marble, which has been quarried here for many years. The white dust produced from this quarrying brightens the beaches along this shore of Loch Slapin. At Kilbride, just before Torrin, a track goes off to the left. Following the loch shore it reaches Suisnish. The members of this once-thriving community of crofters emigrated to Canada after the clearances of the nineteenth century.

Loch Slapin is a very sheltered sea-loch. The main road follows the shoreline, and crosses a river in the upper reaches. Immediately before this, a path leads inland. This follows the river through a succession of lakes, to the head waters. It then leads down to Luib, on the main road to Portree. This relatively easy walk of 5–7km passes through the spectacular glen of Strath Mor. The ornithologist will find that this walk through the Red Cuillins is a chance to see a number of raptors, including Golden Eagles. The seashore species of Loch Slapin are limited by the steepness of the edges. Eider and other sea ducks are common. Beyond the hamlet of Kilmarie, just after the left hand bend, a gate marks the beginning of a track which takes the walker across the hills towards Loch Coruisk. This is a slightly shorter route than following the coast from Elgol, 7km further on at the end of the A881.

Elgol provides excellent views across to the Cuillins and south to the islands of Muck, Eigg and Rhum, the last of which is the nearest. The limestone on the beach has been eroded into a variety of shapes but it is essentially a shingle-boulder shore. From here you can take a boat journey across Loch Scavaig, to the base of the rapids which flow from Loch Coruisk. The walk is excellent – but tiring! This loch is in the heart of the Cuillins and is most impressive. The peaks of the mountains on the western side are the highest in Skye. Glen Brittle is one of the best bases from which to climb Sgurr Alasdair and the other Cuillin peaks. This glen is particularly beautiful, especially if you approach from Carbost at Easter time, when the slopes of the mountains are still covered in snow. The Ordnance Survey maps show the paths up Sgurr Alasdair. Remember that the weather can change rapidly, so climbers must be prepared for the worst. It requires experience and skill to reach the peak.

Loch Bracadale and the West Coast:

The road from Sligachan to Drynoch climbs through a very wet area of moorland. This is reflected in the numbers of midges.

The Cuillins, from Elgol, looking towards Loch Coruisk.

They can form very dense swarms in summer. After a mile or so the road levels out slightly. The area to the right is worth visiting, from the botanist's point of view. The top of the hills here are dotted with lochans and a plateau of peat dissected by large pools of Sphagnum Moss. In the damp Sphagnum grow the insectivorous Butterwort and delicate Bog Pimpernel. A variety of non-flowering plants can be seen. These include the Stag's Horn Clubmoss, and the Rhachomitrium Moss, which is more typical of tundra landscapes.

As you descend through Glen Drynoch, a succession of waterfalls can be seen flowing down its steep sides. The water has cut into the rock in places where the glen is already relatively steep. In these sites, the V-shaped hollows are very well protected, and hence support a large flora and fauna. Birch and hazel trees can be seen lining these humid areas. Among the cascades are beautiful mosses and liverworts – *Conacephalum* is the most prolific of the latter. The change in vegetation from the barren sides to the wetter and more luxuriant zones is most fascinating. In late spring this region is coloured by bluebells and primroses, while the wetter parts support Golden Saxifrage.

The River Drynoch slows as it reaches the sea-loch. Sediment has accumulated to yield a well-grazed saltmarsh. Cattle are a common sight in spring, feeding on the seaweeds at low tide. Just before reaching the loch take the B8009 along to Carbost and the Talisker Distillery.

Behind the distillery a road goes west to Talisker Bay – a wild and beautiful spot. Fulmars, Kittiwakes and Cormorants nest in the nearby cliffs. Just before the distillery, on the B8009, a minor road turns off very sharply to the left. It is signposted to Glen Brittle. This is a spectacular road and for the first few miles it aims straight for the Cuillins, with Sgurr Alasdair in the centre. When the slopes are covered with snow, during the spring, this is a breathtaking sight.

The A863 from Drynoch follows the shore of Loch Harport, passing delightful small bays such as Gesto Bay. The road bends around the headland and passes over a causeway and bridge, spanning the narrow estuary of Allt Mor. The B885 to the right takes you across moor and peatland, to Portree. Under the bridge are some marine rapids, with large mussel beds, but they are only worth a fleeting visit. The most fascinating feature here, not to be missed by the naturalist, is the small sea-loch of Loch Beag. It narrows towards the seaward end, before entering the extensive

Common Starfish feeding on a mussel, Loch Bracadale.

sea-loch of Loch Bracadale. At the far end is a very sheltered loch where waves are a rare sight. It empties at low tide, leaving a shingle-mud shore. The unique feature of this loch is that the majority of the seaweeds are an unanchored form, called ecads. Biologically, they are seaweeds that have become affected by the shelter and the dilution of the seawater. There is a large flow of freshwater down the hillsides. As a result, Yellow Flag Iris is a common species at the top of the seashore.

Ascophyllum nodosum var. Mackii (a variety of "Egg" or "Knotted" Wrack) is the most prolific ecad. It grows in large, round balls. Much of the Saw Wrack on the lower shore is free floating, simply moving up and down with the tide. Undoubtedly, some of the seaweed consists of fragments that have been washed in from Loch Bracadale. This becomes caught in the other weed and begins to grow. Many unusual animal species are present here. The burrowing sea anemone, *Peachia hastata*, is especially noteworthy. These lie in deep water on the lower shore and when the tide drops their tentacles can be seen above the surface of the mud.

The A863 passes through the village of Struan, where there is a craft shop. Less than a kilometre beyond the village, a sign points left to Ullinish. The minor road turns a right angle at the

Ullinish Lodge Hotel. This is an excellent establishment to visit for refreshment – especially in early spring when there is a roaring log fire. The road climbs onto a ridge from where there is a superb view across Loch Harport to the Cuillins. The road descends to skirt the upper shore of the sea-loch. The ledges of rock shelter a diverse range of marine species – sea urchins and starfish, for instance. The rocks of the splash zone are colonised by large orange, green and white lichens.

A group of flat-topped mountains, called Macleod's Tables, provide a superb backdrop on the other side of Loch Bracadale. The mountains lie on the remote peninsula of Glendale and can be reached by turning left onto the B884, about 9km further along the main road. Climbing is best done from Osdale. Just beyond the village of Glendale, a minor road goes west to Neist Point, from where there are excellent views.

There is another excellent marine site near Loch Bracadale – Pool Roag. At the tiny hamlet of Roskhill, on the main road, take the first minor road on the left to Vatten. (The second road goes to the other side of the water and to Roag village.) The pool fills with seawater at high tide and partly empties through a narrow channel at low tide. These tidal rapids are dominated by kelp *(Laminaria digitata)*. Around their bases are starfish, feeding on the abundance of attached organisms. These are also consumed by large numbers of yellow Sea Lemons, a type of sea slug. Below the rapids the kelp is replaced by clumps of Sea Oak *(Halidrys siliquosa)*. These dense plants have an abundance of animals sheltering in their fronds, from large crabs and sponges to an assortment of fish. The whole area shows a wide range of seashore habitats.

A few miles on from Pool Roag is Dunvegan. This is famous for its castle and grounds – interesting, but a little formal. Inland, it is surrounded by some of the finest woodland on Skye. Low-growing trees are covered in epiphytic mosses and lichens. The ground flora grows amid rocks and boulders. A walk through here is recommended. The main road terminates at the far end of the woodland, where it deteriorates into a narrow lane. The rocky islets just offshore are favourite basking places for Grey Seals. The road crosses Loch Suardal, which is quite good for spotting the occasional migratory wildfowl. It leads on to Claighan, where the beach is covered with a substance known as "coral". In reality, it is the hard, red, lime-based seaweed, *Lithothamnion*.

Portree and the Trotternish Peninsula:

Portree is the administrative centre of Skye. It has a good selection of shops and hotels. Loch Portree lies to the south. It is well silted, and provides another chance to see ecad seaweeds, among the vast lugworm "hills". There are several garages here and on the road to Uig. There is also a tourist information centre. Going into the town from the south, there is a car park near the shore. A portacabin houses a fish and chip bar here. Their fried haggis will put hairs on your chest.

Trotternish is a long peninsula to the north of Portree. Around its periphery runs a main road which has been improved considerably in recent years. Progressing anti-clockwise, the road climbs steeply out of Portree. As the route begins to flatten, it is worth stopping to take in the view. The Storr stands straight ahead, and there are two lochs on the right. The first of these is Loch Fada which is connected to the larger one, Loch Leathan. Both are good places to see Red-throated Divers. At the far end of the lochs is a hydroelectricity generating station, which supplies the Isle of Skye. A road to the right gives access to a difficult path which leads down to the stony shore of Bearreraig Bay.

Loch Fada, with Red-throated Divers, and Storr in the background.

Along the main road there are several places to park and take various routes up the slope to the Old Man of Storr. The walk takes about an hour and on a clear day the panorama is stupendous. The Old Man of Storr is a pinnacle of rock. It is 50m in height, and is surrounded by many smaller examples. The rock here lies on top of clay. As it has collapsed, an uneven landscape of boulders and rock needles has been formed. A variety of unusual arctic-alpine plants can be found in the sheltered areas. Sightings of the Iceland Purselane have been reported here, as well as in The Quirang, in the north of Trotternish. Climbing the 719m of The Storr requires both experience and equipment. It can be tackled further south than this ridge, but the easiest route is to walk the 7km from Rhenetra, on the other side of Trotternish.

Eight kilometres further along the road, there is a turning to the left, leading to Lealt. Just before this, the road makes a sharp turn up a hill (with parking to the right), as it crosses the River Lealt. Below the road, the river plunges down the cliff in a cascading waterfall. Beyond the hamlet of Lealt the track deteriorates. It follows the line of a dismantled railway track that once connected with the road. The track stops beneath the cliffs of Cuithir. This was once a thriving mining area – hence the railway. Cuithir is a huge amphitheatre of cliffs. In the basin below, a partially raised bog has developed because of the high humidity. Several artificial lochs are nearby. Their rich invertebrate population supports many (disappointingly small) trout. On a clear day, there are delightful views – northwards along the huge rocky ridge, and over the sea to the Torridon Mountains, on the mainland. The area around Cuithir is wild and remote with grouse, wheatears and a range of different raptors.

The main road passes the edge of the cliff where the water from Loch Mealt cascades into the sea. This is a well known tourist spot and the parking area is extensive. The waterfall tumbles down a cliff of columnar basalt. The shape of the columns has given it the name of Kilt Rock.

A mile on from the settlement of Staffin, a tiny road descends steeply to the right. This crosses the river and follows the base of a cliff.

At Brogaig, a few kilometres further on from Staffin, a minor road cuts across the wild moorland interior to Uig. (The main road continues along the coast.) The road climbs steeply as it traverses the rocky ridge. There are several parking places from where to admire the views, especially over to The Quirang in the north. The naturalist will find much to explore. In a similar way to The Storr, hard volcanic rocks on top of clays have slumped to produce a series of pinnacles and outcrops, with names like "The Needle" and "The Prison". The geologist and botanist will both be kept happy here – rock crystals and rare alpine plants abound.

The road to Uig passes through peatbogs of Sphagnum and insectivorous plants. The view is impressive as it descends into the fishing harbour of Uig. Caledonian MacBrayne ferries cross the Minch to the Outer Hebrides from here. Beyond the bay you can see the Ascrib Islands. Local inquiries about a fishing boat should be made well in advance if you hope to visit these islands. It is the main seabird breeding area in Skye, and supports most species of auk, including the Puffin.

The north of Trotternish is a good place to see Golden Eagles. At Duntulm there are the remains of a fifteenth-century castle. The nearby footpath provides an excellent view of Tulm Island, with the Outer Hebrides beyond. The island is long and narrow with steep sides where seabirds nest. The sand below has a greenish tinge, because of the presence of olivine – a mineral which combines silicate of magnesia with protoxide of iron. A few kilometres on towards Uig, near Kilmuir, is the Skye Cottage Museum. A number of restored black houses depict early life on the island. This area is steeped in history – from stone-chambered cairns to monuments for Flora Macdonald. It is all set in a wild coastal setting.

The Outer Hebrides

This chain of islands extends for well over 150km, from the island of Mingulay in the south to the Butt of Lewis in the north. We will concentrate on the southern and central islands, which each have a distinct character and a diversity of habitats. You can catch the ferry from Oban, just north of Islay, and cross to Barra. This is the southernmost island that can be reached from the mainland. From there you can travel by ferry to South Uist. This island has high mountains in the east and superb machair dunes to the west. It is possible to drive the length of South Uist and over a road bridge to the islands of Benbecula and North Uist. The latter is fairly mountainous but has more lochs and freshwater than land. From here a ferry crosses back to the Inner Hebrides and docks at Uig, on Skye. It is then easy to reach the mainland and travel back towards Glasgow via Fort William and the Grampians. The boat from Oban leaves at about midnight and arrives at Castlebay on Barra at 0930 on the following morning.

Barra

Getting there:

The ferry service to Barra leaves from Oban. As discussed earlier, the A816 from Lochgilphead passes some spectacular scenery. The route from Glasgow starts in a similar way, winding around the western shores of Loch Lomond on the A82. Instead of turning off at Tarbet you should continue on this road to Crianlarich and then left to Clifton. The routes are well signposted and the main road has been extensively improved in recent years. From the other side of Clifton, the A85 goes west through Glen Lochy on the way to Oban.

It is worth allowing time to make a diversion here in order to visit the wilderness of Rannoch Moor. The Grampians provide spectacular mountain surroundings to the whole area. The A82, which turns off just before entering Glen Lochy, crosses this desolate region. Forty kilometres further on is the infamous Glen Coe. However, well before then, the road crosses the edge of Rannoch Moor. You will be able to see Red Deer and Golden Eagles, as well as a number of rare flowers and grasses. If you decide to visit the region, then bear in mind that snow flurries are not uncommon, even at Easter.

An alternative to this route is to fly by Loganair in a Trilander plane from Paisley Airport, near Glasgow. On a clear day this can be exhilarating. The one and a half hour flight crosses the Clyde, the Isle of Mull, Staffa, Coll and Tiree. The plane lands on a sandy beach in the Sound of Orasay.

Where to stay:

A number of cottages are available for rent by self-caterers. Full details can be obtained from the Scottish Tourist Board or from the tourist board in Castlebay. The latter is open from May until October. They will also be able to provide details of Bed and Breakfast accommodation. There are several hotels and guest houses on the island. These include the Isle of Barra Hotel at Tangusdale, and the Castlebay Hotel.

You will be able to camp on the west coast in places where the machair has developed. On the opposite side of the road from the airfield, there is a large area suitable for camping. Another can be found at Borve – about 3km from Castlebay. If you are considering a stay on any other islands in the region, such as Vatersay, then a tent is vital as no other accommodation is available.

Castlebay and the south islands:

On an island in the middle of Castlebay stands the twelfth-century Kisimul Castle – the stronghold of the MacNeils. A rowing boat crosses regularly with visitors from the town. The port was once the centre of a thriving herring fishing fleet, but this has sadly now declined. The town's main street runs up towards the Catholic church. This is in contrast with the northern Hebridean islands, which are Protestant.

In the summer months, boats regularly depart from the pier to take travellers and naturalists to the islands south of Barra. For information, you can consult the tourist office near the petrol pumps at the top of the main street.

Vatersay is the nearest island and lies just across the bay. A few people live there but the village is in decline. As the boat lands, it is worth keeping an eye open for swimming animals. The water is so clear, and the sand so white, that visibility is amazing when the sun is out. The island is really two islands that are joined by a stretch of machair dune in the centre. Harebells tend to dominate the machair. The deserted beach is beautiful here with its backdrop of dune. A lack of disturbance means that nesting birds such as the Skylark are easily spotted. The desolate appearance of the island is enhanced by the wreckage of a Second World War fighter plane that crashed near the schoolhouse. From the boat it should be easy to spot Black Guillemots in the bay. Eider Ducks are also fairly abundant.

Mingulay is the island most worth visiting. The boat trip passes close to the other islands, all of which look like mountain peaks. The first that you will pass is Sandray. White sand is blown off the beaches by the wind to cover the lower slopes of the hillside on the eastern edge. Pabbay is smaller, although it has a large cove. There are signs of habitation which include the remains of an old fort and carved stones.

Mingulay lies another 2km to the south-west. The bay on the eastern side of the island possesses a small dune system and the remains of a village deserted in 1934. On the west coast the towering cliffs echo to the noise of seabirds. This is the reason that most people visit the island. Kittiwakes, three species of gull, Fulmar, Guillemots, Razorbills and Puffins can all be seen. At night, you will also find shearwaters and petrels. The flying insects here can be unique where they have developed in isolation. For example, butterflies tend to be much larger than on the mainland. Dun Mingulay is a fort on the west coast, from where you can see natural arches and stacks carved out of the cliffs by centuries of erosion.

Coastal Habitats in the west and north:

Leaving Castlebay and travelling in a clockwise direction around the island takes you to the exposed west within a few kilometres. Just before you reach Tangasdale there are several shallow lakes. Both contain reed beds of Phragmites and are good nest sites for wildfowl. The invertebrates are fairly rich with damsel and dragonflies, snails and sticklebacks. The water is less acidic than most on the island as it is near the machair at Tangasdale.

From this sandy cove a flat headland juts into the sea to the north. This is Borve Point. There is a track off to the left of the main road, just beyond the right-hand turning to the village of Borve. This will take you along the headland. Again there is a

Greian Head, with the dunes of Allandale in the foreground.

great deal of machair vegetation present. The edge nearest the sea is dominated by Sea Pink. Further inland it is Silverweed and then the rich yellow of the Lady's Bedstraw. Tread carefully along the fringe bordering the rocky shore, as a variety of birds nest here. Oystercatchers and Arctic and Common Terns make their nests amongst the pinks, from a collection of dried seaweeds and grasses. If there are young about they will leave the nest when they hatch. Their colours blend in well with the lichens. As you walk across the rocks the proximity of chicks will be indicated by mobbing adults, which scream as they dive-bomb the intruders. The wave-torn rocks are home for some interesting seaweeds. For example, you can find the stunted bladderless bladderwrack (*Fucus vesiculosus var. linearis*).

Another excellent site is at Allasdale – about 3km on from Borve. The machair is very well developed here and the strong wind carries it up the side of the hills. Ladies' Bedstraw is also abundant as it is a calcicole (calcium-tolerant plant). The shell sand produces a soil which is strongly alkaline. The site is similar to Borve – Terns and Oystercatchers nest here and the seaweeds are present. Grey Seals are very common offshore, with their heads bobbing up and down. They are very inquisitive and are said to be attracted by whistling!

Greian Head protects and helps guide sand on to the beach at Allasdale. Almost a mile inland along the A888, a minor road to the left goes to the settlement of Grean. Turn left again within a hundred metres and you will be taken back towards the headland, along a deteriorating track. Greian Head is interesting botanically and also for birdwatchers. Rose Root, Vernal Squill, Pearlwort and Dark Green Mouse-ear Chickweed can all be found among the typical cliff plant communities.

As the road bears to the right at Allasdale to go inland, there is a ruined prehistoric tower on the right called Dun Cuier.

The main road continues inland and then descends towards a reservoir, Loch an Duin. The protected valley produces an excellent site for insects amidst a bog of Marsh Orchids, Bog Asphodel, Pennywort and insectivorous Sundews. Damselflies and the Black-Legged Sympetrum can be seen flying over the water. The latter is a yellow bodied darter dragonfly with a wide distribution in the Hebrides but which is found less frequently on the mainland. This is also a good spot for the green-eyed, yellow bodied horseflies, *Chrysops*. Perhaps the most fascinating species here is the Dark Green Fritillary butterfly. Although this is found in many parts of Britain, the wingspan is much greater on the Barra specimens. In some cases this may be by as much as 25 per cent. The great abundance of plants on Barra (400 species) makes it especially good for butterflies.

The main road descends to join up with the minor road from the airfield. The sheltered area here is Northbay. Above the little hamlet, a plantation of trees is composed of Sycamore, Hazel, Alder, Scots Pine and Spruce.

An excellent piece of coast for studying seashore life is on the Ardmor peninsula. Follow the minor road towards Eoligarry. Within half a mile, there is a right-hand turning to Northbay pier. Ignore this and take the second right to the settlement of Ardmor. Park at the end of the road and continue for a few hundred metres. At high tide a pool of water collects. As the tide recedes, it empties through a narrow gap between the rocks. The shore along this northern strip is protected from the Atlantic gales. The large expanse of rock encourages the attachment of seaweeds.

The pool basin is filled with sand and mud. It is home for some very large lugworms. Around the edge, Knotted Wrack, with its huge fronds, is the dominant seaweed. The exit point for the water is the most interesting area as a set of tidal rapids form here. This phenomenon is a common feature in the Hebrides. Sea-lochs fill and empty through a narrow gap. This produces very different features from other types of habitat. The rapids here are short. They grade from sand where the flow is slight, to rock at the fastest point. In the gravel areas, the tubes of the Sand Mason and Peacock Fan worms are often seen. The rapids have a large number of encrusting forms fixed to the rock. Great growths of Bread Crumb Sponge, Purse Sponges, Dahlia Sea Anemones and red seasquirts (such as *Dendrodoa*) attach to the boulders. In addition to the usual crabs and crustaceans, the delicate Little Cuttlefish, Pipefish and 15-Spined Sticklebacks swim in the basin. Other fish that can easily be seen are Sand Eels, Scorpion Fish, Wrasse, Gobies, Blennies and even Gurnards. One of the most abundant species along all these shores is the bright yellow sea slug called the Sea Lemon.

However, there is another sea-loch on Barra that has perhaps the most spectacular tidal rapids that you are likely to see. You should return to Northbay Inn and continue along the main road towards Castlebay. After a mile the road curves around the upper reaches of Loch Obe. Carry on up the hill and stop near the telephone box. Walk down the slope and the short distance up the other side. The rapids should be just below. At full speed the noise can be deafening. Loch Obe is a fairly large body of water and it empties through a very narrow ravine, which is about half a mile in length. The difference in height from one end to the other is about 5m and the sides are steep. If you arrive as the tide is going out, the kelp in the middle can be seen to bend over with the flow. At low water the flow slowly stops. The channel never completely empties and lies still for approximately 30 minutes. The flow then reverses, the kelp flips back and the water pours back into the loch. On a clear day the shelter and atmosphere are superb, as insects buzz through the scrub vegetation. The shallower parts of the rapids abound in hydroids – four species of sponge and seasquirts such as *Dendrodoa* and *Clavellina*. The Purple Starfish, *Henricia*, can be found among the kelp. Progressing towards the sea, the communities undergo changes that are typical of exposed sites – barnacles and Thongweed are prevalent. Moving inland, the high degree of shelter means that the lower shore species disappear under the silt and mud that is deposited.

Eoligarry lies to the extreme north of Barra. This was once an island, but it is now joined to Barra by sand dunes and the Great

Cockle Strand (where the Loganair planes land). On the edge of the hill, there is a tiny cemetary which looks out to the north-east. It is near the site where island chieftains were traditionally buried. The grave of the author Compton MacKenzie can be found here. From the point of view of the naturalist, this is one of the best areas on the island for small mammals. Possible finds include the Hebridean subspecies of Field Mouse, House Mouse and Pygmy Shrew.

The dunes and the well-developed machair are impressive here. Sea Rocket and Orache grow on the beach. Beyond the growing dunes of Marram Grass you can spot Sand Sedge, Ladies' Bedstraw, Trefoil and Thyme. In spring, a yellow carpet of primroses covers the hills of Eoligarry.

A passenger ferry crosses to South Uist from Eoligarry Pier.

The road that passes through Eoligarry touches the west coast at Clach Bay. This small, rocky bay lies below Dun Scurrival, which is the remains of a lookout tower built by the Picts. It provides a superb view along the west coast of Barra. Further on, the rocks of Scurrival Point show the greatest degree of exposure to wave action. Consequently, the lower shore is dominated by Thongweed and Dabberlocks.

The moorland interior:

Much of Barra's interior consists of barren moorland, populated by grouse which feed on the young heathers and moor grasses. A good overall view of the island is the reward for the 383m climb up Heavel – Barra's highest point. The climb is not a difficult one. It is best approached from the bend in the main road, 3km east of Castlebay. There is no specific northward path through the Ling and Bell Heather. En route, keep your eyes open for Hairy Stonecrop. A statue of the Virgin Mary with child stands on Heavel and faces Castlebay. The view stretches as far as Mingulay in the south and the mountains of Uist to the north.

The Magpie Moth is a day-flying species. On the mainland it would feed on blackcurrant bushes, but here it has adapted to feed on heathers. The moth is predominantly white, with black and yellow spots. It is common over much of the island, but is particularly abundant in this area.

There is an excellent walk from the west to east coast. The 7km crossing starts at Craigston, near Borve, climbs the ridge between Grianan and Hartaval mountain and descends to the east by following the stream, Allt Heiker. The stream enters the sea by the main road near to Harbour Cottage.

Several small, acid lochs lie half a mile's walk northwards along the main road. The first, Ruleos, has a number of species of dragonfly but few visible plants, with the exception of the Water Lobelia. This rare plant is a northern species and is fairly widespread in the Hebrides. A single stalk grows out of the water, with pale lilac flowers. The area around the edge of the loch is quite boggy, and thus it supports the Bog Pimpernel with its pink flowers and creeping runners. Also present are the Bear Berry and Creeping Willow, many of which are galled. In addition, sundews and butterworts are common in the wetter parts. You may also find a freshwater sponge under some of the stones in the water. The area provides shelter for a range of butterflies and other insects. These include the rusty brown bumble bee, *Bombus smithianus*. This is found on many of Britain's offshore islands, and is the bee most often seen on Barra.

South Uist

Getting there:

A passenger ferry service leaves from Eoligarry. However, the usual route is the Caledonian MacBrayne sailing from Castlebay. It departs soon after arriving from Oban and then takes several hours to reach Lochboisdale, on South Uist.

The nearest flight is to Benbecula, to the north of South Uist.

Where to stay:

There are two hotels in Lochboisdale. The tourist information office in the village will give details of self-catering and Bed and Breakfast accommodation in the Uists.

Camping is relatively easy on the extensive machair which runs along the length of the west coast. On the other side of a bog area, the east is mountainous and remote. The closest machair area to Lochboisdale is near Kilpheder, approximately 8km away. Follow the main road to Daliburgh. The B888 goes south and the main road north. A minor road continues west. Where this road reaches the machair, after about a mile, take the track to the left. The dunes between here and the sea are an excellent place to visit as well as to camp in.

There is only one main road on South Uist. This covers the 35km from Lochboisdale to Benbecula. It stays on the west to follow the flatter coastal land.

Lochboisdale Area:

The MacBrayne Ferry docks at the tip of a rocky peninsula which is dotted with crofting communities. There are few settlements in the Uists as all fertile land is cultivated and cottages are spread out on rocky outcrops. Lochboisdale boasts one of the few supermarkets and banks of the Hebrides. However, mobile versions of both are a common sight along the north–south road. The Lochboisdale Hotel is the centre of the sporting fraternity. Hunting and fishing trips are organised from here. It is also the place for a good meal. There are sheltered conditions afforded by the loch, and extensive rocky inlets and small islands. These combine to make the shore here one of the richest areas in South Uist for marine life. Calvey is an island at the entrance to Lochboisdale, on which stands a thirteenth- century castle where Bonnie Prince Charlie once lived.

The dunes to the west of Daliburgh have some of the best machair in Scotland, dominated by calcium-loving plants. On a

Typical western coast of South Uist, with crofts between mountain and machair dunes.

warm summer's day it is alive with butterflies, skylarks, pipits and rabbits. The beach is one of pure white sand made from wave-crushed shells. Near the dunes where camping was recommended there are the remains of a second-century wheelhouse. This is worth a visit. Crofts are dotted along the minor road which runs southwards and parallel to the machair. There are several lakes with rich invertebrate fauna. The road passes through North Boisdale and a short deviation onto the machair takes you around a circular track. The map and local signs will indicate the presence of an alginate factory. Until 1980 it was a common sight to see seaweed spread out in large pens to dry. Algin could then be extracted from this. This is used to create the smoothing agent in lipstick, ice cream and non-stick paints. Sadly, the industry here has failed. There is another factory in the north. Hence, it is still possible to see lorries loaded with seaweed travelling the roads of the outer isles.

The sandy beach here is dominated by the Scentless Mayweed. In 1977 a male Sperm Whale of some 19m in length, was washed up on the beach in front of the factory. The smell was pungent for quite some time! Years later, bones could still be found spread along the strand-line. The huge skull is now partly buried by the windblown sand.

At the southern tip of South Uist the B888 stops at Pollachar. There is a traditional pub here, which (on a clear day) affords a good view across to Barra. A minor road winds its way along the south coast. It passes Ludag Jetty where the passenger ferry lands from Eriskay and Barra, and ends at South Glendale.

Northwards:

Nine kilometres on from Lochboisdale, there is a left turn to Milton. A number of turnings all along the road take you across the wet machair to the drier dunes beyond. The damp areas are dominated by small lochs which teem with dragonflies and wildfowl. Some of the larger lochs are now used for fish-farming. This is common practice in these isles – especially in Skye.

Six kilometres further on, a left turn brings you to the area of Bornish. Like many other sites along this coast there appears to be more water than land. Carry straight on and the minor road deteriorates into a track. This crosses machair which has joined up with a rocky outcrop at Rubha Ardvule. This exposed rocky shore projects beyond the normal coastline to produce the only real break in a 32km stretch of white sand. There are the remains of an ancient fort here and a small loch which has been affected by the salt spray. It is a good site for wildfowl.

Loch Eynort is a sea-loch which virtually cuts South Uist into two halves. In some of the shallower areas of the seashore, there are preserved trees and roots. These are remnants of a forest which once dominated Uist until the water-level rose and covered it. One of the few right-hand turnings off the main road leads down to the loch. After about a mile, turn left over the "bridge". After a further mile, the road stops on the northern shore of the loch, near Arinambane. To the north is the mountain region of Beinn Mhor (620m) and Hecla (606m). The latter is the less accessible, and would be better climbed from Lochskipport.

This massive region of diamond hard, Lewisian gneiss is highly recommended as a place for exploration. There are few paths and the flatter areas are bogs. A good map is essential as picking your route around bogs and over rocky crags soon disorientates the walker. Cloud cover can descend very quickly on the mountain. The southern slopes of Beinn Mhor are criss-crossed with streams, one of which is Allt Volagir. It is about an hour's hard walking from Arinambane. Once the stream has been located it can be followed to the top of Spin (356m) or up to the top of Beinn Mhor.

Allt Volagir is a delightful place. It has a protected valley, incised into the mountainside. It supports species that are more typical of a woodland: hazel, rowan, aspen, dwarf willow and sallows. Below these trees grow Crowberry, Bearberry, Wood Sage, Herb Robert, Golden Rod, Foxgloves, Royal Fern and Hard Fern. On the drier and more exposed rocks, above the stream, are Dwarf Junipers lying prostrate across the ground. All of these plants are the remains of a forest which once clothed the Outer Hebrides. In springtime the bluebells make a fine show.

The summits of these peaks present some spectacular vistas. On a clear day, the view extends from the Inner Hebrides, to Barra and the isles beyond, and to St. Kilda and the Monachs to the west. You can also easily appreciate the extent of the machair and freshwater lochs. The flanks of these mountains are the haven for a diverse alpine flora: Alpine Sawwort, Viviparous Knotgrass, Alpine Rue, Cushion Pink, Alpine Willow Herb, Mountain Sorrel, and Mossy, Starry and Purple Saxifrages. Even the rare Yellow Saxifrage is here. In addition, Filmy Fern grows in the wetter areas with a variety of Spleenworts, Paisley Fern,

Beech Fern, Brittle Bladder Fern and the Scented Buckler Fern. Several large dragonflies hawk up and down the streams.

Returning, you meet the main road at a crossroads. Continuing straight on brings you to Ormiclate, which only consists of a few crofts. Turn left at the T-junction and at the next junction you will see the ruins of Ormiclate Castle standing in a farmyard. This was built in 1710, only to burn down in 1715. A track leads northwards from here, across the machair. However, it may be more convenient – especially for the farmer – if you turn round and follow the road to Stoneybridge, where you should then turn left. The road passes close to the sea and a track to the left goes even closer.

There are some rocky outcrops lying offshore, which are linked at low water. At high tide, only a few blobs are visible. Nonetheless, Oystercatchers and Arctic Terns do occasionally breed here. It is also often possible to see large groups of Eider Ducks, which favour the area. The rocks support a good seashore fauna. Across the sandy ridge, there is an impressive zonation of plants from Oraches, Saltwort and Mayweed to Ladies' Bedstraw, Fescue and Silverweed. Twenty metres further on, the diversity increases, to yield Wild Carrot, Yellow Rattle, Eyebright, Red Bartsia, Bistort and the occasional orchid.

The track/road continues to Howmore. The church here has an interesting interior with a very unusual Communion altar. There are also several pre-Reformation chapels, with some interesting artefacts.

Along the main road, especially between here and Loch Druidibeg, keep an eye out for Short-eared Owls. These are common in the Uists and can be seen hunting by day. They have a gentle zig-zag flight about 4m above the ground. By looking under the telegraph poles in the area, you may be able to find their regurgitated pellets. They feed on the small mammals which can be found nearby, namely Bank and Field Voles, Pygmy Shrews and Field Mice. These are distinct subspecies, as we have already pointed out in the Barra section. The smaller bird species also have distinct forms where they have become isolated from the genetic stock of the mainland. These include the Song Thrush, Stonechat, Hedge Sparrow, Rock Pipit and the Wren.

The island species of bumble bee (*Bombus smithianus*) is found here and so is a unique species, *Bombus jonellus*. Stilligarry and Grogarry are good areas in which to look for all these species. The

Short-eared Owl, often seen flying over moorland in the day.

former is the home of the warden of Loch Druidibeg Nature Reserve. Across the road is the extensive freshwater Loch Stilligarry. The site is well known for its wildfowl – especially the Greylag Geese and herons which nest here. It is also a good place to spot Red-throated Divers and migrant White-fronted Geese.

Following the northern edge of Loch Druidibeg is the B890. This can give good views of the loch and also goes down to the very sheltered sea-loch at Lochskipport. En route, many delightfully sheltered valleys and gorges are passed. Rhododendron has developed here but has not had a great impact on the natural vegetation. The gorges bear some resemblance to Allt Volagir (as discussed above) especially in terms of the prolific growths of Royal Fern. This loch also almost slices Uist into two. At its highest point a flood gate prevents seawater entering an extensive network of freshwater lochs. This includes the vast Loch Bee which exits on the north of the island. The only trace of humanity at Lochskipport is a derelict pier, built for Victorian steamers but never really developed.

The main road north crosses a causeway over Loch Bee. The loch is famous for its Mute Swans, which breed on the hundreds of tiny islands here. Occasionally, Whooper Swans can be seen feeding on the loch.

This area is famous for several other reasons. The "Danger" signs in red, both on land and on the Ordnance Survey maps, indicate a military presence. This is the centre of the army's guided missile range. Secondly, there is the Hebridean Jewellery Workshop. This lies at the end of the minor road which passes through Eochar – the left turning after Loch Bee. Visitors can watch the craftsmen at work. A right turning after Loch Bee leads down to Loch Carnan. This almost empties at low tide to leave large pools and small tidal rapids. The variety of seashore life is quite remarkable, but over the water on the southern shore of Benbecula the best is yet to come.

Benbecula

Getting there and where to stay:

Benbecula is connected by causeways to both North and South Uist. Until a short while ago, the only way to get there was to ford the dangerous quicksands at low tide. The island has an airport in the north-east, at Balivanich. This has been developed for military purposes. Finding accommodation is not as easy as on the other islands. However, it is quite practical to stay on North or South Uist and simply visit Benbecula. Details of accommodation can be obtained at the tourist offices in Lochboisdale (South Uist) or Lochmaddy (North Uist). The Creagorry Hotel is on the main road, quite close to the crossing from the south. The island is very flat and almost completely waterlogged. Consequently, camping is limited to a few areas near the west coast where there are sand dunes. For example, Borve is a suitable site in the south-western corner.

The island:

Just beyond Creagorry, the B892 branches off the main road to the left. It circles round to Balivanich, closely following the coastal strip. A short distance past the junction near Creagorry, the B891 leaves the main road on the right. The road is 7km in length and has a dead end. Nonetheless, it is one of the best spots for the naturalist to visit.

In common with the other outer isles, the land of Benbecula is covered with freshwater lochs. However, they are largely eutrophic. This means that they are shallow and contain a high concentration of nutrients. They tend to be dominated by Bog Bean and White Water Lily. Half a mile down the B891 from the junction with the main road, there is a small loch to the left. At one end, the growth of vegetation across the water has been so prolific that the plant matter will support human weight – quaking as you walk across it. This is another example of a hydrosere (see Islay, page 31). Probing the surface shows that the vegetation is less than a metre thick. This type of environment is fairly typical of the small shallow lochs in Benbecula. Amongst the Bog Bean around the edge of the loch, you will be able to find Marestail, Horsetails and the red flowered Marsh Cinquefoil.

The rest of the B891 uses a succession of islands like stepping stones as it follows the edge of Loch Kilerivagh. The region is an archipelago of tiny islands. At low tide the sheltered rocks are a haven for seashore communities. Seals are a very common sight, while terns and Eider Ducks can also be seen feeding here.

A short trip across the water to Wiay brings you to a bird sanctuary with raptors, wildfowl and seabirds. The most impressive feature for the seashore naturalist is the gentle tidal movement that occurs between Loch Kilerivagh and the sea. This sea-loch does not completely empty at low tide. The rocks on the edge are covered by communities typical of sheltered seashores. However, it is at the low-water level that the incredible variety of life is most apparent. The floor of the channel is covered with a loose, red, coral-like seaweed – on occasions to a depth of 30cm. Most of the animals are encrusting species. The fauna includes hydroids, Horse Mussels, Saddle Oysters, anemones and four species of sponge. These provide food for a large number of molluscs, including cowries and several types of sea slug. Sea urchins, Purple Starfish and large brittle-stars are also present. Feather stars (a crinoid) can be found amongst the brown fronds of the Sea Oak (*Halidrys siliquosa*). These are filter feeders, which can obtain adequate material where seaweed grows in the flowing waters of the channel. Swimming amongst the seaweeds at low tide are 15-spined Sticklebacks, the colourful Lumpsuckers, Scorpion Fish and Cornish Suckers.

The B892 provides good views of the aerodrome at Balivanich. The aircraft are not particularly interesting, but Short Eared Owls are fairly common there.

North Uist

Getting there and where to stay:

The long causeway fords the mud and sand from Benbecula to North Uist. It touches the western tip of the island of Grimsay, where there is a Harris Tweed weavery open to the public.

On the sheltered eastern side of North Uist is Lochmaddy, the main settlement on the island. It is here that the boat docks after its two-hour journey from Uig on Skye. The ferry continues to the isle of Harris in the north. The Lochmaddy Hotel is devoted to the angler and hillwalker. Fishing permits can be obtained there. There is a tourist information centre located near the quay, from where details of self-catering and guest house accommodation can be obtained from May to September.

There are no official camping sites on North Uist, but the dunes and machair in the north and west of the island are ideal for rough camping. Baleshare is a beautiful island of machair, but it provides little shelter against a westerly gale. Opposite the church at Balranald, a minor road takes you across the dunes. After a mile this deteriorates into a number of tracks. This area contains a nature reserve, and hence camping should be restricted to the dunes in the south. Machair Leathann lies to the north of Grenicote. There is less grazing here, but this means that the ground is somewhat rougher for camping. In addition, the flies can be a problem.

Around the island:

As with Benbecula, the island is dotted by hundreds of lochs while its coast has a succession of tiny islets. The shelter that these provide has yielded vast expanses of sandy shore. In the east there is an indented coastline of sheltered rocky shores and sea-lochs. One of these – Loch Eport – virtually cuts North Uist into two halves. The land is relatively flat and boggy, but in a few parts rises to over 200m.

The highest point is Eaval in the extreme south-east. You can see this massive bulk of Lewisian gneiss as you cross the northern ford on the causeway from Benbecula. The road to the right will only take you a short way towards it. To reach Eaval, you will need a good map because there are numerous sea-lochs and only narrow gaps between the freshwater ones. It requires a good day's walking to navigate the bogs and climb the 347m. However, there are superb views and the craggy southern slopes are excellent for alpine plants.

There are many sites of historical interest on North Uist. One of the most famous is at Carinish. Take the first turning on the left, after the causeway. The ruins here are an ancient seat of learning. Chieftains were educated here, but it was largely destroyed during the Reformation. The nearby pub is also well worth investigation!

A few kilometres further on, there is another left-turn from the main road. This takes you to Baleshare Island. Beyond the bridge, the road bears to the left before crossing the machair. A left turning at the next cross-roads will bring you onto a huge sandy beach which stretches as far as Benbecula. This is a beautiful place, with numerous birds nesting on the short machair turf. Ringed Plovers and terns are especially common. Arctic Skuas can often be seen harassing the terns for food. You should also have no difficulty seeing Eider Duck, Sanderling, Curlew and Oystercatchers. The outcrop of rock in the middle of the beach merits exploration. Most of these rocks are small boulders. They provide effective shelter for small animals. Large periwinkles move across the sand, leaving trails behind them. Huge sponges and seasquirts encrust under the boulders. The Purse Sponge can be seen attached to the rocks among the Dahlia Sea Anemones – some growing over 8cm in diameter. These are fed upon by the Sea Lemon – a large, yellow sea slug. One of the largest possible finds is the Lesser Octopus. This is typical of the animals which take refuge here. There is also a wealth of fish, crabs, starfish and brittle-stars.

Once more travelling on the main road, within a few hundred metres there is a track on the left to Carnach. Take the right-hand road at the fork. Walking onto the sand at low tide, it is possible to follow the course of a freshwater stream at Claddach Cumhang. It flows from the sea and through a series of lochs. The progressively declining salinity produces a number of interesting marine habitats, with corresponding changes in species. The water flowing over the sand contains vast numbers of Oppossum Shrimps which are eaten by the Plaice and Flounder. Fifteen- and 3-spined Sticklebacks are common. Even Lump-suckers and Scorpion Fish can be found. Moving inland the stream can be seen flowing into Oban Irpeig. The exit is through a narrow tidal rapid where large mussels, sponges and sea squirts grow. With the drop in salinity, many organisms disappear. The few which remain include the 3-spined Stickleback and another species of Opposum Shrimp. The transition into the next loch, Loch Leodasay, is marked by the large brown seaweed called Horn Wrack. All the species here are those able to tolerate the diluted seawater. Typical of these is a small snail, *Hydrobia*. There are also caddis fly larvae which are more typical of freshwater. Within the loch is a fairly rich freshwater community with dragonflies and water beetles.

Returning to the main road and turning left brings you to a junction with the circular road around North Uist. At the junction is Clachan Stores, one of the few "supermarkets" on the island. There is also a mobile fish shop which regularly stops here, selling locally caught fish. Behind the stores is a 40m incline. From its top, there is a good view over the flat land, along the B894 to Loch Eport. This road is dotted with thatched cottages and crofts. The yellow lichen, *Xanthoria*, is common on the rocks above the high-water mark. For centuries it has been used by the local weavers for dying cloth into a reddy brown colour.

The seashores along the edge of Loch Eport are fairly steep but the calm waters are good for birds. A number of tidal rapids empty the contents of brackish sea-lochs into the loch. An excellent one can be found just beyond the end of the road. This is the water flowing from Loch Obisary, a substantial loch that dominates the waters around Eaval. The rapids can be reached from the road.

The road to Lochmaddy crosses a desolate plain of peatbogs and freshwater lochs. In these lochs nest Red-throated Divers which can usually be seen from the road. Black-throated Divers are present, but are less common. Much of the water to the north of the road is linked to one vast body, Loch Scadavay. This is believed to have more than 80km of shoreline. Some of the backwaters are rich in divers, swans and skuas. These nest here because of the solitude. In the shallow waters grow water lilies, Milkwort and Water Lobelia. Insectivorous plants, such as the butterwort and Greater Sundew, grow on the peat.

Ben Langass is the highest point in the area – at only 90m. There is an impressive view from the top. Near the road, it has a Neolithic chambered cairn on its slopes. Despite appearing to be little more than a pile of stones, this cairn is in good repair. An opening takes you into a chamber of flattened rocks. The relatively dry heathland soil of the southern slopes is good for nesting birds. Among these, the Twite makes its home amongst the Ling heather. The track at the side of the hill leads to a guest house with good bar food.

To the east of the flat peat-lands are the two peaks of North and South Lee. At 250m and 281m respectively, they are well worth the climb. Waiting for a clear day is the most difficult problem. As well as offering incredible views, the slopes are grazed by Red Deer and support a range of arctic-alpine plants. Golden Eagles can often be seen hunting over the Lees. Lochmaddy is a village on a small peninsula. For the naturalist its most important features are the sea-lochs to the north and south. Although small, they possess some of the best examples of tidal rapids in the Hebrides. At Stromban, just before the main road bears to the right, a path crosses the short distance to Leiravay Bay. With its long narrow exit, this is reminiscent of Loch Obe on Barra. The most dramatic tidal rapid is at Sponish, where there is an alginate works. In the centre of Lochmaddy there is a minor road to the left, just past the petrol pumps. At the staggered cross roads, go straight on to the end of the road, approximately 400m. A track continues on to a "suspension" bridge over the Sponish Rapids. This water is flowing from Loch Houram along a wide and twisted channel. From the bridge, looking up the channel, a

The mountains of North and South Lee, from the peat bogs of central North Uist.

small bay can be seen to the left. This is a sheltered area of seaweed-covered boulders, beneath which an incredible diversity of organisms live.

The rapid ebb and flow of so much water through the channel provides a rich supply of oxygen and nutrients. However, most of the organisms have to be able to hang on tightly because of the scouring effect. At Sponish there are Cup Corals, as well as five species of sea anemone. Large numbers of marine molluscs, including scallops, cowries, Saddle Oysters, Keyhole Limpets, Bearded Horse Mussels and sea slugs, are also common. Sea urchins, starfish and brittle-stars abound at low water. Sponish is highly recommended for the naturalist with an interest in seashores.

The shores around Lochmaddy are rich in invertebrate species. As a consequence, birds come in to feed here. After driving northwards from Lochmaddy for about 7km, there is a road to the right. This poor quality route winds for 13km across a large peninsula. More like an island, it produces sheltered shores to the north and south which are the haunts of otters and seals. Some of the best shores are around Cheese Bay near the end of the road.

The junction between this minor road and the main road is a good vantage point for bird-watching. Arctic Skuas are a common sight. They have two phases, the light and dark. The former is the more likely type to be seen in Scotland, but the dark phase can sometimes be seen here. Golden Eagles and buzzards are also often seen.

The B893 to Newtonferry lies a mile further along the A865. The ferry in question takes passengers to Harris, Lewis and Berneray – a delightful machair island lying just offshore. A mile along the B road, you will see a series of flat saltmarsh areas on the left. Like most of the saltmarsh on the Uists it has been grazed by crofters' sheep. This keeps the turf well cropped and allows only the most tolerant species to grow. One of these is the Sea Pink. Their display ensures that the saltmarshes are a beautiful sight in the early summer. Creeks and pans break up the "lawn" appearance. The latter are formed by a concentration of salt, which prevents plant growth.

The two peaks to the east of the road are Beinn Bhreac and Beinn Mhor. These afford superb views across to Lochmaddy, as well as being a home for Golden Eagles. The beginning of the walk crosses boggy ground carpeted with sundews and butterworts. In summer it can be yellow with Bog Asphodel. The

Fulmar with chick, nesting on the sand dunes.

best route is to aim for the gap between the two peaks. Several species of club moss are present on the upper slopes.

Sollas, in the north of the island, is an area of crofts and some cultivation. The cry of the Corncrake, a harsh ratchet sound, can occasionally be heard here (although the best spot is at Balranald). There is a supermarket at Sollas. This area suffered greatly during the Clearances in 1850. Many crofters were being evicted from the land to make way for more profitable sheep farming. Sollas was the scene of one of the bloodiest confrontations as the crofters stood their ground against the landlord and police. Those that died were buried on the machair field behind.

At Grenitote a track goes down to the sheltered strand and along the edge of the Machair Leathan. This is a lovely area of dune and beach. The dunes near Huilish Point are particularly interesting, as Fulmars nest in scrapes amongst the Marram Grass. The machair has been cultivated behind the dunes, and the rare Corn Marigold grows among the pesticide-free barley. Udal lies at the far end of this zone of machair. Archaeological excavations here have revealed a settlement which was inhabited from the Bronze Age through to the Clearances of the mid-nineteenth century. A number of valuable artefacts have been discovered.

To the west of Sollas there is an expanse of sand covered only by spring tides. This is Valley Strand. It must be forded at low tide in order to reach the island of Vallay which protects the bay. This area is one of the most beautiful spots in the Hebrides. The whitewashed walls of the old thatched croft cottages glisten in the sun, against a backdrop of shell sand and islands.

From Vallay, you can follow the A865 around the coast or take a potholed minor road which cuts across the desolate interior. There are good views as this road climbs inland. Near the middle, a plantation of conifers can be seen up on the hillside of Ben Aulasary. Although the road is narrow there are places to park so that you can make the relatively easy walk to the top. Voles and Field Mice live near the plantation. On sunny days large dragonflies hawk over the heath in search of the midges which flourish in the area.

Peat extends as far as the summit. It has been heavily eroded to form a number of pools and steep banks. In the sheltered parts there are colourful bog plants and flowers, which support damselflies and the Large Heath butterfly.

The north–west corner of North Uist has exposed rocky headlands and small sandy bays. The waves crashing at Griminish Point can be a spectacular sight, especially through the 10m high natural arch which has eroded from the cliff. From the coastline here there are good views across to the seal breeding nurseries and seabird colonies of the Heskeir Islands. On a clear day St. Kilda can be seen on the horizon.

The shallow lochs at Scolpaig and Griminish are choked with Bog Bean, Marsh Cinquefoil and Marestails. Nesting swans are common – usually Mute Swans, with the occasional Whooper. The several kilometres of coast between Scolpaig and Raikinish consist of steep cliffs. If you park near Kilphedder, then there is a splendid walk along the cliff-tops from there. You will almost be able to touch the Fulmars, which nest just below the edge. They have dramatically increased in number in recent years. They are present in many parts of Uist, but this is one of the best places in which to see the family groups – parents with a single, large fluffy chick. If you get too close, then they regurgitate their last, oily meal. Beware – their aim is exceedingly accurate!

A mile or so on from Kilphedder is a cross-roads. The right turning is signposted to Tigharry. To the left the track is one of many which ascend the slopes of South Clettraval (133m). There are several standing stones and chambered cairns. As well as impressive views, this area is good for nesting Golden Plovers and Red Grouse.

Corn Marigolds at Balranald, growing on the machair dunes.

Tigharry is a delightful village of crofts extending round to Hougharry. All this area comes within the boundary of the Balranald Nature Reserve, run by the RSPB. The information centre is a small cottage near the cemetary at Goular, and the warden should be consulted before entering the reserve. The cemetary is on a slight rise and is a good place to start looking for birds. Hen Harriers are a common sight, hunting over the marshes. Even the occasional Sea Eagle can be seen. Warm weather is often accompanied by the sound of the Corncrake and Corn Bunting. The shallow water in the marshes is home for a variety of water birds. These include the very rare Red-necked Phalarope, the presence of which is one of the main reasons for the reserve. Tufted and Shovellor Duck are often seen on the lake below the cemetary. Traditional methods of crofting are encouraged on the reserve, in order to help preserve the Corncrake and the Corn Buntings, which are on the decline in other parts of the country. Early in the morning is a good time to watch the movement of seabirds off the reserve headland. Shearwaters and Gannets feature prominently.

The dunes and machair here are excellent. They are well grazed by rabbits in the south, but a diverse range of plants and insects can still be found. Butterflies and beetles are abundant.

There is an interesting transition from the young dune plants, through developed machair to the marsh. The back of the marsh meets Loch Paible, which empties at low tide. Waders tread carefully along the sheltered bank. You may well see an Oystercatcher. When disturbed, they dive into the clear water and swim under the surface for as much as twenty seconds, using their wings as paddles. Waders favour this area because of the abundant food which is buried in the sediment of the loch. Bivalves, huge lugworm and ragworm, shrimps and crustaceans attract a variety of birds. Arctic Terns are often seen hovering over the shallow water and diving for the small flatfish and young bass.

Paible is a scattered settlement area with the largest secondary school on the island. Numerous local industries have been tried to supplement the crofters' way of life. Tulips were grown for many years on the rich machair soils. A knitwear factory survived for just a short while.

The Monach Isles: *no reg. sailings*

These islands form a small group about 13km offshore. There are no regular sailings but you can ask a local fisherman to take you over. The greatest problem is finding a suitable day, as there are few good places to land and a swell can make it very difficult. The islands present a superb machair habitat, and support a large bird population. Numerous seals bask on the beaches. When the weather is fine they are an idyllic place to visit.

In common with many isolated islands, the Monachs once had a thriving fishing community. The main island, Ceann Ear, still has the remains of a village with sixteen buildings. The restored schoolhouse has been used by fishermen and it is a good source of fresh water. It is best to camp near the village. The ruins are now home for Fulmars that nest in the walls. Domestic cats now run wild on the islands. They have been studied at some length, but their population fluctuates considerably.

Fulmars, Oystercatchers and Turnstones nest in the dunes and on the shores behind the village. The small bay west of the village has a dense covering of *Zostera,* the Eel Grass. Large flocks of Knot are common. Ceann Ear and the islands of Shivinish and Ceann Iar are linked by sand at low tide. Shivinish is dominated by the yellow Ragwort. On the beaches, extensive strands of Sea Rocket (a member of the cabbage family) produce a pale pink colour on the sand. Short-eared Owls, Buzzards and Herons are widespread.

ADDRESSES

Caledonian MacBrayne Ltd.,
The Ferry Terminal,
Gourock,
Scotland,
PA19 1QP.
Telephone: (0475) 33755

Highlands and Islands Development Board,
Bridge House,
27 Bank St.,
Inverness, IV1 1QR.

Mid Argyll, Kintyre and Islay Tourist Board,
The Pier,
Campbeltown,
Argyll,
PA28 6EF.
Telephone: (0586) 52056.

The Warden,
Loch Gruinart Nature Reserve,
Grainel,
Gruinart,
Islay.
PA44 7PS. I

Islay Field Centre,
Port Charlotte,
Isle of Islay,
Argyll,
PA48 7TX.
Telephone: (049 685) 288.

Tourist Information Centre,
Meall House,
Portree,
Isle of Skye. I
V51 9VZ.
Telephone: (0478) 2137.

Loganair Ltd.,
Glasgow Airport,
Abbotsinch,
Paisley,
PA3 2TG.
Telephone: (041) 889 3181.

Tourist Information Centre,   [Main Tourist Information
South Beach Quay,   Office for Outer Hebrides]
Stornoway,
Isle of Lewis.
Telephone: (0851) 3088 or 2941.

IRELAND

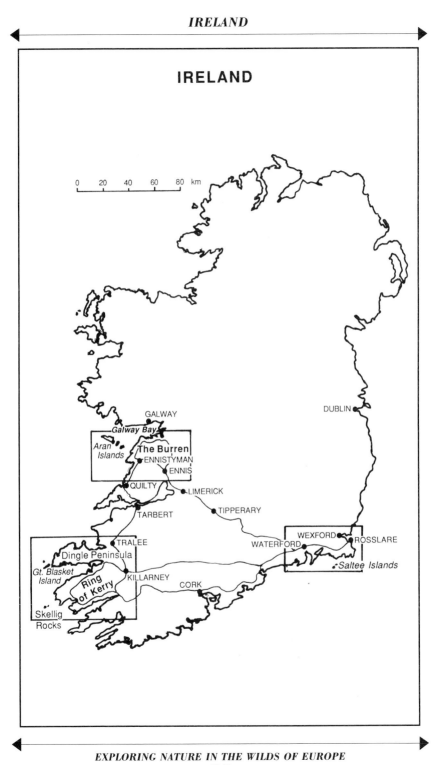

IRELAND

0 20 40 60 80 km

GALWAY
Galway Bay
Aran
Islands
The Burren
ENNISTYMAN
ENNIS
QUILTY
LIMERICK
TARBERT
TIPPERARY
TRALEE
Dingle Peninsula
Gt. Blasket Island
Ring of Kerry
KILLARNEY
CORK
Skellig Rocks
DUBLIN
WEXFORD
WATERFORD
ROSSLARE
Saltee Islands

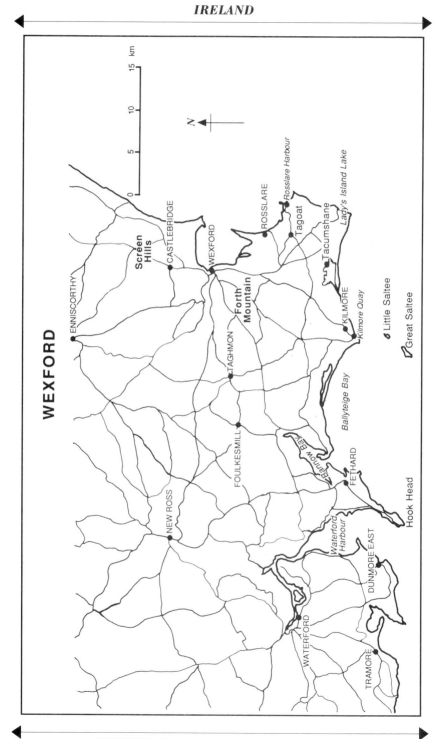

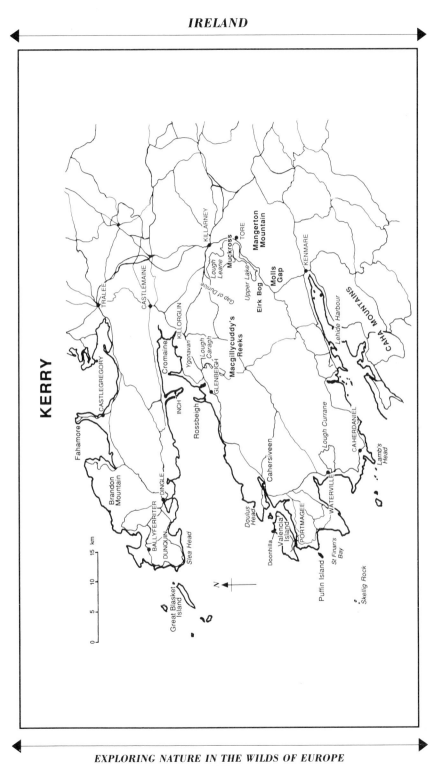

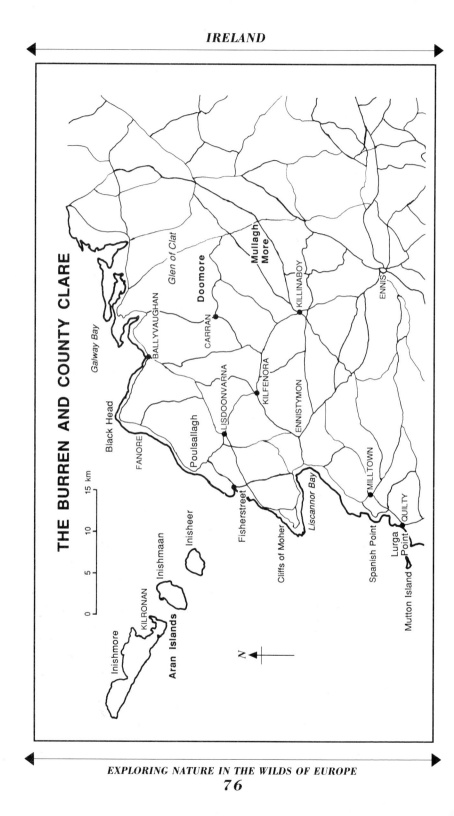

THE BURREN AND COUNTY CLARE

Galway Bay

Glen of Clat

Mullagh More

Doomore

BALLYVAUGHAN

CARRAN

KILLINABOY

ENNIS

Black Head

LISDOONVARNA

KILFENORA

FANORE

Poulsallagh

ENNISTYMON

MILLTOWN

Fisherstreet

QUILTY

Liscannor Bay

Cliffs of Moher

Spanish Point

Lurga Point

Mutton Island

Inisheer

Inishmaan

Aran Islands

KILRONAN

Inishmore

15 km

0   5   10   15

N

Introduction

To the naturalist, Ireland is perhaps best known for its bogs! Certainly, these are an important feature of the wet, western regions. But for anyone who actually visits the Republic, it is the friendliness and hospitality of the people that is the enduring memory. You will often be treated like a long-lost friend, and rarely be left with no-one to talk to.

The country is divided into four provinces: Leinster to the east, Munster in the south-west, Connacht in the west and Ulster to the north (three counties of which lie in the Republic). This chapter considers the first two of these provinces. They show a remarkable variation as you move from east to west, with the land becoming more rugged. For the traveller, time barely seems to pass. You can drive for a whole day in parts of the west and never see a soul. The biology and archaeology are rich and varied. Both remain relatively untouched. Only recently have the public authorities begun restoring some of the ancient sites.

Ireland is undoubtedly the country for anyone who loves islands. The southern and western coasts are liberally scattered with inhabited and uninhabited isles. Even those which are apparently most remote are accessible with local help.

Geography

Several thousand years ago Ireland was covered by forest. Felling by the Celts was accompanied by a change in climate. The warmer, moister weather encouraged the growth of Sphagnum Moss. Today there are few original woodlands remaining, as much of the country is under the Sphagnum. This moss does not decay when it dies, but instead builds up to form peat. This is a vital component in the weak Irish economy. Cut on a commercial scale it is used in peat-fuelled power stations as well as being burnt for domestic purposes. The trees killed by the rising tide of moss are uncovered when the peat is cut for fuel. They are bleached on exposure to the sun. An industry has now grown up using this wood. In Killarney you can buy carvings and jewellery made from it.

The coast of Kerry is very indented. The great inlets in the rock are rias. They are formed when the Earth's surface subsides, and river valleys are flooded by the sea. Hard rocks are the most resistant to weathering and these stand out at the tips of the peninsulas eg. Puffin Island and the Blaskets. County Clare is famous for the huge sheet of carboniferous limestone which breaks its surface like the blunt end of a wedge. The thinner end disappears under the peat bogs of Roscommon. At the seaward margin the limestone forms rounded hills which descend from over thirty metres to the sea. This region is called The Burren. The west coast is rarely troubled by frost and snow because of the proximity of the Gulf Stream. This allows rare plants and animals to survive and flourish.

Flora and Fauna

The overall number of plants and animals is lower than in Great Britain. This stems from the retreat of the Ice Age. Recolonisation of the British Isles occurred from across the channel, via a land bridge. The organisms then spread across the country. For some it was too late to cross into Ireland as it had already become separated by rising water, as the ice melted. This is why there are no snakes in Ireland.

Spotted Kerry Slug.

However, the remoteness of the west has enabled many species of animal to survive while elsewhere they have declined – the Corncrake, for instance. The numerous offshore islands make it a haven for seabirds, with some of the best colonies in Europe. Little Skellig supports 40,000 gannets and has over-wintering sites second to none. Some of the islands are quite large. Their plant and animal populations have become isolated, producing a number of unique subspecies.

One of the most fascinating aspects of the natural history of Kerry is the range of Lusitanian species. Such organisms normally live in areas close to the Mediterranean. These include the Strawberry Tree, the Spotted Kerry Slug and the small spiny sea urchins which dominate the rockpools of the limestone coast. Mountains encourage arctic-alpine species. A number of such plants are found only in a few locations in the south-west.

Motoring in Ireland

Although motorways and dual carriageways are a rare sight, there are few traffic problems in the areas we describe. There are far fewer people on the roads, than in Great Britain. However, your journey can be slowed by the bumpy roads and their infuriating bends. Many roads have been widened and modernised in recent years, but this can be a problem in itself. For miles the road will be straight and wide until you suddenly, and without warning, meet an old stretch with a narrow right-angled bend! Most of the major roads have a hard shoulder and heavy lorries will often use it to allow overtaking.

High excise duties mean that petrol is very expensive. However, it is worth shopping around, as prices tend to vary.

Camping and Accommodation

There are few official camp-sites, but fortunately there is little need for them, as the opportunities for rough camping are numerous. Some sites, inevitably, tend to be boggy, but there are a large number of sand dune systems around the coast, and these are ideal. You should never assume that what appears to be a remote green pasture is actually wild – always ask permission from the local farmer. This will almost always be given, although you should be prepared to pay a token amount for the use of the land. Youth hostels are mentioned in the text where appropriate. Details of self-catering cottages and hotels can be obtained from tourist information centres.

Food and Drink

Small supermarkets cater for most needs, although some can be quite expensive. In the far west it can be difficult to obtain fresh fruit and vegetables. Eating out varies greatly in cost, and is just not possible in some areas. Bars, however, are prolific. Even the remotest hamlets have at least one. If a settlement has only a few houses, then one of them may have a bar in the front room. (There will usually be a Guinness sticker in the window.) They are often run by tradesmen, so the bar may be in a grocer's shop, for instance. In Killarney, there is one in the undertaker's! Bars may also serve coffee and food.

Maps

These are easily obtained before your visit, through the Ordnance Survey or specialist map centres. The most useful maps are the half inch to the mile. They are based on old surveys but are generally accurate. Place names may vary from map to signpost.

Money

The Irish currency is the *punt*. Currency can easily be obtained from Irish banks in the UK. Credit cards are increasingly being used and most garages will take them for petrol.

Passports

British citizens do not need their passports when entering the Republic.

The South-east

Getting there:

Our suggested base is on the southern coast, at Kilmore Quay, 25km from Rosslare Harbour. There are no official camp-sites in this area, but the sand dunes which border Ballyteige Bay to the west are ideal. However, access can be difficult, depending on the size of your vehicle. From the quay, follow the road past the large parking area. Within a few hundred metres, the dunes will lie to your left. In order to reach them it is necessary to cross a small stream. There are several bridges – the first is the most suitable for vehicles. Please remember to shut the gate on the other side. To open and shut it may require the use of a spanner! It is not recommended to take vehicles onto these dunes unless you have four-wheel drive. There is a great deal of loose sand. In addition, the soil of the dunes is very fragile and driving should be kept to a minimum. Drinking water is available from the public toilets in the car park near the quay. The village has a number of bars, a hotel and a small shop.

For those requiring an official camp-site, there is the Ferrybank Camping Park between Wexford and Castlebridge. This is only open from April to September. There are plenty of Bed and Breakfast places but the nearest hostel is at Rosslare (IYHF).

The camp-site area:

Hollows in the dunes provide well-drained areas in which to set up camp. They can be a bleak landscape in the wind and rain, but in the sun the profusion of flowers offers a colourful backdrop. The sand itself has a high shell content, which makes it alkaline. This 10km stretch of dunes is the finest in the county. As well as including the typical dune species such as marram and sea couch, the rich flora has examples of Wild Asparagus, Dewberry and a rare clover, *Trifolium campestre*. Hares are particularly common on the grassland behind the dunes. In addition, there are numerous insect communities. Several thousand pairs of Golden Plover and Lapwing also breed here.

The original, rugged, south coast of Wexford county has been smoothed out over the years to produce long sweeping bays (see map, page 74). The westward drift of sand and pebbles along the

Close-up of cottonweed, on shingle ridge near Lady Island Lake.

coast, has turned rocky inlets into brackish lakes, such as Lady Island and Tacumshin Lake. Most of these lakes have outlets to the sea on their western edges. These produce estuarine conditions. They provide ideal refuge sites for migratory seabirds. Behind the Ballyteige Dunes, the saltmarsh is well developed. It supports the rare Glasswort plant, *Salicornia perrenis*, found nowhere else in Ireland. The Cull, as this region is known, is renowned for its large numbers of wading birds. The small island is a favourite roost. At the western end of the dunes, a small group of islands – the Kerragh – supports a colony of almost 200 cormorants and other seabirds.

The narrow Tacumshin dune system, east of Kilmore, is relatively inaccessible. The lake behind it is composed of sandy inlets at the seaward end. It is possible to get down to the lake at the outlet point, via Talladavin. The sand is firm enough to drive over. At low water you can get across to the islands and bars, from where birdwatching will reveal wildfowl and waders. The former include Brent Geese, Pochard, Scaup and Widgeon.

A more interesting region is that around Lady Island Lake, cut off from the sea by an extensive shingle spit. This has been breached in recent years, so the freshwater lake has become brackish in its lower reaches. The lake is shallow, with many fascinating communities of marshland. Hence, it is an important breeding ground for wildfowl. Terns and gulls are particularly numerous on the islands. The south-eastern part of the spit is the most interesting. You can easily reach it by the following the road, which then deteriorates into a track as it approaches the shore. The first sight out to sea is a dense mat of what appears to be cottonwool. In fact, it is the very rare Cottonweed (*Otanthus*). This is the best location in the British Isles for this species.

Wexford:

The L29 is the fastest road to Wexford, taking about 30 minutes. A more scenic route is via the Forth Mountains, an area of upland a few miles west of the town. On a clear day there are excellent views from the tors at the top, with the flanks covered with heathland.

In 1169 the Normans conquered Wexford. The name comes from the Viking word for "harbour of mudflats". It is a quaint, old town with narrow streets and a fishing harbour. The Westgate Tower is the sole remnant of the original Norman walls. To the north is Selskar Abbey, a twelfth-century priory. The Bullring, in the centre of the town, was originally used for bloodsports by the Normans. There are several car parks near the shopping area, which is quite substantial. The building which Cromwell stayed in at the start of his bloody Irish campaign is now occupied by Woolworths! Numerous bars abound, many with music and dancing. The Crown Bar in Monck Street has good food. Early closing is on Thursday.

The River Slaney is estuarine here – the deeper parts are used by shipping. Seaward of the road bridge, it widens to form the tidal Loch Garman. Behind two peninsulas – the Raven to the north and the Rosslare to the south – the area has been reclaimed. This has produced the most important wetland in Ireland, known as the Slobs. During the winter months White-fronted Geese, Brent Geese, Bewick's Swan, Pintail, Teal and Mallard are here in huge numbers. Over 15,000 waders feed at low tide. They include Godwits, Curlews and Dunlin.

The L29 continues out of Wexford, passing through Castlebridge. The river here has an excellent flora of reedswamp and sedge. The Strawberry Clover is common. Seven kilometres beyond the village, a right-hand turning leads to Screen. Keep bearing to the right. Less than 2km further on the road forks. Go left and shortly, left again. The road winds across the Screen Hills for several miles before meeting the L30A, just north of Curracloe.

This deserted, sandy coastal strip marks the point where the Irish Sea ice-sheet was once stationary and a glacial morraine built up. The lagoons here are rich in flora (e.g. the water parsnip) and fauna. The map shows a series of small lakes and ponds among the Screen Hills. Undulation characterises the scenery. This is a kettle landscape, marking the end of a morraine from the last ice age. The ground consisted of great blocks of ice which created depressions as they melted. There are also a number of deep lakes shaped like kettles, with narrow openings at the top. In early summer, the land is carpeted by bluebells. The animals form unique communities from one lake to the next. They are especially rich in dragonflies, notably the Hairy Dragonfly (*Brachytron pratense*) – a scarce species. Some of the flatter areas contain small patches of water. The perimeters have become colonised by Sphagnum Moss, which then grows across the surface of the water. Rich communities of fen plants can grow in this, even including trees. As you walk across this floating bog, it quakes, and trees some distance away will sway from side to side. Doo Lough is the largest lake. Surrounding it is an example of a raised bog.

Hook Head and Bannow Bay:

Take the L128A west, from Kilmore to Wellington Bridge. A castle and abbey stand here on the banks of the Bannow Estuary. Tintern Abbey was built by William the Marshall after he survived a storm at sea. It stands on the site of the first Norman landing, in 1169. The banks of the river have numerous ancient sites of interest – mainly ring forts. There are mudflats in the lower reaches of Bannow Bay. Their importance for wildfowl and waders is second only to Wexford Slobs. The road after Wellington Bridge becomes the L159. At Poundtown cross-roads, turn left to Fethard and Hook Head. A mile before Fethard, turn left to Wood Bridge. This part of the coast is a raised beach. The area where the level of the present shoreline is lower than Hook Head, marks the junction of sandstone and limestone. As well as being an excellent rocky shore for seashore organisms, it contains numerous fossils of marine creatures.

Waterford and Tramore:

To reach Waterford from Kilmore or Wexford it is necessary to go via New Ross, where the river narrows high up the Barrow Estuary. The main road, the T12, passes along the picturesque tidal river. It then goes south to Waterford – famous for its crystal glass. This takes one and a half hours from Kilmore. Traffic is slow on the bridge crossing the River Suir but you can usually park along the quayside. The shopping centre runs parallel to the river. There are two cathedrals worth seeing here. It is also possible to arrange visits to the crystal factory, which is in the western part of the town.

Take the L158 out of Waterford to Dunmore East. Ten kilometres on, Belle Lake lies to the right. There are several places to park and a number of paths take the walker around this large, shallow lake. In parts, it is thickly wooded. These areas are the haunts of the large hawker dragonflies. At the southern end is an excellent reed swampland. Back on the road, a turning to the left, only a few hundred metres on from the lake, takes you up a hill towards a well preserved megalithic tomb. These stone structures date from about 2,000BC, and are the work of early settlers from Brittany. The road can be followed for a few kilometres to Dunmore. The cliffs here are nesting sites for Kittiwakes. With over a thousand breeding pairs they are hard to miss!

There are numerous minor roads which can be followed to reach Tramore. Alternatively, you could backtrack on the main road for several kilometres – turning left at the Kilmacomb cross-roads. The 5km stretch of sandy beach is famous for its safe bathing and golf course. The sand dune system is also well known for its wealth of plants, which include Dewberry and privet communities. The rare bistort (*Polygonum maritimum*) is not found anywhere else in Ireland. The flats behind it are rich in wildfowl, and wintering seabirds such as Dunlin.

The Saltee Islands:

The Saltee Islands lie off the coast from Kilmore. They can be reached by hiring a fishing boat from the quay. The person to contact is Bill Bates (Tel. 296 44) who will take you to the islands in the "Mystical Queen" for about £6. It is best to stay for at least one night if possible. However, that does involve two trips for the

General view northwards across the Great Saltee, covered by Bluebells and Sea Pink.

fisherman (£12!). The uninhabited island does not have a proper landing stage and the boat anchors offshore. You then transfer to a flat-bottomed boat in which Bill ferries the passengers to the shore. Remember that it may be impossible to land (or be picked up!) if the weather is unfavourable.

The Great Saltee is the best island to visit. It belongs to the self-proclaimed "King of the Saltees", who lives in Dublin. When you land you will see a large stone tablet inscribed with a message from the King. There is a house on the island, belonging to him, with a large kitchen/diner and five or six rooms. If the King is not in residence, it is open for use by travellers (details and key from Bill Bates). Water is available from a well just outside the kitchen, but you will need to bring food and cooking utensils with you. Do not expect a palace – the house is very spartan! There is a grassy area close to the house which is suitable for camping.

Great Saltee is a magical place. The time to come is from May to July, when the land is carpeted with bluebells and ringing with the call of thousands of seabirds. The relief is relatively flat, with the once-cultivated interior now a mixture of bracken and grassland. Cliffs border the island and form important breeding sites for the countless seabirds. On the north-west side of the house, there are avenues of palms leading up to a high point where the stone throne stands. Walking from the throne towards the cliffs, you reach the main puffin colony. One and a half thousand pairs nest in burrows at the top of the cliff. On the ledges it is possible to creep very close to the guillemots (13,000 pairs) and razorbills (1,500 pairs). Along this eastern edge, you can follow a fascinating path south, with the ledges becoming increasingly more populated with these birds, as well as the Kittiwake – a cliff nesting gull.

At the southern end, the interior is one vast Herring and Black-backed Gull colony. Their alarm calls create a deafening noise. Around Whitsuntide it is a common sight to see the chicks hatch, calling to their parents from within the shell. The most southerly point is the Gannet colony (250 pairs). If someone strays too close to the colony, the Shags nesting amongst the rocks brazenly threaten the intruder. There are few birds on the gentle western side, except for a few Oystercatchers. However, to the north, the Fulmers and more Puffins breed.

No description can do the Great Saltee justice. The colours and beauty must be seen to be believed – clifftops ablaze with the pink of the thrift, the white and red campions, and the dry stone walls covered by pennywort.

The Blackstairs Mountains:

Thirteen kilometres west of Enniscorthy is Killoughrum Forest, a beautiful and very extensive woodland of oak, birch and hazel. The soil is acidic, thus heathers and broom are supported. There are rich populations of insects – especially butterflies and moths. The forest lies to the south of the L127. It has to be crossed on the way to the Blackstairs Mountains. These rise to over 800m at Caher Roe's Den. The entire area is blanket bog. Near the summit of Mount Leinster are species of arctic-alpine plants. The moorland supports large populations of birds, particularly grouse. Several tributaries of the River Urrin rise here, flowing eastwards. At its headwater in the north of the mountains, the blanket bog supports two rarities – the Bell-flower and the Lusitanian Butterwort. The latter is an insectivorous species.

The Journey West

County Cork

There are two main routes to the south-western coast. The T12 goes via Cork city, and hence tends to be congested. The T30 is a faster route which runs 25km to the north. If you are going direct to Killarney the latter road is better. It can be joined a few kilometres before Dungarvan, after taking the T12 from Waterford. Sixteen kilometres on from Dungarvan is the small town of Lismore, on the spectacular River Blackwater. It is a town with a modernised medieval cathedral and monastery. A detour north will take you on a steep climb into the desolate Knockmealdown Mountains, which are over 850m high. From the main road on Sugarloaf Hill, there is a spectacular view across the Galty Mountains, as far as Tipperary. The road west will take you through the modern towns of Fermoy and Mallow – good bases from where to visit the Nagles Mountains to the south. The T30 follows the valley of the River Blackwater (famous for its salmon fishing) almost as far as Killarney.

If you are in no great hurry then you can set a more leisurely pace by following the southern route through Cork. The first diversion is to the pleasant town of Dungarvan. It has a fishing harbour which is particularly exciting biologically. There is a vast expanse of mud, sand and shingle colonised in parts by the Eel Grass (*Zostera*). The area is protected by the Cunigar – a long, narrow spit. Within this, huge flocks of seabirds such as Godwits, Knot and Grey Plover, spend the winter. It is believed to support the largest concentration of waders in the country. Leaving on the Cork road, the T12, turn left onto the L177 to Helvick Head. This is a rocky headland where Razorbills, Guillemots, Kittiwakes and other seabirds nest. Back on the T12, it is worth making a short visit to Ardmore on the coast. Here stands one of the best preserved Round Towers in Ireland. This 30m tall structure dates from the twelfth century. The nearby church-yard contains two Ogham Stones – well worth seeing, with their ancient runic inscriptions. In fact, there are many fascinating sites around Ardmore – from the seventh-century lead mines to St. Declan's Oratory. There is also an excellent sandy beach.

Following the minor roads along the coast brings the traveller through delightful sandy bays and backwaters, like Cabin Point. Eventually you will come upon the Blackwater Estuary, with Youghal on the other bank. There is a small ferry boat for foot passengers only. Cars must go onto the T12. Before you leave this eastern bank, look at the profusion of Yellow Horned Poppies colonising the shingle. Youghal is a busy town, made famous by its appearance in the classic film, "Moby Dick". The next bay on from Youghal is Ballycotton Bay. The western area has been cut off by the sea to create salty lagoons and swampland. Gadwall and other wildfowl feed here. Several rare plants can be found, including the Beaked Tassel Weed (*Zannichellia*). The choice of route from Cork to Killarney depends on how much time you have free. The further west you travel the more spectacular the scenery and the more temptations there are to deviate from your planned route! The coast of County Cork is very indented. Each harbour has a character of its own.

The T29 from Cork goes direct to Killarney. At Macroom the T64 provides an alternative itinerary, linking up with the Ring of Kerry at Kenmare. This route takes you over the Shehy Mountains, through the spectacular Pass of Keimaneigh and down to Bantry Bay. Turn right onto the T65 and within 8km you will enter Glengariff Harbour. The beauty of this region is legendary. The mountain river flowing into the harbour has a backdrop of colonising woodland. This consists of oak, birch, rowan and the Strawberry Tree. The dampness encourages the growth of a myriad of mosses, liverworts and ferns, particularly the Filmy Fern. Continuing over the Caha Mountains you will cross the border into County Kerry.

The South-west

Killarney

Camping sites:

There are many rough sites available in the mountainous regions but most tend to be boggy and need careful selection. If you want to use better, grassy areas then it is necessary to ask the permission of the local farmers, who are usually friendly and helpful. You may prefer to use an official site. The White Bridge Camping Site is a mile from Killarney on the Cork road. The Fossa Site lies to the west, on the Kilorglin road just before the left-hand turning to Beaufort. There is also a hostel nearby. Both camping areas cost about £5 per night. You will also find an excellent youth hostel close to the Upper Lake, to the south of the Gap of Dunloe. This makes an ideal base from which to explore the wilderness of the upper reaches of the Killarney valley.

Rather than staying near the busy city, you can try the Rossbehy dunes. These lie half an hour's drive away, near Glenbigh. This is an ideal place for rough camping. Just through the village of Glenbigh, which has a garage, hotel and a number of shops, the main road bends to the left. Follow the sign straight on to the Strand. Take the road along the beach and follow it round behind the dune system, where it is more sheltered. You have to pass under height barriers to get onto each road. This places a restriction on caravans or overheight vehicles. Fortunately, the right-hand barrier can usually be moved. The main reason for such precautions is to stop the removal of the sand for commercial purposes. The ground is firm and dry with superb views across to the Dingle Peninsula. There are litter bins and several standpipes by the track, from which to obtain water. Near the entrance to the beach there is a hotel with a series of bars. As well as providing liquid refreshment, it is useful if the weather is bad as it provides pool tables, video films and, occasionally, traditional music. Camping here gives an ideal base for exploring the northern part of the Ring of Kerry – the road which circles the Kerry peninsula. Alternatively, you can turn right at the Strand Hotel and climb around the mountain to the main road. The views back to the Strand are excellent. On the rough ground there are dozens of Butterworts.

The lakes and mountains:

The Killarney region is renowned for its breathtaking beauty –
high mountains, cloaked in natural woodland, and a series of
large lakes at various altitudes. It is not only unrivalled for
walkers but also for the naturalist who will find many species
unique in the British Isles. The warm, moist climate produces
an environment similar to southern Europe. As a consequence,
a number of Mediterranean species are easily found. *Arbutus*,
the Strawberry Tree, is a common species in the Killarney
forests and the Spotted Kerry Slug (grey with white spots)
abounds in the damper places. The lakes are unusual in many
ways and there are two species of fish – a race of Char and a
land-locked Twite Shad (*Alosa fallax*) – which are particularly
interesting.

The drive from Kenmare to Killarney on the T65 is a
dramatic start to your journey through this region. The first
9km take you from sea-level to an altitude of nearly 300m at
Molls Gap, where the scenery really begins to unfold. To the
north, the U-shaped valley of Eirk lies before you. The floor of
this valley is carpeted with an unusual bog. To reach it, you
should turn left at Molls Gap and on to the minor road which
winds to the bottom. Once on the valley floor you should take a
right turn at the junction. The unfenced road follows the river,
which you have to cross to reach the bog. The best place to stop is
about 4km from the junction.

The middle of the bog is higher than the surrounding wetland
because the very humid conditions greatly stimulate the growth
of Sphagnum Moss. It is one of the best examples of a raised bog
in Europe and has several rare species present. The Large
Marsh Grasshopper is the largest species in Europe and the most
impressive. It likes very wet places and can travel 12m or more
in one flight. It can be found on warm days in late summer.
Frogs are very common. You will notice that they are melanic
forms – surprisingly dark. Three species of insectivorous
sundew grow on the Sphagnum Moss. The area demonstrates a
good transition from raised bog to boggy pools with reeds and
Bog Bean. Continuing along this road brings you to the southern
end of the road through the Gap of Dunloe, just beyond the youth
hostel. It is possible to travel this road by car. However, this is
not recommended because of the large number of horse-drawn
carriages. The drivers resent the use of motor vehicles on the

road, and their reactions can sometimes be violent! The Gap of Dunloe is one of Ireland's most visited tourist attractions. It is a picturesque valley through the eastern end of the country's highest mountain range – MacGillycuddy's Reeks. In a succession of hairpin bends, the road from the youth hostel continues for some 8km, before emerging at Kate Kearney's Cottage. The northern stretch can be very crowded in summer.

After returning to the T65, a few kilometres on, the road runs next to Loch Luascanaigh before entering a small conifer plantation. Just beyond this is Ladies' View, so called because carriages would stop here to allow the gentry to take in the spectacular panorama across to Killarney. There is a large souvenir shop and a place for refreshments, with adequate parking. From here there is a strenuous but interesting walk of about a mile, down towards the lake. There is no marked pathway, and the terrain is very bumpy, with long grass. Walking to the right brings you into an oak woodland called Derrycunihy Wood. This is one of the most natural woodlands in the British Isles with a very rich variety of ferns, mosses, birds and insects. There is a particularly interesting green spider which can be found amongst the long grass.

You can walk to the lake from the wood. Alternatively, drive on over Galway's Bridge and stop a kilometre later, near Queen's Cottage. From here you can follow a path through the wood, down and along the side of the lake. Upper Lake is typical of those in upland country with its numerous small islands. These are difficult to visit unless you have brought your own dinghy, although it is possible to hire one from Lord Brandon's Cottage. Arbutus Island is one of the most interesting, so-called because of the predominance of Strawberry Trees. The density with which these cover the rock is a result of the lack of grazing. Rhododendron threatens to invade most of the Killarney woods but these islands are free from their scourge. The island is steep sided, which makes landing awkward. The trees (over 6m in height) and dense undergrowth make it difficult to move about. However, on the western, windward side their growth is a little more stunted. The bitter fruit, which gives the Strawberry Tree its name, ripens in October. The bark is attractive with its flaky, peeling outer surface.

The edge of the Upper Lake is one of the places in which you are most likely to spot the Strawberry Tree. As the road winds around the lower part of the lake, climbing towards Ladies' View, there is

Ladies View, showing the Killarney Woods and the Upper Lake.

a point at which the road turns sharply and passes through a short tunnel in the rock. There is a place to pull in immediately beyond this tunnel. Between here and the water there are a number of Strawberry Trees, some hanging onto the sides of the rock.

Near the outlet of the Upper Lake is a large flat region of blanket bog dotted with heath and Strawberry Trees. This is the Newfoundland Bog and access can be obtained by stopping further down the T65 at Cromaglan Bridge. This is an excellent place to stop to explore the 400m Cromaglan Mountain, which stands to the south. Initially, you should follow the smaller river which forks to the right. This takes you across boggy land where small pools are home for the large, white-striped, chocolate coloured Raft Spider. The terrain is very rocky. It is also steep in parts, so it may be easier to follow the cascades of the river. Demoiselle Dragonflies flutter nearby and numerous Tiger Beetles fly around in the sunshine. Eventually you will reach a delightful corrie lake, cradled by the sheer rise of the mountain behind. This is Lough Crincaum, with a rich variety of dragonflies and an exceptionally rare species of pond snail. The surface of the pool is covered by white water lilies, Common Reed and Bog Bean.

Muckross Lake is surrounded by forest. It is famous for the

nearby abbey which is always open. The abbey was ruined by Cromwell but the gothic cloisters remain. The grounds are remarkably beautiful at dusk, when the sun sets on the other side of the lake. Muckross House is worth a visit. It is a nineteenth-century manor house with splendid gardens. Amid the woods south of Muckross is a signposted pathway to Torc Waterfall – a series of cascades which are impressive after heavy rainfall. The humidity is very high, allowing a profusion of mosses, liverworts and ferns to grow on the rocks and trees. There are a series of paths which wind up the hillside. Occasionally they open out in clearings with views across the Killarney lakes. Opposite Muckross House there is a minor road. This runs into a track which passes near Torc and onto the moorland of Mangerton Mountain. To reach the summit you must leave the track and follow the river south east. Between the two peaks of Mangerton is the Devil's Punch Bowl, with a large corrie lake. The cliffs here have concentrations of arctic-alpine plants and many other rare species. The vast area of blanket bog and upland heath covering the western slopes is grazed by herds of Red Deer, one of the few Kerry populations.

The lowest lake is Lough Leane. Its close proximity to Killarney means that it is the most visited. However, its size means that there are plenty of quiet backwaters. For the naturalist, two places stand out. Tomies Wood on the wild western side is made up of oak and birch and contains a population of Sika Deer. Ross Island (in fact, a peninsula) is easily accessible from Killarney and is sign-posted to the left on entering the city from Kenmare. There is a large car park area for Ross Castle – a sixteenth-century ruin with excellent views. It is possible to hire a boat and visit islands in the lake, such as Innisfallen where there is a fifth-century abbey.

For the naturalist, a walk along a small path from the car park (away from the castle) brings you through a dense alder swampland to the shore of Lough Leane. Ross Island has a rich soil which supports an impressive flora. There are also several fascinating outcrops of rock. Along the edge is swamp and fenland, criss-crossed by streams and dotted with ponds. One large pond near the car park is covered by water lilies. On drier ground the trees are ash and beech. On a warm sunny day in summer it teems with life. There are also several Bronze Age mines with spoil heaps, reworked for the cobalt and copper. Artefacts are still being found.

The Ring of Kerry

The ring consists of the main road which circles the Iveragh Peninsula. It takes in some breathtaking scenery but requires several days to do it justice. For the north coast, a base at Rossbehy is ideal. The southern area is more rocky, and camping places are not as easy to find. However, the upper shoreline of Lough Currane has some well drained fields which are suitable, but do not forget to ask the farmer. The indented coastline of Kerry is made up of rias – drowned valleys which let the sea flow far inland.

The north coast:

Follow the T67 from Kilorglin to Killarney. There is a tourist information centre here, as well as a good place for ice cream! The route runs alongside the River Laune which drains the lakes to the sea. Within a mile, as the main road bears left, take the minor road straight on to the village of Cromane and along the shingle spit to Cromane Point. There are good views of Dingle and it is often an ideal vantage point for watching wading birds. An excellent saltmarsh has developed on the sheltered side of the point, as well as extensive mudflats.

Returning, there is a T-junction on the other side of Cromane village. Turn left and in less than a mile, turn right. This will bring you back to the main road, but also take you through an area of peat bog. To your right is Lough Yganavan, a low-lying lake surrounded by bog pools and drying peat. Large swathes of Royal Fern grow in the damper places. Dragonflies hawk and dart across the water. Natterjack Toads and Spotted Kerry Slugs live around the lake, especially on the north side and under large stones. On the other side of the road there is an extensive peat bog. Where the peat has been cut, ancient tree trunks and branches are exposed. These are the remains of the forests which dominated Ireland several thousand years ago, but were engulfed by the Sphagnum as the climate became wetter. An industry has now developed, carving this preserved wood. Examples can be purchased in Killarney.

When you reach the main road, turn right. Then, after a short distance, take the left-hand turning which is signposted to Lough Caragh. It is possible to circle the lake, which is set amongst

Lough Caragh from the south.

glaciated hills and woodland. Many of the trees are in plantations, although there are some good natural oak woodlands on the southern edge. The lake is very rich in aquatic communities. A good place to stop is at Blackstone Bridge, which crosses the River Caragh as it enters the lake to the south. If you look in the pools between the boulders near the bridge you can find large freshwater Pearl Mussels. Do not bother to disturb them – it is highly unlikely that you will find any pearls! The boulders above the road are covered with London Pride, a sight that will become increasingly common.

The conifer wood next to the bridge has several delightful walks. Because pesticides are used infrequently here, you can often see the magnificent Giant Wood Wasp. It is completely harmless to us but a serious pest to pine forests. Lough Accose lies a few miles to the south of here by road. It is a mountain lake containing a unique race of Char. Following the road clockwise around Lough Caragh eventually brings you back to a left-hand turning to Glenbeigh. Follow the signposts to Glenbeigh. Just beyond the village the main road veers to the left. Carry straight on, along the road signposted to Rossbehy Strand.

As well as being the suggested camping site, this is an excellent sandy beach and dune system. The flowers in early summer are superb. These include several species of orchid, including the Bee and Pyramidal varieties. The Sea Pea is in flower in June. In the same month, Burnet Moths emerge in large numbers from their cocoons in the Marram Grass. There is an abundance of snails on the dunes. These show considerable variation in colour and banding. Choughs can regularly be heard calling as they fly over the dunes. Behind the dune spit is an extensive area of mudflat and sheltered outcrops of seaweed-covered rocks.

The road from Rossbehy offers magnificent views as it hugs the coast and skirts the mountains. It enters the town of Cahersiveen, where there is an information centre. Cahersiveen is the main town along the coast and is a good centre from which to walk across the mountains of the interior. The town lies on the Valencia Estuary. A road bridge crosses it to reach Doulus Head from where there is a splendid view of the Blaskets (see page 106).

The west:

A few miles on from Cahersiveen the main road runs inland. Turn right on to a minor road to Portmagee. The vegetation is dominated by Yellow Flag Iris, an indication of the boggy terrain. Portmagee is a small fishing village consisting just of a row of cottages. A bridge connects the mainland with Valencia Island, from where the first Atlantic cable was laid in 1866. Dohilla, to the west of Valencia Harbour, has several small quarries where Choughs breed. London Pride grows on the damp rocks. One of the quarry caverns is now a delightful grotto. The climate here is moist but warm. Frost is a rarity. Near the church in the harbour grows a sub-tropical garden with tree ferns, fuchsias and other exotic plants.

The slow climb out of Portmagee towards Waterville passes over vast blanket bogs. From the top, the view north-eastwards is quite spectacular. A right turn at the top opens up a panorama across the fossil-rich coast of St. Finan's Bay. If you intend to visit Puffin Island, then this spot provides the only view from the mainland. There are hundreds of Choughs in the area. This cliff and those on this side of Ballinskelligs Bay are some of the best anywhere for seeing their flocks. Waterville is a fishing and seaside resort town. Behind the long sandy beach is the large Lough Currane. A dead end road winds along the southern edge of the lake.

On the main road from Waterville to Caherdaniel there is a National Park at Darrynane Abbey. This lies on the coast, and it is possible to walk across to Abbey Island at low tide. Just beyond Caherdaniel there is a right turning to Lambs Head. The rockpools around these headlands are excellent sites in which to see the Mediterranean species of sea urchin. They dominate the pools and are a unique sight.

The offshore islands:

This part of Ireland is famous for its offshore islands. No trip to these parts should pass without a visit. Portmagee is one of the best departure points. A drink in O'Shanahans Bar is one way of making contact with someone to take you there. From the pier, Joe Roddy regularly carries passengers on the "Thanet Queen". He will take you down the channel and across the open sea to the Skelligs. He can also arrange fishing or trips to the other islands.

Puffin Island:

The crossing from Portmagee takes just over half an hour. You pass below 300m high cliffs as you enter Puffin Sound. The longest

The camp on Puffin Island, looking towards Puffin Sound and the 300 metre high cliffs of the mainland.

part of the trip is probably the landing. On the north-eastern side of the island there is a small inlet. Its so-called "landing stage" is only capable of coping with dinghies – and even their manoeuvres must be timed to perfection. Consequently, the boat moors just offshore – the proximity depending on the wind direction. As the baggage has to be transferred onshore, you are advised to keep it to a minimum and ensure that it is waterproof! Once on dry land, there is a path which zig-zags up the cliff.

The island is uninhabited except by thousands of seabirds. It is a recent acquisition of the Irish Wildfowl Conservancy. There is a flat area in the northern part, a few hundred metres from the inlet, which is suitable for camping. It is close to a profusion of Sea Pinks, which make the island very beautiful in the early summer. It is worth staying for at least one night, if possible. However, you must remember that there is no fresh water on the island. Hence, you have to take enough for your stay, plus extra supplies in case the return boat is delayed.

The island is like two steep hills joined in the centre by a narrow ridge. The western cliffs are sheer and, in parts, eroding badly. There are a number of rabbits, and bluebells carpet the upper regions. The vegetation varies considerably. The steep hill behind the camping area is very acidic, with marsh orchids and heathers. To the west of the camp is a Lesser Black-backed and Herring Gull colony. Their droppings and regurgitated pellets contain a great deal of shell material which in turn creates a strongly alkaline environment. This ensures that the vegetation is very sparse. Under the stones there is also quite a community of invertebrates. The southern slopes are dense with the white Sea Campion and Mayweed.

Although the island is named after the Puffin, numbers have dropped considerably in recent years to less than 4,000 pairs. They nest in old rabbit burrows on the slopes to the south. The western cliffs are the best place to see the Guillemots and Razorbills (200 and 700 pairs, respectively). Fulmars nest in any small ledge around the island but the Kittiwakes are mainly in the south.

The main reason for visiting Puffin Island is that it is one of the main breeding grounds for the Manx Shearwater and Storm Petrel. These birds only land during the night, so it may not be necessary to bring a tent with you, as you could be up all night watching them! They only fly close to the land when it is time to breed. The Manx Shearwater is a sleek black and white bird. Shearwaters begin to circle the island a few hours after dark, calling to their young who are deep in their burrows. This eerie, haunting call can be very unnerving in the darkness. On land they are most ungainly and cannot easily take flight, requiring a high point to launch themselves from. With a torch, they can easily be seen picking their way through the campion. They will be gone before dawn. The awakening gulls will try to pick them off as they try desperately to take to the air. Hence, several dead bodies can be found, picked clean of flesh. It is believed that over 15,000 pairs of Manx Shearwaters breed on the island. The Storm Petrel is barely six inches long, and its fluttering flight would make it easy prey for the gulls during the day.

The burrows of these two night flyers are set in two main areas: one to the back of the camp and another on the south-east slope. The openings make any trek in the middle of the night somewhat hazardous.

Grey seals are often seen in the boat cove and in other inlets on the sheltered north. While you are in your tents, their calls can often be heard in the distance.

However long you stay, please leave the island as you found it – any fires should be kept very carefully under control, within large stones. Take all litter away with you.

To the south of Puffin Island lie the Skelligs, a pair of rocks towering out of the sea like the peaks of two mountains.

The Skelligs:

Camping is forbidden on the Great Skellig unless special permission is granted from the lighthouse keepers. On the Little Skellig it would be virtually impossible. Day trips are fairly frequent in summer from Portmagee, usually departing at around 1100 hours. The journey takes about one and a half hours. The boat will dock on the Great Skellig, passing the Little Skellig en route.

The Little Skellig towers over 200m in height. It has very steep slopes and no place suitable for landing. However, it is still important for its inhabitants – 40,000 gannets! From a distance the rock appears white because of the guano. Consequently the smell downwind is quite incredible! The spectacle is amazing, with Gannets flying all around. On a very calm day (when the swell is less than two metres) it may be possible to land by jumping from boat to ledge, but the rocks are steep and crumbling. Gannet nests are set just outside pecking distance and walking

Nesting Gannets on Little Skellig.

between them can be quite dangerous. Kittiwakes, Razorbills and Guillemots also breed here.

The Great Skellig also has a good variety of seabirds nesting on its 300m flanks. There are more Puffins than on Puffin Island but it is also especially good for Storm Petrels, with over 10,000 pairs. They nest not only in burrows but also in the island's main attraction – one of the earliest known monastic settlements in the British Isles. The monks moved to the island as a refuge from the marauding Vikings, although it is believed that King Olaf of Norway was baptised here. They later established a community on Holy Isle in Northumberland.

It is a long climb up an open rock stairway to reach the monastery. The buildings consist of small beehive huts, made with dry stone in the sixth and seventh centuries. A small church was added later and is made with mortar. There is a small well and a cemetary where the monks are buried. The soil on the rock is very shallow and so it must have been collected by the monks and placed here to produce a sufficient depth for burial.

The Kenmare River:

The coastal strip from Lamb's Head to Kenmare is beautiful, with its indented rocky and sandy shores. Several kilometres on from

Caherdaniel there is a signpost to Staigue Fort. Three kilometres of minor track take you to the best preserved prehistoric fort in Ireland. Visitors are asked to place a donation in a box for crossing a farmer's field. The fort is circular (35m in diameter) with dry-stone walls 9m high and up to 4m thick. It is possible to walk from here, over the Windy Gap pass (which lies above the fort), to Lough Currane, and thence to Waterville. This is an excellent trek, but fairly strenuous.

Grey Seals are a common sight in the sheltered coves around here. The wet heathland bordering the Kenmare River is the habitat of the very rare Blue-eyed Grass. This is not a grass at all, but it has a tall thin stem from which develops a delightful blue star-like flower. This can best be seen in the coastal area on the other side of the river, between Lehid Harbour and Ardgroom Harbour. (The former is a good locality to camp and explore.)

The Dingle Peninsula

Getting there and camping:

Like the Ring of Kerry, there is a circular route around the Dingle. For the purposes of our description, we will assume that you are travelling in a clockwise direction. In addition, several islands to the west are worth a visit. There are a number of possible camping areas to consider. We recommend the Inch sand dunes on the southern coast.

Follow the T29 out of Killarney to Tralee. After a mile the road curves to the right and a minor road goes off to the left at a tangent. This is more direct than the main road but both will eventually join the L103. This starts the circular route around Dingle and is signposted first to Castlemaine. The road is straight as it skirts the extensive mudflats of Castlemaine Harbour. When you reach Inch, go into the beach car park, where there is a small track that runs behind the dunes. However, this eventually peters out, so you should beware of getting bogged down. There is ample space for camping. At peak times of the year, such as Bank Holidays, there may be a small charge made for facilities near the entrance (water, toilets etc). However, if you camp far enough away, this need not affect you.

Alternatively, you can camp in any one of several sites on the coast of Tralee Bay. These lie on the T68 out of Tralee town, where there is a tourist information centre from which you can get details of other sorts of accommodation. Bicycles can easily be hired here or from a number of places on the Dingle. Most of the roads are around the coast. A few, such as the Connor Pass, would be difficult cycling terrain. There is also a good bus service from Tralee to Dingle, travelling on the north road.

Inch:

The strand runs out at right angles to the Dingle. The spit is over 3km in length and 1500m at its greatest width. The sand dunes are very extensive and those in the south are mobile. To the north they are eroding on the seaward side to produce a high dune cliff. Marram Grass is the dominant plant with Sea Twitch, Sea Holly and Sea Spurge. Further inland the fixed dunes have abundant flowers including Lady's Bedstraw, Sea Pansy, Pyramidal Orchid, Dune Sweet Pea, Red Bartsia, Biting Stonecrop, Kidney Vetch and Century. There is also the rare grass, *Catapodium*. The grasses in summer are buzzing with insect life, notably butterflies and moths. Larvae of the Six-spot Burnet number 100 per square metre in June. By midsummer the pupae are clearly visible in white cocoons on the grass stems, as are the red and black adults visiting the flower heads. Other species include Grayling butterflies, Dark

The Natterjack Toad, Inch dunes.

Green Fritillaries and Garden Tiger Moths. Rabbits and hares can usually be seen and in the late evening, badgers as well.

When the dunes stabilise, the hollows between them become very damp and are known as slacks. The dominant plants become Dwarf Willows, the beautiful pink Bog Pimpernel and uncommon Yellow Bartsia. In the larger wet depressions you find the Natterjack Toad. This is one of the best colonies in the area. Behind the dune system is a vast expanse of sand and mudflats, exposed at low tide. It almost seems possible to cross over to Cromane Point on the other side, but a deep tidal channel prevents this. Much of this depositing shore is dotted with Eel Grass, one of the few species of flowering plant which uses water to carry its pollen. At the lowest point is a mussel bed with patches of cockles. This area is of considerable importance to wildfowl in autumn and winter. Widgeon, Teal, Pintail, Shoveler and Brent Geese can all be found feeding in this sheltered backwater. The last of these feeds on the Eel Grass.

Around the Dingle:

The scenery of west Dingle is quite superb. It is also an area of special note for archaeologists. There are over 400 beehive huts, of Celtic origin. The best examples are at Fahan, near Ventry. The fishing town of Dingle is located on the edge of an almost landlocked harbour. It is a delightful and busy town with a good tourist information centre from which details of the archaeological sites can be obtained.

On a clear day you should try walking to the summit of Brandon Mountain. At over 1000 metres, this is the second highest in Ireland. As you climb from almost sea-level, there are splendid views across Dingle and to the Blaskets. Seven kilometres north of Dingle on a minor road there is a no-through-road to the right, signposted to Ballybrack. From here a path worn by pilgrims, called the Saint's Road, climbs to St. Brendan's Oratory at the top. An alternative start to the climb is at the end of the road to Brandon Creek, by the sea cliffs. Brandon Mountain is covered by blanket bog through which outcrops of rock project. There are cliffs near the summit which hold an abundance of arctic-alpine flora.

On the way back from the mountain by road, there is a right turning to Ballynanna. A signpost at the village cross-roads will direct you to the Gallurus Oratory. This is an eighth-century hut. Architecturally, it is the successor to the beehive style. Rectangular and exceptionally well preserved, it is constructed entirely from dry stone. Kilmalkedar is a nearby village. In its twelfth-century church there is an Ogham stone, containing ancient runic script. The western tip of Dingle ends with the magnificence of Mount Eagle and Slea Head. From Ventry it is possible to take the coast road. Alternatively, by crossing the high ground to the north of the mountain you can see a spectacular panorama over the Blaskets as you descend towards Dunquin on the coast. Turning right brings you close to Clogher Head, a volcanic rock rich in fossils. The wild scenery of peat bogs and isolated crofts along to Ballyferriter is stunning. It was in this region that the film "Ryan's Daughter" was shot, making use of the natural backdrop. One sequence takes place on the steps down to Dunquin Quay – from where you can travel to the Blaskets (see page 106).

Returning from the town of Dingle, take the mountain route past the Sugarloaf and high through the Connor Pass. There are several spots where you can stop on the road and admire the scenery as you wind between Shevanea (400m) and Ballysitteragh (400m). By following small streams at the side of the road it is possible to find a number of interesting species. You are likely to come across several species of Butterwort – a plant which uses its outstretched leaves to trap insects. By walking further afield from the road, you will see corrie lakes and cliffs that are abundant with alpine plants.

From the Connor Pass you can look down on a huge sand bar which joins a rocky outcrop to the mainland. This feature is known as a tombolo. Once on the coast road to Tralee take the left turn signposted to Castlegregory. This is next to the lake trapped by the tombolo – Lough Gill. The dunes are exceptionally rich and the nutrients which enter the lake make it particularly good for invertebrates as well as a large Natterjack Toad population. The lake is a breeding ground for wildfowl.

At the end of the tombolo are the Magharee Islands, some of which were once joined to the mainland. The rock is limestone and the most northerly tip of the shore, just beyond Fahamore, has fascinating sculptures which have been eroded by the sea. As a seashore it supports an extensive community – the rockpools are well worth exploring. Look out for the unusual purplish crab, *Xantho*, with its large pincers. Echinoderms, such as sea cucumbers, brittle-stars and sea urchins are prolific in the area. Beachcombing is often rewarded with items that have become caught on the rocky outcrop. The corpses of Basking Sharks are not an uncommon find.

The islands immediately offshore have breeding colonies of gulls and other communities suited to the more exposed seashore. Several kilometres out is the lonely island of Inishtooskert with its colony of Storm Petrels and Greater Black-backed Gulls. Seabirds breed on most of the islands and these includes Common and Arctic Terns. It is possible to hire a boat to take you out to the islands. Along this stretch of coast some fishermen still use the traditional curragh type.

Rejoining the T68 on the way to Tralee, the naturalist should stop at Derrymore and walk out to Derrymore Island, which is actually a peninsula. This is a compound spit built up by a series of shingle ridges behind which there is a well developed saltmarsh. The mudflats have large growths of the Cord Grass (*Spartina*) and the Eel Grass which help to support a large wader population. Especially in winter, these include Brent Geese, Pintail and Widgeon.

The Blasket Islands:

These islands off the coast of Dingle are the last parish before America. They have inspired many literary works. One of the most famous is *Twenty years agrowing* by O'Sullivan, in which

The ruined village of Great Blasket, amongst the Ragwort.

he describes the hardships of living on the Blaskets. There are six main islands, but by far the largest is Great Blasket. On the eastern slope are the ruins of a village, evacuated in the 1950s. Many of the local people have repaired their houses to return in the summer months. During the summer there is a small guest house open. To stay a few nights is a memorable experience. It is possible to camp on the island, but you would be well advised to take advantage of the shelter of the ruins.

The boat which will ferry you across to Great Blasket leaves Dunquin Quay in the middle of the morning – weather permitting. It takes just 15 minutes. During the crossing, it is a common sight to see gannets fishing. The boat lands at the foot of the village, and it is only a short walk up the slope to the guest house. This is usually open for food even if you are not staying. Everything is freshly home baked and some food is collected wild from the island. Choughs are a common sight for the birdwatcher. The village is bright yellow in summer because of the ragwort. This supports a large population of Cinnabar Moths and also an interesting brown sub-species of the bumble bee.

Isolation is an important feature of evolution. On these lonely islands many species have become isolated from their populations on the mainland. In most cases they have had little competition with similiar species. Hence, they have been able to occupy habitats from which they would normally be excluded. This opportunity has enabled them to develop into unique forms. This is especially so for the insect population. On Great Blasket the Field Mice have evolved almost rat-like features in the absence of that species. Over many years some have left the grassland to become associated with areas of human habitation. They are very large individuals and more aggressive. All the islands here have unusual species.

In addition to the Great Blasket there are a number of other islands worth visiting. However, special arrangements with the boatman will be necessary. Inishtearaght is an exposed pinnacle of rock. It is the furthest out and is very inaccessible. The steep, loose scree covered edges make climbing very hazardous. It is home for 25,000 Storm Petrels, with Puffins, Kittiwakes and unique species of insects. Nearer at hand is Inishvickillane with grassland and unusual butterflies. Seabirds include Shearwaters, Razorbills, Guillemots, Fulmar, Greater Black-backed Gulls and 10,000 Storm Petrels. Very close to Great Blasket is Beginish with a tern colony and Black Guillemots.

Western Ireland

County Clare

Getting there and camping:

From Dingle or the Ring of Kerry, go to Tralee and follow the T68 to Listowel – about 23km away. A couple of kilometres beyond the town, at Bolton's Cross-roads, there is a fork. Bear left to Tarbert. This small fishing port has a car ferry which crosses the Shannon and avoids the lengthy route via Limerick. If you do travel through Limerick and then on to Ennis, it is worth looking at the Fergus Estuary, which runs into the upper reaches of the Shannon. Turn off at Clarecastle, just before Ennis, and follow the minor road along the estuary. The mudflats and saltmarshes are rich in animal life. This in turn feeds the thousands of waders which flock here in autumn, notably Godwits, Redshank, Widgeon and Dunlin. The car ferry leaves from a pier a few miles beyond Tarbert. It lands near Killimer where there is a camp-site. We recommend that you follow the coastline up to The Burren.

A good place to camp is on the extensive dunes at Fanore, in the north of that region. The land belongs to a farmer. He lets mobile homes which are scattered over the site. It can clearly be seen from the road. However, you can camp well away from these – continue along the track, past the farmhouse and down to the rocky beach. Tents can be pitched on the grass above the shore. Campers are expected to pay a nominal amount. Toilets, water and other facilities are provided near the main site. This is not a normal camp-site and you can isolate yourself from other campers.

The coastline here is very striking. Sitting outside your tent, you can watch dolphins playing offshore. Alternatively, you may decide to camp in the wilderness of The Burren. Although dry, the terrain is invariably hard and rocky. There are some suitable spots near Carran, or in the area around the Glen of Clab. The latter requires permission from the farmer. There are a few official camp-sites. These are on the coast – there is a large site near Lehinch. A small quiet site can be found at Fisherstreet, a lovely fishing village on the south of The Burren. Most of the larger towns have hostels. The summer information centre in Lisdoonvarna will help with addresses.

Purple Sea Urchin, dominating the rockpools of the Burren coast.

Loop Head to Lehinch:

Leaving the Tarbert ferry, you should take the road to Kilrush. Loop Head is the southernmost point of County Clare and can be reached by following the road to Kilkee and then the L51 to the head. The coastline is very wild and exposed. Even the grass looks stunted. However, there is a well developed flora and the cliffs afford protection for nesting Kittiwakes and nearly 3,000 Guillemots. If you are not visiting Loop Head take the L54 out of Kilrush. This is a turning off the main T41 road, near the school. Go straight on at the Creegh cross-roads, until you meet the sea again at Quilty. Take the sharp left turning to go southwards. The sea is the livelihood for most people living here. The seaweed on the beach is still harvested for fertiliser. Carefully stacked bundles of dried kelp can be seen above the cliff, near the car park in Quilty.

Almost 3km further on is Lurga Point. Beyond it lies Mutton Island, with a small chapel dedicated to St. Senan. The island is important geologically. It can easily be seen that it is composed of moraine debris, left over from the last ice-age. In addition, it is a vital overwintering site for Barnacle Geese and other wildfowl. It has a particularly large population of hares. This windswept stretch of coast is renowned for its number of shipwrecks. These include many vessels from the Spanish Armada, which sailed around Scotland and down this side of Ireland to avoid the British. Several galleons were sunk here. One sinking on the reefs of Lurga and Mutton Island killed more than a thousand men. Others were wrecked on Spanish Point, at the other end of the bay. The sailors were then buried there.

The rock from Lurga to Spanish Point is limestone. This has eroded to produce an amazing shoreline with an incredible richness of species. Here again you can find rockpools choked with the Purple Sea Urchin. It thrives along this western coast and is found elsewhere only in the Mediterranean. In the more sunlit pools the urchins pull shells and seaweeds over themselves with their tube feet. This serves like a parasol – shading them from the burning rays. In parts the beaches are sandy. Where the sand has dried and blown, dunes have developed which are dominated by sea holly. A few miles south of Lurga Point is an interesting lake, Lough Donnell. This was once an inlet, but has now been cut off from the sea by a storm beach of pebbles. The area is excellent birdwatching territory.

Continuing up the coast takes you into the long sweeping bay of Lehinch – a favourite tourist town in these parts. From here you can reach The Burren by carrying on along the coast or by going inland to the lovely market town of Ennistymon. This is situated on the River Cullenagh which cascades towards the sea. It is known as the gateway to The Burren.

The Burren:

"No water to drown a man; no tree to hang a man and no soil to bury a man." With these words, the pillaging Cromwell described the unique landscape of The Burren. It certainly should not be missed! The entire area is characterised by spectacular limestone scenery which produces a moon-like landscape stretching down to the sea. Where the rock has been eroded by water, deep clefts (called "clints" and "grykes") have formed. These are ideal sites for the rich flora. To see the plant-life at its most beautiful, you should come in early summer when the bright colours contrast with the stark land. Any vegetation trying to grow out of these grykes is flattened and stunted by the Atlantic winds. The water drains away underground, and has carved out a cavern and cave system, which extends over more than 40km. Some parts are open to the public. One of these, the Pol-an-Ionain Caves, contains one of the largest stalactites in the world – 10m in length. The Kilwee Caves are the most visited and the easiest to view. The area includes some unusual lakes, which are known as "turloughs". In dry weather they vanish underground but may reappear after rain. So be careful where you place your tent – by morning you could be in the middle of a lake! Wherever you go on The Burren there is plentiful evidence of the presence of early man. In the centre of the region to the north of Caherconnell, there are several burial chambers or "dolmens".

The coast:

The journey along the coast from Lehinch to Ballyvaghan – in the north of The Burren – is a memorable one. There are many places worth exploring. The first stop is at the Cliffs of Moher – an awesome 206m in height. The population of nesting seabirds is one of the most important in Ireland. There are thousands of Kittiwakes, Fulmar, Herring Gulls, Greater Black-backed Gulls, Guillemots, Razorbills, Puffins and Shags. One of the best views is from O'Briens Tower, reached by following the coastal path.

From the cliffs, follow the signpost to Fisherstreet. The shore along here – opposite Crab Island – abounds in Purple Sea Urchins. The rock pools are some of the best examples along the coast. The limestone above the shore has an excellent flora.

A trip inland will bring you to the spa town of Lisdoonvarna. The town lies among some very remote and wild scenery. To the south are vast tracts of acidic peat bogs. This is being cut in the area around Lough Coller. In recent years some dragonflies rare to Ireland have been discovered here. To the north of Lisdoonvarna is the limestone of The Burren.

Take the L54 to the coast at Poulsallagh. The windy road suddenly brings you to a magnificent view of the Aran Islands. Gradually, you move into the area where the scenery and flora are limestone based. At Poulsallagh the botanist will find a unique region. The maritime and limestone influences combine with a range of plants characteristic of zones from the arctic to the Mediterranean. At their peak the Bloody Cranesbill produce a riot of colour to combine with Spring Gentians, Orchids and Rock Rose.

The transition of species from the seashore, on to the limestone and up the slopes of Knockaums Mountain is fascinating. The climb, with splendid views to the Arans, not only reveals changes in the plants but also in rock formations. This is the boundary between soft shales and limestone, producing a varied landscape with sink holes and caves. There is a minor road which winds up the mountain here. It gives a good start for the higher climb to the summit of Slieve Elva. The slopes are dotted with stunted woodland and ancient tombs. Further along the coast road are a series of sand dunes at Fanore. It is here that the River Aher drains from the limestone to the sea. This is the only permanent river in the Burren. The dunes are fascinating. Look out for the limestone pavements. They often show through near the sea or in the slacks.

The northern tip of The Burren ends with the magnificent Black Head. Superficially it appears to lack any vegetation. In fact, like Poulsallagh, it possesses a marked transition of species from sea-level to the highest point. The range of habitats here is even greater, because of the considerable influence of the glaciers which helped in the shaping of Galway Bay. The climb is strenuous but unmissable! The views on a clear day are superb. There are several plants to look out for: the Bearberry, the Mountain Avens, Dark Red Helleborine, Maidenhair Fern and a species of Cotoneaster at the summit. There are several species of

A carpet of the rare arctic-alpine Mountain Avens, common on The Burren.

saxifrage. The conditions become more sheltered on the other side of Black Head. On the seaward side of the road you should look out for wild or feral goat herds, as this is an area where they survive particularly well. (They can also be seen fairly easily on Ross Island, near Killarney). You will pass through Ballyvaghan – a small village with some excellent "watering holes".

As a result of the high degree of shelter there is an extensive saltmarsh with mudflats and rocky outcrops. This makes it good for seabirds. A short distance outside the village, on the landward side, is the Ballyvaghan Turlough where a superb growth of the Shrubby Cinquefoil can be seen. This is a spindly bush with yellow flowers. At the end of this coastal stretch is a small village called Burren, about 9km from Ballyvaghan. The main road makes a ninety degree turn to the right. By going straight on you travel down a minor road to Finavarra village and Lough Murree. The sheltered inlets and freshwater lake ensure good birdwatching.

The inland limestone scenery:

From Ballyvaghan it is a impressive journey back towards Ennistymon. The road forks after a mile. The right-hand turn will take you up Corkscrew Hill, and then to Lisdoonvarna. The left turn to Kilfenora is more interesting. This will take you past a number of well preserved megalithic tombs, such as Poulnabrone on the left-hand side. There are also forts such as Caherconnell. You should also look out for the caves at Kilcorney, which are associated with a nearby turlough. On this route you cannot fail to see the signs for the well-known Ailwee Caves. During the height of the season the caves may be quite crowded, while The Burren is deserted – especially if it is raining! These are the only commercialised caves on The Burren. At Kilfenora there is a good display of artefacts from the area in The Burren Centre. It also provides further details of the region, although the entrance fee is a little expensive. The ancient church nearby has a twelfth-century cross. This is 4m high, and is covered with clear carvings and inscriptions.

The eastern side of The Burren is more remote. Carran is a good base from which to explore this part. The most interesting feature in this area is Mullagh More. This rounded bulk is 190m in height, and can thus be seen from a great distance. It is an excellent climb. There are Mountain Avens at the top, and the

The Glen of Clab.

flanks are dotted with stunted trees that grow out of the grykes. A pothole-scarred road leads east from the cross-roads at Knockaunroe. The route passes some exceptionally good limestone pavement and small turloughs. The flora is a naturalist's dream. It includes bushes of Shrubby Cinquefoil and a profusion of smaller varieties. The stunted woodland of elm and hazel is home to dark green Fritillary butterflies. The folding limestone of Mullagh More provides a superb backdrop.

From the summit of Mullagh More, Lough Bunny can be seen to the east. This deep lake has a well developed fenland, with orchids. The rare Dropwort plant can be found nearby. Many bird species come here to feed, including gulls, wildfowl, terns and waders.

An exploration of The Burren would not be complete without a visit to the remote regions around Slievecarran – even higher than Black Head. Taking the minor road eastwards out of Carran village, you will come across a water-filled turlough. At this point, take the very minor road to Doomore, on your left. After a few miles the road becomes hemmed in by hazel thickets. A track to the left, through the woodland, appears very quickly. This is the entrance to the Glen of Clab. Once inside this dry ravine, there is a distinct transition of vegetation on either side. The very steep sides are thickly wooded with hazel, ash, rowan and birch. The branches are covered by rich growths of mosses and lichens. This woodland is one of the finest on The Burren. A track climbs to the right until it reaches the top end of the Glen. The track then gradually disappears. On this stretch, the rocks and shallow soils are carpeted with Mountain Avens and other rarities. Just over the brow from here a huge depression can be seen in the ground. This is a "doline" – formed by a collapsed cavern deep in the limestone. It is called Poullavallan.

Back on the road, you wind on upwards towards Slievecarran and Eagles' Rock. If you have any energy left, the climb to the top is well worth it. On a clear day, the view spans across Galway to the Twelve Bens and Connemara. The stunted woodland on the slopes is excellent. It supports a rich bird fauna.

The Aran Islands

If time allows, a visit to the Aran Islands is an unforgettable experience. A famous early documentary, made by Flaherty in the 1930s, chronicled the old ways of Aran. Even today, they almost seem to live in another time. These islands are part of County Galway. To reach them, you will first have to visit Galway city.

Walking across Inishmore, the largest of the Aran Islands. On top of the cliff to the right is Dun Aengus.

There are two ways to travel to the islands – by boat or plane. The latter is certainly more convenient. A twelve-seater Islander plane, operated by Aran Air, makes the journey in thirty minutes. The views are breathtaking from the air. Your plane lands on a stretch of dune. Ferries are quite numerous. Crossings vary in length, from an hour and three quarters to three hours. The average cost is about £12 return. If you are going only for the day, careful consideration of routes is therefore needed. It is best to contact the tourist information office in Galway to receive an up-to-date guide on the different ferries – their costs and times. Once on the main island, Inishmore, there is another information centre at the pier in Kilronan. Maps are sold with details of sites, as well as information on the twice daily boats to the other islands of Inishmaan and Inisheer.

Transport consists of old taxis (occasional), hired bikes (very bumpy) or walking. It is possible to walk from Kilronan to Kilmurvy and back again in a day and still see the sights. If you stay, there is little trouble in finding Bed & Breakfast accommodation. Camping is officially illegal, but many people ignore this without difficulty.

The island is a huge limestone platform, set 100m above the sea. There are sheer cliffs and little natural soil. Over the centuries, the islanders have broken the rocks into fragments and mixed them with seaweed and what little soil they could find. By placing dry stone walls around it, a landscape of walls and tiny fields has been created. It is a bleak existence. The lack of soil produces problems with burials. As you enter Kilronan, there are several large, upright stone coffins with crosses on top. Most fresh water is collected rain water. Few houses have electricity.

The island is famous for its well preserved prehistoric forts. Dun Cathir stands on a lonely promontory, with a single wall and beehive huts. Near Kilmurvy is Dun Aengus, the finest fort of all. It has a commanding view over the island. The approaching invader would have to pass through the chevaux-de-frise – a series of very sharp, outward-angled stones. The wall is 6m thick and once again there are beehive huts. Food is expensive to buy on the island, and the best bet is to visit a tea house. These are local houses with a handwritten sign outside. There is an excellent one in Kilmurvy – try the homemade soup, bread and cakes.

Before going to the Aran Islands, it is interesting to have read something about the life of the people. Try Thomas Mason's *Islands of Ireland*. Several authors have come from the island –

J. Bynge, for example, who wrote the play *Riders to the Sea*. Better still, try to see Flaherty's original documentary.

ADDRESSES

Irish Tourist Board,
Ireland House,
150, New Bond St.,
London W1.
Telephone: 01-493-3201.

An Foras Forbartha, [For details of Sites of Special
St. Martin's House, Scientific Interest]
Waterloo Road,
Dublin 4.
Telephone: Dublin 764211.

Irish Wildbird Conservancy,
Southview, Church Road,
Greystones,
County Wicklow.
Telephone: Dublin 875759.

NORWAY

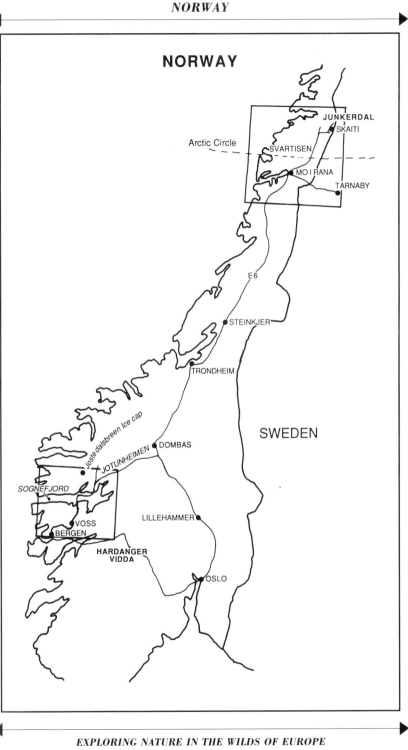

NORWAY

JUNKERDAL

SKAITI

Arctic Circle

SVARTISEN

MO I RANA

TARNABY

E6

STEINKJER

TRONDHEIM

SWEDEN

Joste dalsbreen Ice cap

JOTUNHEIMEN

DOMBAS

SOGNEFJORD

LILLEHAMMER

VOSS
BERGEN

HARDANGER
VIDDA

OSLO

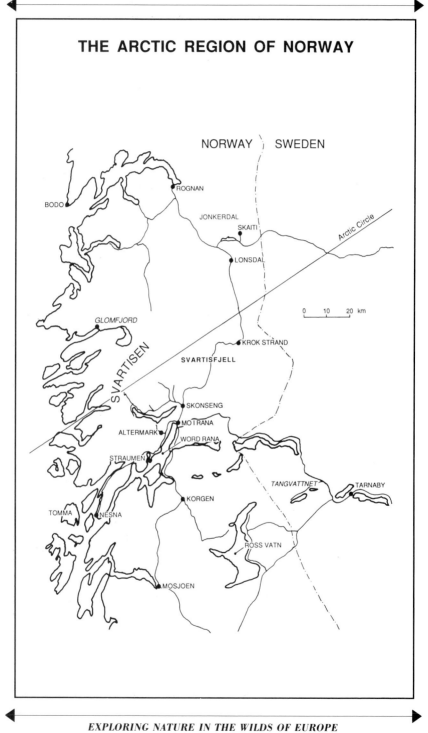

THE ARCTIC REGION OF NORWAY

NORWAY) SWEDEN

BODO

ROGNAN

JONKERDAL

SKAITI

Arctic Circle

LONSDAL

GLOMFJORD

0   10   20 km

KROK STRAND

SVARTISFJELL

SVARTISEN

SKONSENG

MO I RANA

ALTERMARK

WORD RANA

STRAUMEN

TANGVATTNET

TARNABY

KORGEN

TOMMA

NESNA

ROSS VATN

MOSJOEN

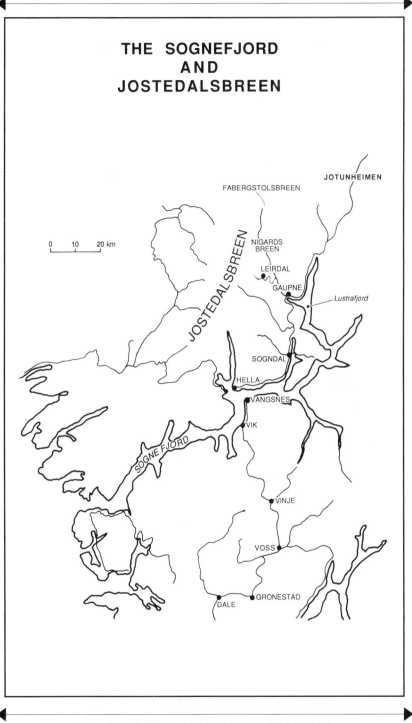

THE SOGNEFJORD
AND
JOSTEDALSBREEN

JOTUNHEIMEN

FABERGSTOLSBREEN

JOSTEDALSBREEN

0   10   20 km

NIGARDS
BREEN

LEIRDAL

GAUPNE

Lustrafjord

SOGNDAL

HELLA

VANGSNES

VIK

SOGNE FJORD

VINJE

VOSS

GRONESTAD

DALE

Introduction

Norway combines easy access from the United Kingdom with a wealth of unfamiliar landscapes, natural history and culture. The remote scenery offers a spectacular backdrop to the serious hill walker and casual hiker alike. From the desolate mountain regions to the wooded slopes of the fjords there is an impressive variety of locations to explore. The naturalist will find that Norway's plant life is one of the most varied and exciting in Europe. Birdwatching too, will reveal much that is new to the foreign visitor. The Norwegian people, like most Scandinavians, are welcoming and open, while the Lapps of the north are proud of their separate identity.

Geography

Norway stretches for a grand total of 1770km, while its width varies from 435km to 6km. Like a spine running along its back, the Scandinavian mountain chain extends for approximately 1700km (this is about half as long again as the Alps). Much of the land is characterised by high plateaux. These often lie over 1000m in altitude, and are scattered with small lakes and peat bogs. At a higher altitude still, lie the many mountain peaks – sharpened by centuries of glacial activity. The highest of these is Glittertinden in the Jotunheimen, which reaches 2481m. The plateaux are slashed by a large number of long valleys. The lower ends have become fjords, while the upper reaches often contain freshwater lakes. This series of lateral gashes is a major factor in slowing down any north-south journey. The action of the ice carves out the typical U-shape of a glaciated valley. Towards the coast, there is a relatively narrow strip of flat and well cultivated land. The subsidence of the western edge of Norway means that the peaks of old hills now form offshore islands.

Climate

The climate of Norway is far less extreme than its latitude would suggest, because of the warm Gulf Stream which passes the coast. The proximity of the sea and the long mountain chain mean that rainfall is considerable – over 2m a year in Bergen. Visitors to the country should be prepared for a wide variation in temperature. The high plateaux and ice fields can be bitterly cold even in high summer, while inland reaches of Lapland can have temperatures of over 30 degrees centigrade.

Vegetation

Three main vegetation zones can be distinguished: tundra, taiga and the lowlands. The last of these consists primarily of deciduous woodland and is generally the most heavily populated. Tundra is a treeless region because of the cold winds and permafrost (a permanently frozen subsoil). The characteristic vegetation is of lichen, a prime source of food for reindeer. When the upper layers of soil thaw in spring, boggy pools form on the surface – a breeding place for mosquitoes. Tundra is not restricted to the area north of the Arctic Circle, but is related more to altitude. Large areas of the Jotunheimen conform to this pattern.

Taiga is a region of coniferous forest, bordering the inhospitable tundra. The trees are primarily larch and spruce, rarely reaching maturity because of the shallow soils and flooding in spring.

Motoring in Norway

The roads in Norway are generally well built and well signposted. It should be remembered that their priority is to get you to your destination, but not necessarily at high speed. Crossing fjords and climbing hills will dramatically slow your progress. In a day's driving, you can only expect to cover half the distance that you would in the UK. Bear this in mind when planning your route. The vast distances and frequent narrow and winding stretches of road mean that experienced and careful driving is required.

Drivers need to ensure that they have their licences, vehicle registration documents and "green card". Law also requires a red warning triangle and a spare set of light bulbs.

The speed limits in Norway are 90km/h on motorways, 80km/h on open roads and 50km/h in towns. Alcohol limits are very strict and random police checks are standard practice. It is also customary to drive with dipped lights at all times.

Visitors should be aware of the extensive network of vehicle-carrying ferries which serve the fjords and islands. Possible delays of an hour or so waiting for these should be borne in mind when planning routes.

All octanes of petrol are available, as is DERV. The former is particularly expensive.

Maps

A good general map of the whole country (1:1,000,000) is available from Esso petrol stations. The best regional maps are the 1:250,000 – Series 1501, which display geographical features and contours in good detail. For hiking and detailed exploration the 1:50,000 – Series M711 is very accurate. Both series are available from Stanford's, but the latter may need to be ordered in advance.

Language

The Norwegian language has two principal dialects. Bokmal is spoken in the towns while Nynorsk is used in the countryside. Gradually, these two are fusing into a single form, Samnorsk. This process will take many years. In addition, the Lapps have their own language, Samisk.

English is almost everyone's second language. It is widely spoken, except in the north and more rural areas of the country.

Currency

The Norwegian *krone* is divided into 100 *ore*.
Banknotes: 10, 50, 100, 500 & 1000 kr.
Coinage: 5, 10, 25, 50 ore; 1 & 5 kr.

The only currency restriction is a limit of 800kr (including no 500kr notes) to be taken out of the country.

Foreign banknotes and Traveller's Cheques can be exchanged on North Sea ferries, in many ports, all airports, large railway stations and some big hotels. Banks are open from 0900 until 1500 hours on weekdays. In rural areas banks may only open on particular days. Major credit cards (including Access and Barclaycard) are widely accepted, as are Eurocheques. In general, prices in Norway are rather higher than in the UK (especially for clothing and alcohol). All prices and costs given in this section are calculated on the basis of an approximate exchange rate of £1=10kr.

Camping

The right of visitors to camp on uncultivated land ("outfields") was recently confirmed by the "Open Air Act". Thus, Norway is an excellent country to camp in – as long as you can find somewhere flat! Hence, we lay very little emphasis on official sites, as free alternatives of similar standard can usually be found nearby. Most official camp-sites are quite sophisticated, with cabins that can be hired for £2–£4 per person per night. This restricts your choice far less than relying solely on scarce youth hostels. As a result, it is possible to make a fairly lengthy journey without needing tents. A common problem when camping in Norway is rocky ground. It is a good idea to bring a spare ground-sheet which can be placed under the tent. This minimises the chance of puncturing the sown-in ground-sheet. It is also wise to take plenty of spare pegs, and when possible to reinforce them with rocks in order to provide greater stability.

Gas for cooking is often difficult to find in remote areas. If you cook by petrol then burners will need regular cleaning, as even low-octane fuel contains lead.

Fishing

Fishing in the sea is unrestricted, although a licence is required for freshwater. This is obtainable from local Post Offices.

Food and Shopping

There is little difficulty in buying food in Norway. Supermarkets or general stores are common in most towns and large villages. You should, however, be prepared to pay proportionately more than you would in the UK. Fish is one of the more reasonably priced commodities, and is widely available in the coastal or fjord areas. Most foodstuffs are fairly familiar, although we would like to recommend the powerful "Salt og Pepper" crisps, and strongly warn against the sickly "Brygg" beer!

Restaurants are often of good quality, but they can be very expensive. A cheaper alternative is to eat at the railway stations, which offer good food at subsidised prices. Wine can only be purchased with a meal and will cost between £8 and £10 a bottle.

Most shops are open from 0900 until 1700 hours on weekdays. Some remain open late on Thursdays, but almost all are closed on Saturday afternoons and all day Sunday.

Medical

The most apparent medical problem in Norway is that of biting insects, and mosquitoes in particular. (See Planning and Preparation chapter, page 5 for suggested precautions and cures.)

The climate is another source of problems. Climbers should be aware that ultra-violet light from the sun is much stronger at altitude. Thus a good barrier cream is advisable on bright days. At the opposite extreme, hypothermia is a very real danger in areas like the Jotunheimen, especially if you become wet.

No inoculations are required for Norway, although it is always a good idea to have a tetanus booster before travelling.

The Health Service in Norway is very efficient. However, you should be sure to take out suitable insurance (such as that offered by the RAC or AA), before departure.

Jostedalsbreen

Leirdal

Getting there:

The journey from the port of Bergen to our suggested base in the Jostedalsbreen region is straightforward and yet spectacular. The necessity of crossing the Stolsheimen mountains means that the 250–300km route cannot be comfortably completed in a single day. In a sense, this is not a bad thing, as it would be a shame not to fully appreciate the scenery by rushing. On leaving the town of Bergen, you should get straight onto Route 13 which then snakes its way north and away from the coast. For about 25km it hugs the wooded edge of the Sorfjord, which affords excellent views.

Some 50km along Route 13, you reach a group of four deep, clear lakes near the village of Gronestad. These have been dammed in order to provide the area with hydroelectric power. If you decide to break the journey to Leirdal, this is an ideal spot in which to do so. The engineers have created several small flat plateaux at the side

The reservoir of glacial water, Leirdal.

of the lakes. These are accessed via small tracks off the main road (a sharp eye is needed to spot them). They are good, if somewhat rocky, sites for tents.

The deep, glaciated valley is covered with luxuriant vegetation because of the very high rainfall in the Bergen area. The hillsides are steep and covered by birch scrub, with an undergrowth of heathers. This is typical of a highland heath with a covering of bog. Walking around the site, you can find the Tiger Lily, Arctic Catchfly and a wide range of wintergreens. Stag's-head Club Moss is also common here, often growing to over a metre in length.

Beyond the town of Voss there is a spectacular crossing of the Stolsheimen.

Selaginella, the Club Moss.

This long and steep route takes you up to the snow-line, even in summer. You pass a succession of rivers and waterfalls, before being greeted with a photogenic panorama down to the Sognefjord, and the town of Vik. Contrary to the impression given by some tourist literature, the cross-fjord ferries do not leave from here, but from Vangsnes, which lies another 10km along the shore. Vangsnes is one of several towns which are served by the wide variety of ferries and cruises which criss-cross the Sognefjord. Any such trip provides a splendid new perspective from which to view the impressive fjord scenery.

The range of different routes mean that it is important to get into the correct lane for loading – in this case the crossing to Hella on the opposite shore. The cost is between £3 and £5 for a vehicle.

Once in Hella, it requires another three hours driving to reach Leirdal. Initially, you follow Route 5 along the edge of the fjord for 25km and then join Route 55 for a similar distance. You then have to leave this road and join Route 604 for 10km, and then take a turning to the left, signed for Leirdal. At this point the road curves upward in a succession of steep hairpins. You can follow the road almost to its conclusion, before taking a dirt track for 3km which brings you close to the edge of the large Lake Tunsburgdalsvatnet, with Mount Sala towering above it. A variety of possible camp-sites then present themselves. These are flat and not too hard, although the most suitable are unfortunately covered with dried and flattened sheep dung.

The camp-site area:

Several factors recommend this spot as a suitable centre for your exploration of the Jostedalsbreen area. As well as being reasonably flat, it is remote from civilisation and is a beautiful landscape in which to camp. In common with much of the area around the inner reaches of the Sognefjord, Leirdal is blessed with a relatively dry climate – an important fact to consider when touring the western fjords. The access road follows a river valley. Hence there are lakes which provide fresh water for drinking and washing – hardy (and mosquito-proof) souls can also find some spots which are deep enough for swimming. The rivers and lakes will also provide much of interest for the naturalist.

If you need to purchase food in the area, then small supermarkets can be found in Fossoy and Gaupne, 10km north and south along Route 604 respectively. At Gaupne, there is also an excellent medical centre which serves the region.

Moving away from the centre of the valley, you soon find yourself in quite substantial areas of Norway Spruce-based woodland (in which Bilberries, Twin Flower and various wintergreens can be found). On a practical level, this provides good quantities of firewood, but it is also a productive source of small mammals. These include Grey-sided Voles, mice, shrews, Red Squirrels and the Norway Lemming.

Lemming populations are subject to marked cyclical fluctuations. If you arrive soon after one of these mass migrations has taken place, then it will prove particularly difficult to see (let alone catch) any live specimens. Conversely, if you come during a "Lemming Year", then you will have difficulty avoiding them.

The area around the camp is also home for flocks of Fieldfares and a smaller number of Redwings.

Alternative camp-sites:

The main advantages of Leirdal are its relative seclusion and central location for visits to the Jostedalsbreen ice-cap and the Sognefjord. It should be possible to retain these factors by exploring any of the roads which leave Route 55 and follow the course of glacial valleys northwards between Fardal and Hauge.

Mount Sala:

Mount Sala provides an impressive backdrop to the Leirdal site. It is 1701m in height, and towers above the valley and Lake Tunsburgdalsvatnet. It is well worth climbing up to the snow-capped ridge – both for the scenery and for the wide variety of plant life on the slope. An energetic walker could complete the ascent and descent in five hours or so.

The climb can be fairly steep at times, but there is certainly no need for special climbing equipment, although strong boots are a good idea.

The distance to the foot of the mountain depends on how far along the river valley you have camped. However, the climb starts about 150m before the dirt track reaches the lake. Initially you follow the paths which climb up through the region of birch wood at the foot of the slope. Once above this point, the vegetation is far less constricting and the most direct route can be selected. Sheep are

A Fritillary butterfly on mosses, Leirdal.

grazed on the slopes and the shepherds' hut provides a pleasant area of shade in which to rest and gaze down on the bright turquoise of Tunsburgdalsvatnet far below.

If you have the time and inclination, it is worth making your way through the snow field, to the top of the ridge. This affords a splendid panoramic view to the west. The other side of Mount Sala leads down to a flooded glacial valley, which has become Lake Veitastrondvatnet. Beyond that lie another set of snow-capped ridges, about 150m lower than Sala.

In addition to the obvious beauty of the glaciated landscape, the naturalist will find great interest in exploring the flora of the mountain slopes, and in particular, investigating the way in which the plant types vary as altitude increases – from the birch woods at the foot to the very sparse vegetation as you near the summit.

If you trace the path of the river of melt-water through the birch forest, various small clearings open out. In these, Norwegian Cudweed, Wood Cow Wheat and Alpine Sow Thistle can all be found – these are rare species in Britain. Amid the profusion of flowers fly Heath Fritillary butterflies and dragonflies. The latter hawk up and down the clearings catching flying insects which live in great numbers here. As you ascend, the birch gives way to a mixed community of Bilberry and Mat Grass. In this area it is possible to spot the rare Blue Heath. A large species of Formica ant lives here. As you approach the snow-line, the vegetation is considerably limited. However, a cliff below the summit, which has not collected snow, produces a good selection of acid alpines. These include Alpine Rivulet Saxifrage and Hairy Rock Cress, although the most interesting is the scarce Frog Orchid. Towards the summit, the vegetation is naturally very sparse, although it is possible to find Alpine Catchfly and Glacier Crowfoot – the latter holds the altitude record for a plant in Norway.

Above the treeline of birch, the bird species to be seen are Ptarmigan and Snow Buntings.

Sognefjord

Vik and Hopperstad:

Vik itself is a picturesque town on the edge of the Sognefjord, but the principal item of interest lies about a mile further up Route 13 – the renowned church of Hopperstad.

Hopperstad church was built in the thirteenth century in the "stave" style for which Norway is so famous. The distinctive

The town of Vik on the edge of the Sognefjord. The boat crossing to Hella is just visible in the background.

features of a stave (or "standing wood") church are the corner posts and wall planks standing on sills, and the covered walkway which encircles the building. The roofs are particularly steep, in order to prevent snow standing on them for long periods. The whole building is blackened by a covering of pitch.

Both inside and out, the church is intricately carved. Particularly interesting are the dragons' heads which gaze out from the roof like the prows of Viking longboats. Visitors should note that there is an admission fee of £1.

While you are in the Vik area, keep a sharp eye out for Pine Martens which can often be seen running across the road, and Red Squirrels in the surrounding woodland.

The Fjords:

"Fjord" is a Norwegian word which refers to a long, narrow inlet from the sea. Geographers believe that they were originally river valleys. During the ice-age, glaciers making their way to the sea scoured out deep troughs. Generally very deep, fjords are shallower towards the mouth because the glacier loses some of its erosive power.

The Sognefjord is Norway's longest fjord. It stretches 185km inland to the base of the Jotunheimen Mountains. In places it can be 1250m deep, with the sheer rock face rising over 500m above the water-line. There are three factors which dictate the plants that inhabit the fjord edge: the salt-water from the sea, the fresh-water inflow from the retreating glaciers and the shelter afforded by the distance from the sea.

Ness, on the Lustrafjord (a tributary of the Sognefjord), can be found about 20km from Leirdal on Route 55. Tidal movement is slight and the rocky shores along here are unsuitable for beach combing, due in part to the steepness. However, the shoreline does bear many similarities to the shores 185km away on the Atlantic coast. It shows a typical banding of seaweeds as you start at the top of the shore and move down to the bottom. The most fascinating feature of this is the way that the seawater, diluted by the glacial meltwater, has caused the larger seaweeds to deform into unusual varieties. For example, the Bladderwrack is curly instead of flat. The extent of deformity varies from Hella (where the species are normal), to the upper reaches of the Lustrafjord (where malformation is most extreme). Above the bands of seaweed, a narrow but dense belt of lichens grow. The soil is thin between here and the road, but you can find Alpine Woodsia, Oblong Woodsia and Perennial Knawel.

Gaupne, about 5km back towards Leirdal, provides a different type of habitat. It lies at the head of the Gaupnefjord (a small branch off the Lustrafjord). The vegetation is dramatically affected by the fact that all the melt-water from the nearby glacial and valley systems flows into the fjord at this point. Thus, a muddy delta has formed, which is slowly being transformed into saltmarsh.

The Vernal Sandwort is present on the upper shore – this is an extremely rare species in this part of Norway. The white Grass of Parnassus is less rare, but is particularly pretty.

As well as the plant life, the saltmarsh is also a fine place for bird-spotting. The glacial river deposits provide a breeding ground for Mallard, Arctic Terns and Arctic Skuas. Herring Gulls, Red-necked Phalarope and Redshank can also be sighted. Further offshore in the fjord you can see Slavonian Grebes, Saw-billed Ducks, Red and Black-throated Divers and even Black Guillemots.

The Glaciers

The Jostedalsbreen Ice-cap:

The Jostedalsbreen icefield is the largest in mainland Europe. It covers an area of some 777 square kilometres. A total of 24 named glaciers emerge from the main mass of ice and fall down into narrow valleys. A visit to this spectacular natural phenomenon will undoubtedly be one of the highlights of a trip to Norway.

The glaciers in Norway are described as retreating – this means that the wastage at the snout (through melting and evaporation) is greater than the addition of new ice at the head of the glacier.

The two glaciers which we go on to describe are offshoots of the main Jostedalsbreen field. They can be accessed with reasonable ease from Leirdal, and they also illustrate many of the classic geographical and biological features that one associates with glacier systems. There is a marked contrast between them, because of the lake at Nigardsbreen – hence it is a good idea to try and visit both. The sites are certainly more suitable than those found at Svartisen.

Nigardsbreen:

The Nigardsbreen glacier is at present the most easily accessible. Unfortunately, this does bring the problem of considerable tourist interest in the summer. Thus, if you have a reasonably robust vehicle it is worth concentrating most of your time at Fabergstolsbreen.

The site is reached after a 40 minute drive up Route 604. There is a turning to the left off the main road which takes you up to the edge of Glacier Lake. This lasts for only a few kilometres but a toll of about £1 is required for cars. There is a newly enlarged parking area with excellent views over the lake to the massive snout. There are then two options if you want to reach the ice: firstly, there is a well marked footpath along the edge of the lake which will take about 80 minutes for good walkers; secondly, and more relaxing, you can catch the boat "Jostedalsrypa" (the Jostedal ptarmigan). This takes you to the far edge of the lake, from where it is a half hour walk to the ice-tongue. The boat operates between 1000 and 1800 hours between 20 June and 20 August. The fare is approximately 70p.

On days when the boat is operating, it is also possible to join easy 2¹/2 hour hikes on the glacier. Crampons (ice-spikes) and ropes are required, but these can be borrowed from the experienced guide. This will give an unforgettable impression of the colossal and fantastically shaped ice masses. The hikes leave at 1115 and 1400 hours – groups would be wise to book beforehand by telephoning (056) 83 117.

The road which leads from the lake to Route 604 is also interesting, because of the impressive terminal moraines which stretch across the valley. These are huge ridges of rock debris which had been pushed down by the advancing ice and then left as the glacier retreated back. There are two main moraines – the lowest dates from 1748 while the largest was left in 1875. By climbing the moraine it is also possible to find a particularly good vantage point for photographs. Moraine debris is also responsible for the existence of the lake as it provides a natural dam for the melt-water.

Fabergstolsbreen:

The Fabergstolsbreen glacier is less easy to reach than its southern neighbour. However, this fact in itself means that it is

The Fabergstolsbreen Glacier from about a quarter of a mile away.

rarely visited and hence is unspoilt by the trappings of tourism. This is especially useful if any serious botanical studies are intended.

The area is reached by continuing north along Route 604, past the exit to Nigardsbreen. About 8km later you reach the minute settlement of Bjornstegene. At this point another toll is required. There is a small hut next to a gate across the road. Two tickets have to be completed with the registration numbers of the vehicles. One is kept and the other placed in a small box, together with about £2. Beyond the gate, the quality of the track deteriorates significantly, eventually becoming a simple set of tyre marks. The series of rickety wooden bridges need to be crossed with care. Some 5km later the track passes through a large area of waste ground, just after the main melt-water torrent – an ideal spot in which to leave the vehicles.

The walk along the glacial valley is deceptively long and fairly arduous. Before entering the valley, the terminal moraine has to be negotiated. This has been colonised by birch and willow scrub, together with many Frog Orchids. As you get closer to the valley, large boulders and rocks make the walk slow and unsteady. Bearing to the right it is not long before you reach the mouth of the valley, and the boulders are replaced by a comparatively flat-bottomed U-shape with tall scree sides. A gushing river of ice-cold melt-water splashes over the rocks in the centre of the valley. As you follow the curve of the sides you are greeted by an awe-inspiring sight. For miles ahead you can see the glacier swerving between the rock peaks like a vast ivory motorway, 200m in width, before taking up the entire head of the valley.

As you approach the snout, the wind becomes appreciably colder. This is a phenomenon known as "glacier breeze" – a wind formed because the air next to the ice is cooled by it, and then flows along the course of the valley under the influence of gravity.

In order to reach the ice itself, it is necessary to cross the fast flowing river of melt-water. This emerges from beneath the glacier at two points, scouring out caverns of ice. By following the torrents you can enter these caves – that on the right being the more substantial. By examining the blue, glass-like walls, you can appreciate the enormous pressures which act on the frozen crystals.

It is also possible to walk up the glacier itself. However, the ice is so hard that it is impossible to make any impressions with the feet . Hence, if any substantial walking is planned, crampons are indispensable. As you reach the glacier, one of the most surprising things to appreciate is the amount of dirt and grime that is present within the ice itself, made up of dust and other pollutants. In Iceland, many of the glaciers are virtually black because of the ash deposited by the volcanic activity on the island.

There is an absence of lichens near the glacier and this reflects the fact that a thaw in the spring releases ice and water into the valley, which then scours the rocks. As a result, only very fast colonisers such as Viviparous Fescue are able to inhabit the area close to the snout. They manage this by developing complete young plants, attached to the parent. As you move further down the valley, the change in species becomes increasingly dramatic. Tufted Saxifrage and Plum-leaved Willow can both be found, as can the Woolly Willow which is remarkable for its stunning white leaves. The area outside the main valley is also worth investigating – Alpine Sow Thistle, Northern Monkshood and the Lesser Butterfly Orchid are all present, together with three species of Wintergreen.

The Journey North

The Jotunheimen

Getting there:

Having left the Jostedalsbreen area, our suggested route takes you further north-east and away from the coast. In essence, this is to meet the E6 – the main north-south artery of communication in this linear country. Leaving Leirdal, you travel south along Route 604 and then turn left to follow Route 55. This road continues for 170km until it joins the E6 at Otta. For much of the distance, you are climbing up and over the Jotunheimen – Norway's highest range of mountains. Hence, you should be prepared for sections of steep and winding road. This could make things very slow for less powerful vehicles, and certainly no one should expect to progress with any great speed. However, this is not a trip to be rushed. The scenery is a striking and desolate change from the lush green of the fjords, and for those who decide to camp there, it is a first experience of truly Arctic conditions!

The "Home of the Giants":

The poet Vinje christened the highest mountain system in northern Europe as the "Jotunheimen" – this means "home of the giants". The name is apt as many of the peaks are over 2000m in height. The highest is the Glittertinden which reaches some 2481m. The whole area has been granted National Park status and thus the facilities for tourists are better than elsewhere. Fortunately, the ruggedness of the terrain and the climate means that there is no danger of being crowded out.

If you are equipped with your own tents then there are plenty of opportunities to camp and set up your own base around which to hike and explore. You must, however, be prepared for the cold produced by the combination of wind and altitude.

Even if you are simply passing along Route 55 and you do not intend to stay for a night, then it is still possible to appreciate this wide area of snow-capped mountains. It is worth stopping for an hour or so in one of the sections where the road passes above the snow-line in order to explore the geographical and biological features. There is a particularly impressive area of lakes, hills and rocky outcrops to the north of Fannaraki (45km on from Gaupne). This is scattered with patches of snow and mini-glaciers. The lack of soil means that the ground cover is dominated by lichens, within which a profusion of other plants grow. Some interesting species survive in this punishing environment, including various types of arctic grass and an unusual abundance of Arctic Catchfly. Red Snow is a surprising phenomenon that is much in evidence in this area – patches of standing snow are given a pinkish tinge by colonies of red algae which live within them. These plants recover nutrients which are dissolved in the snow. Like a pair of biological ski goggles, the red colour helps to filter out ultra-violet light which would otherwise harm them. Interestingly, no known animals feed upon them.

An ideal climb in this area takes you up the Jotunheimen's second highest mountain. Driving north-east along Route 55, you take a right turn about 3km after the little hamlet of Elvesaeter, and just before the village of Boverdal (approximately 75km on from Gaupne). This steep and winding road will take you south to the little settlement of Gjuvvashytta, which lies on Mount Galdeho at an altitude of 1850m. Leaving the vehicles here you take a path which circles around a small lake to the south and enters a minor ice-field at 2223m. The track then crosses the Styggebreen ice-field to Galdhopiggen. This reaches 2469m – only Glittertinden is higher. This is an incredible vantage point from which to view the Jotenheimen.

Fokstua

Getting there:

When Route 55 reaches the town of Otta, you should make your way north on the E6. The town of Dombas lies 47km along this road. Once north of there, you are in the Dovrefjell National Park. The small settlement of Fokstua is about 15km further on. The surrounding area has a few official camp-sites as well as plenty of opportunities for unofficial stops. The best places are on the eastern side of the road and to the north of a large lake which lies about 5km beyond Fokstua itself. This site is particularly renowned among naturalists and is centred on the Fokstumyra Marshes.

Camping near the Fokstumyra Marshes.

It is a good idea to camp well away from the marshes themselves, because they are infested with mosquitoes. They will be encountered in most stops north of this point. Mosquitoes are a constant irritation when camping – however ingenious your methods of repulsion, one of the little horrors always seems to be buzzing in your ear just as you fall asleep!

The Fokstumyra Marshes:

Although the landscape is unspectacular when compared to the mountains, glaciers and fjords, the Fokstumyra marshes are undoubtedly one of the most important habitats in Norway. They possess the most varied selection of bird life in the country. A total of 87 different species have been observed here, including the Great Snipe, Hen Harrier, Whimbrel, Lapwing, Temminck's Stint and many types of marsh and water bird.

The marshes also represent an outstanding site for botanists, with an enormous range of interesting plant species. There are a number of rare sedges including the Bristle Toothed and Few Flowered varieties. Among the specimens are several that cannot be found anywhere in the UK. It is worth looking out for the Alpine and Slender Gentian, the Icelandic Koenigia, the Norwegian and

Alpine Milk Vetch, the Strict Primrose and the Norwegian Oxytropis. Among the most pretty are the Moss Campion, Alpine Cinquefoil and Hairy Lousewort. This list could be continued indefinitely – the site is a botanist's paradise and most species will be growing next to your tent!

The location of this area obviously has a great bearing on the life that it can support. The altitude means that it is semi-tundra. This encourages the plants that have just been described, as well as ensuring a plentiful supply of lichens, some of which are very large, branched examples. The lakes nearby are fairly numerous and this ensures that there is a rich variety of wildfowl.

Trondheim

Getting there:

Having left the Fokstua area, there is very little choice of route – the E6 is now a constant and indefatiguable companion. You will have to follow it for about 145km before reaching the city of Trondheim. As you progress north, look out for the roadside camps that have been set up by the Lapps (of which there are about 20,000 in Norway). The people can be seen in traditional costume as they tend the reindeer herds on which they depend for survival. A wide range of reindeer products are usually for sale – antlers, skins and meat. The meat can either be bought in the form of a large sausage, or you may even be offered the roasted product – this has a strong flavour and requires powerful jaws to deal with it.

The city:

The city of Trondheim was founded in 997 by the Viking king and saint, Olav Tryggvason, to be his capital. It is built on a triangle of land enclosed by the River Nid. During the Middle Ages it was the religious and political centre of Norway, and today it remains the third largest town. As well as being an important port and industrial area, it is pleasant and spacious with several interesting architectural features. The winter palace of the present King of Norway is also to be found in the region. One of the central attractions is the Nidaros Cathedral, which is dedicated to St. Olav.

If you plan any shopping then it is important to realise that almost everything closes on Saturday afternoons.

Official camping is available at Malvik, 15km north on the E6.

The Taiga

As you move north of Trondheim along the E6, after about 200km or so, it is apparent that a typical pattern of scenery and plant life develops. This is the "taiga". The word describes a sub-arctic region of coniferous forest that lies to the the south of the tundra. The area is hilly, with a large number of lakes and streams. High rainfall means that typical peat bog conditions arise, together with the characteristic undergrowth. This in turn ensures a plentiful supply of midges and other biting insects. Forests of spruce, firs, pine and larch are common. This in turn has a bearing on the bird life. Black Woodpeckers construct very large holes in their chosen trees, while Capercallie are content to nest under the conifer scrub. Lapland Bunting and Yellow Wagtail can also be seen without difficulty.

In practical terms this also means that there is little habitation. One of the the most awkward results is a dearth of petrol stations. Thus, it may be wise to camp near the town of Formofoss. There are relatively good areas for camping here (particularly next to the river), and there is petrol available in nearby Grong. You should certainly avoid the area to the north of Grong as this is largely peat bog, and wholly unsuitable to camp in. The 10km to the south of the village are on relatively well-drained high ground. There will be no difficulty in finding either official or unofficial sites.

Mo-I-Rana and the Arctic Circle

Alteren

Getting there:

The town of Majavatn lies 100km to the north of Grong. It marks the transition into Helgeland. You may like to camp here, and then visit the Borgefjell National Park which lies some kilometres to the east. Mo-I-Rana lies another 170km north along the E6. You should remain on this road until you have passed through the town, and crossed the River Rana. At this point, the road forks. The E6 goes to the right but you should join Route 805 to the left, which then hugs the shore of the Nordranafjord. After about 10km, a small road turns off to the right – signed for Alteren and Little Altermark. Initially, this road is quite steep as it climbs into the hills which surround the fjord. However, the road levels off after a couple of kilometres in an area of quite extensive quarrying. By investigating a few small tracks it should be easy to find a flat and rock free area suitable to camp in. It must be pointed out that biting insects are an unavoidable problem hereabouts.

The camp-site area:

The fact that the site is quite high up and yet close to the fjord, means that it is often covered by the clouds which rise from the valley below. Hence it is also liable to considerable rainfall. If you follow the road a couple of kilometres further, then there is a waterfall near the roadside which is ideal for this purpose, and also for stocking up with drinking water.

Some ten minutes drive from the site, there is a substantial freshwater lake that is worthy of investigation. It is alkaline based and thus provides an interesting contrast with acid lakes to be found elsewhere. In the surrounding marsh and bogland, you can find Coral Root (a rare orchid), Rannoch Rush and the Lesser Twayblade, which tolerate the acid conditions to be found away from the lake. Nearby woodland also supports the unusual Pyramidal Bugle, while White and Fritillary butterflies can be seen in the nearby meadows. On a slightly larger scale, you should

Moor King on the lake, near Altermark.

keep an eye out for Elk and Pine Martens which are both common.

The lake itself is not round. It has several finger-like projections, from where streams flow into it and deposit large amounts of alluvial material, which has been carried from the glaciers. Hence it is an excellent point at which to study the processes of invasion and colonisation by plant species. One of the most impressive specimens to be found is the Moor King, while Lesser Bladderwort, Narrow-leafed Marsh Orchid and Lapland Marsh Orchid can all be found growing in the rich sediments. The area is also a fruitful site for collecting insects (although vicious horseflies may be an unwanted find). In particular, there are many species of dragonflies living in the lake, including large Darters and the Northern Emerald. Both these feed on the hordes of mosquitoes.

The Lapland Orchid, near Altermark.

The bird life of the lake is dominated by the Red- and Black-throated Divers, although White-tailed Eagles can also be seen.

Alternative camp-sites:

There is an official site 10km south of Mo-I-Rana, off the E6.

Mo-I-Rana Town

The town of Mo-I-Rana has a population of 12,000. It lies at the end of the Nordranafjord and owes its livelihood largely to a steelworks and rolling mill, which are served by nearby iron deposits. To the south of the town there is a cable-car up the Mofjell, which gives good views of the town and the Svartisen ice-cap.

As you travel to or from the town, it is worth taking some time to look at the bird life along the muddy edge of the fjord. There are many waders, including Whimbrel, Greenshank, Purple Sandpiper, Dunlin and the Red-necked Phalarope.

Svartisen

The Svartisen ice-field is the second largest in Norway, covering over 450 square kilometres. Access to the glacier is by no means as convenient as the Jostedalsbreen, and it is questionable whether there is much point in trying to visit both. Most of the plateau stands at about 1200–1400m, although individual peaks can rise above 1500m.

To get to the ice-cap, it is necessary to travel about 10km out of Mo, north-east on the E6. You should then take the road to the left which is signed for Svartisen (which, incidentally, means "black ice"). This will take you past the Mo airport. After some 30km you will reach the Svartisvatnet lake. The road terminates at this point in a large car park. This can be packed with tourists in the summer. The snout itself lies at the far side of the lake. As there is no direct vehicular access, it is a very long trek. Alternatively, the lake can be crossed by motorboat – this still leaves you with three quarters of an hour's walk at the other end.

By retracing your journey until the road crosses a large bridge over the Store Raudvatnet, it is possible to follow another route that is signed for the Svartisen. This leaves you no closer to the ice itself, but it passes some interesting sites to investigate flora and fauna. At the end of the road lie some recently colonised terminal moraines, with interesting vegetation. There is an area to park and a signposted path leading to the icecap (2–3 hours). Six kilometres before the end of the road, at Steintjornlia, there is a large area of marsh and peat bogs, to the south of the road. This provides an interesting site to compare to the alkaline lake near the camp at Alteren. Around the bogs there is a cover of Cloudberry, the fruit of which is sold in the market at Mo. Together with this, there are two types of insectivorous plants – Sundews and Butterworts. The String Sedge is found to be dominant in the area of Sphagnum Moss, while the rare Lesser Yellow Water Lily grows in the open water. Small White Orchid and Holly Fern can also be found nearby. Animal life is largely restricted to horseflies, Arctic Emerald and Blue Aeschnid dragonflies, although the occasional eagle can be seen soaring overhead.

The Coast

One of the most interesting exercises around Mo-I-Rana is to compare and contrast the geographical features and plant and animal life that can be found in various coastal sites. The three areas described below provide a wide range of different conditions. From them it is possible to see how these conditions affect the life that inhabits them.

Straumen:

Straumen is about 15km from the camp at Alteren. You drive down the hill onto Route 805, and turn right (away from Mo). After about 12km, you make a left turn, and follow the road for 3km or so. This brings you out on the edge of a sea-loch. This is a pleasant spot to lie in the sun and swim from. Slightly more active individuals may wish to explore the surrounding woods. The limestone substrate of the peninsula means that it can support a wide range of orchids. Twayblade, Common Spotted Orchid, Frog Orchid, Dark Red Helleborine and Broad-leaved Helleborine can all be found. Alpines extend down as far as the water's edge.

The principal focus of interest however, is the set of tidal rapids. These are formed because the sea-loch is, in essence, a large lake, with a small channel of water linking it to the Nordranafjord. Hence, the water is quite salty, but it is also extremely sheltered. The channel itself is particularly interesting. As the tide ebbs and flows in the main fjord, the level rises faster than the water can pass in or out of the loch. Hence, very fast water currents flow through the channel as the level in the loch tries to "catch up" with that outside. This high velocity obviously has a considerable influence on the plants and animals which the surrounding zone can support.

The rapids have three main effects: oxygenation of the water, the removal of small creatures and the scouring of the rocks. As a result of these limiting factors, the dominant life is red algae and mussels. Grey Seals may be seen diving for starfish which abound on the rock at low tide.

In order to complete a fuller study of the rapids it is worth driving around the edge of the loch and seeing them from the other side as well. Here, the alpines are especially in evidence – Wood Vetch, Alpine Clustered Saxifrage and Arctic Bladder Fern. By exploring the mud-flats which are evolving from the sheltered conditions in the lake, it is possible to find the rare Black Vanilla Grass.

Skogsoy:

In order to get to Skogsoy from the camp, you should drive down to Route 805 and turn right. After driving for 40km, you will find yourself following the edge of the Sorfjord. It is worth stopping and climbing up the ridge which runs along the side of the road, as this affords a splendid view down the fjord, westwards towards the islands and the open sea. There is also a very pleasant cafe nearby whose owner is an avowed Anglophile! After a further 13km, you reach the small settlement of Skogsoy.

This is an area which combines rugged coastline with a considerable degree of protection from wave action, due to the many offshore islands. A wide variety of shores exist: mud, sand and rocky. The protection has encouraged large beds of bivalves. As a direct result of this, there is also a considerable population of sea-birds. These include Terns, Common Gulls, Black-backed Gulls and others. The Ptarmigan lives on the adjacent moorland, together with its main predator, the Peregrine. If you feel brave enough, you can also follow the example of the Eider Ducks and eat the mussels – these are perfectly edible, if a bit gritty.

One plant that you will have very little difficulty in finding specimens of is the Eel Grass, *Zostera marina*. This lies in copious quantities in the sheltered muddy regions. *Zostera marina* is the only flowering plant in Europe that makes use of water transport for pollination. The nearby dunes support the parasitic Hayrattle, while salt marshes contain interesting Felworts and Eyebrights.

The shore is a good place for beach-combing. Starfish can often be seen, as well as the fine filigree of the sponge *Leucosolena*.

Tomma:

Route 805 continues beyond Skogsoy for another 10km, when it reaches the little town of Nesna. From here, regular car ferries leave for the nearby islands. The ferry reaches Husby, on the island of Tomma, after a couple of other stops en route. This takes about 50 minutes, and costs approximately £6 for a vehicle with passengers. Despite the apparent unimportance of this service the ferry is equipped with a tea-bar and places to relax. The journey provides a good opportunity for birdwatching, with Puffins, Black Guillemots, Terns and Skuas all fairly common.

Husby contains little more than the landing stage. Leaving the village, you should be sure to avoid going directly inland, but join the main route which skirts the coast. A few kilometres later you will be on the west-facing shore. The preponderance of seaweed will immediately show that the coast is not as exposed as one might expect. In fact, there are several small groups of islands further out to sea, which provide a surprising degree of shelter, together with spectacular views. Plants of interest include Eyebright and Norwegian Whitlow Grass. By exploring the lower slopes of the Briedtinden (which rises to 821m) it is possible to find Diapensia, Norwegian Sedge and the Lesser Butterfly Orchid. The hill also boasts the eyries of several White-tailed Sea Eagles, which can often be seen circling overhead. Various sea ducks are also present – Mergansers, Goldeneyes and nesting Eiders.

The coast road forms a circle of some 20km. Along this stretch, it is always worth keeping an eye open for bird colonies. When you visit the island, remember that the last ferry of the day leaves at 1915 hours (check this at Nesna before you cross). If you can, it is worth waiting for this ferry, as the journey back to the mainland is breathtakingly beautiful when the sun sets over the islands.

Fjord-hopping

A brief examination of a map of Norway will soon show that the north-south traveller is almost confined to one main road – the ever-present E6. There is, however, an alternative – to make use of the country's excellent network of ferries.

The Svartisen area offers one of the best opportunities to try this. The tourist authorities in Bodo are very helpful if you wish to arrange a detailed route. They can provide timetables and prices for the various crossings. If time and finances permit, then you may find the following route helpful. Essentially, it enables you to skirt round the ice-cap on the western side. Of course, if you have time to stop en route, it should be possible to find several points of relatively tourist-free access to the glaciers themselves.

Starting from Nesna, you take the ferry up to Stokkvagen (passing between Tomma and another island, Handnes-Oya), which takes about 50 minutes. Then there is a 25km drive along Route 810 to Kilboghamn, where you catch a ferry to Vagaholmen. This will take you between the islands and the mainland for about two hours. From there it is a 15km drive along Route 17 to Agskaret. From here the ferry takes 80 minutes to get you to Ornes on the Glomfjord. If you have time it is worth making the 24km detour south of Ornes along Route 832, which will take you along this spectacular inlet. The combination of the light green colour of the water, and the ice-field which extends to its shore will provide a memorable sight.

When you leave Ornes, you follow Route 17 north for 110km,

until it meets Route 80. 14km before this junction, you will pass the notorious Saltstraumen – a thin strait where the water velocity is so high that eddies and whirlpools are created. These then trap thousands of fish, making them simple to catch. From the junction you are just 13km from the large town of Bodo.

Bodo is the chief port and airport for communication with the Lofoten Islands. Of particular interest is the small island of Rost, which lies 6 hours away by steamer, and 1 hour by helicopter. This is one of Europe's largest bird sanctuaries, with millions of seabirds. The island has an infamous reputation because of the years 1975–1984 when almost all the Puffins born in those years died, possibly due to overfishing in the North Sea. A recovery in Puffin numbers is now taking place.

From Bodo, you only need travel 65km to the east and you are back on the faithful E6 again in Fauske. The E6 climbs further northwards for hundreds of kilometres, until as Route 6, it meets the Soviet border. If you do opt for this exciting detour, then it is worth moving just 30km or so further northwards from Fauske, to the Rago National Park. The Park extends over 170 square kilometres of wild and occasionally impassable landscape. Deep ravines scar the land – probably drainage channels of glaciers that have now retreated. The Park appears initially to have a poor flora, but there are some places which are surprisingly rich. Interesting plants to be found include Whitlow Grass, Snow Buttercup, Arctic Mouse-ear Chickweed, the Globe flower and the Blue Sow Thistle. Animals are rare, but you may be able to find Beavers, Otters, Mink, Wolverines, Foxes, Pine Martens, Stoats and Lynx. More details are available from the tourist authorities in Bodo.

Tarnaby and Swedish Lapland

Getting there:

From Alteren, a visit to Tarnaby involves a round trip of 300km. After driving into Mo-I-Rana, you should get onto the E79 which travels south-east. The frontier with Sweden lies 40km along this road. There is a place to stop and a large "border stone", but the customs office is in Tarnaby itself. The only indication that you are in a different country is the change in the colour of road signs and centre lines. For the next 30km the road follows the shore of the Overumen lake.

Ten kilometres after you reach the end of the lake, the E79 passes through the settlement of Klippen. There are some beautiful rapids in this area, and the mountains which follow in the next 5km or so are renowned as being some of the richest sites for flowers in Sweden. Gieravardo is particularly notable in this respect. For example, *Diapensia lapponica* and the tiny heather, *Cassiope*, are especially common here and throughout Swedish Lapland. After a further 15km or so, you reach the village of Tarnaby itself.

Tarnaby:

Standing on the edge of Lake Gouta, this village of 600 inhabitants is principally equipped to cater for skiers. Petrol and alcohol are both slightly cheaper in Sweden than in Norway, which is convenient as most places in the town still accept Norwegian currency. The town's nineteenth-century church is worth a visit. It is of classic Scandinavian design, and the interior includes an interesting stone and steel font and a large reredos of the Resurrection. It is also a good idea to drop into the tourist office when you arrive, as it supplies maps, and lists of all the local flowers, birds and animals. The office also stocks an excellent range of Lapp souvenirs.

Although rough camping is possible throughout this region, there are also two official sites near Tarnaby.

Returning about 20km up the E79, you can turn left just after Hemavan and drive down to Lake Tangvatnet. This is surrounded by dwarf and silver birch trees in the centre of a Lapp National Park. The vegetation is dominated by wild Angelica, which seems to attract every fly and wasp for miles around. You can also spot the Giant Arctic Wintergreen and the tall, blue Monkshood which grows in great abundance along wooded rides. It is tragic to see that despite this growth the area is far more afflicted by the effects of acid rain than Norway. About two thirds of the way along the lake, a path follows the course of a river which flows down into it. The river, the Ruttjebacken, dates from the ice age, and it has eroded the rock into a fantastic pattern.

Bird life by the lake is largely made up of birds of prey. Hen Harriers, Peregrines and Golden Eagles all feed on the abundance of lemmings. The lack of waterbirds nearby is probably the result of a shortage of suitable food in the lake. Ger Falcons and Bluethroats are widespread throughout the National Park.

Skaiti and the Arctic Circle

The Polarcirkel:

As the crow flies, Mo-I-Rana is only 30km south of the Arctic Circle. However, as the E6 has to stay well to the east of Svartisen, the distance by road is more than double that. North of the Arctic Circle (66.5 degrees north), the phenomenon of the midnight sun is visible. This means that for a period which varies according to how northerly you are, the sun never sinks below the horizon in a 24 hour day.

The line of the Arctic Circle is marked by a series of stone obelisks, which are topped by metal globes. Throughout the summer, people stop at the line to be photographed by these obelisks (or the "Polarcirkel" notices which stand at the roadside). The E6 crossing is in a desolate and cold area of tundra. It should be emphasised that the conditions have more to do with altitude than latitude – further east the Arctic Circle passes through far more hospitable landscapes.

A few metres north of the line, there is a large Lapp settlement, which sells souvenirs to the tourists. The most popular appear to be sets of reindeer antlers, most of which are still caked with dried blood.

Skaiti:

After leaving the Arctic Circle, continue for 35km up the E6, until Route 77 branches off to the right. Following this for 12km, you reach the Junkerdal Tourist Centre. This is a camping facility equipped with restaurant, bar, shop, television lounge, swimming pool and children's play area – all of which may be found welcome to break camping monotony. Having said this, there are rough sites for unofficial camping nearby. A few yards beyond the centre, a track leaves to the left. Following this for a couple of kilometres, you cross a large and fast-flowing river. A hundred metres or so further on, you find yourself in the middle of a pine forest – there is little difficulty in finding suitable clearings for tents, as the trees are well spaced out because of the lack of soil.

Skaiti is ideal as a northern base. Fondly remembered creature comforts are provided by the tourist centre, while the forest provides plenty of firewood. The river is ideal for water supplies, and for a really bracing wash. Large numbers of mosquitoes are the only practical problem, together with the shallowness of the soil. The latter may render it necessary to strengthen tent pegs with supporting rocks.

The flora of the site is also impressive. Creeping Lady's Tresses and several species of Wintergreen are both to be found nearby. The Lady's Slipper Orchid is present in remarkable abundance – 91 specimens together in one locality. A short way down the track, another rough route climbs upwards and then follows the course of a particularly majestic meltwater river. The cliffs of mica schist which line the roadside are a rich source of many alpines. Mountain Avens, Rock Speedwell, Reticulated Willow, Alpine Fleabane, False Musk Orchid, Dark Red Helleborine, Drooping Saxifrage and Mountain Bladder Fern are all present in this habitat.

The shallow (or often non-existent) soils have placed limitation on the growth of trees. Hence the ground is strewn with dead wood that found itself without sufficient support. Much of the area is covered with layers of mosses and lichens. These are honeycombed with the burrows of small mammals, such as Lemmings and Grey-sided Voles, and also of the stoats which prey upon them. The preponderence of lichens, which take years to grow, means that this is a highly fragile habitat. Thus great care

The taiga forest at Skaiti, north of the Arctic Circle.

One of several beds of Lady's Slipper Orchid, at Skaiti.

should be taken when camping. The atmosphere of desolation is heightened by the huge number of ravens which can be seen and heard all around.

Southern Norway – Oslo to Bergen

The Journey South

The long run south from Skaiti to Oslo can be comfortably covered in two and a half days. Unfortunately, over 500km of this journey simply involves retracing the earlier route along the E6.

Returning on the E6, the first deviation from the northward passage is at Otta. Instead of crossing the Jotunheimen, you remain on the E6 for another 300km to reach Oslo. If you decide to camp on this last stretch, then there is an excellent lakeside area of flat grass a couple of kilometres beyond Moelv (15km south of Lillehammer). The lake is splendid for swimming in and it also supports some interesting plants – Eight-stamened Waterwort, Creeping Spearwort and Water Tillea. Marsh Stitchwort can also be found nearby.

Oslo

Camping:

With the exception of official sites, you must be prepared to go some way out from the city centre in order to find an area in which to camp. It is advisable to head into the lowland agricultural area to the north-west of the city, near Nordby. By finding patches of woodland, it should not be too difficult to locate clearings in which to camp. It is, nonetheless, advisable to check with the local farmer before you set up any tents. There is, however, a large defence installation which should be avoided. Once you have picked your site, keep an eye out for the large population of adders in this region – they are very partial to toilet tents!

The city:

Oslo is the capital city of Norway, with a population of 460,000 people. It is the home of the Parliament (the Storting) and the see of a Lutheran bishop. Founded by Harald Hardrade in the eleventh century, it occupies a magnificent natural setting at the end of the Oslofjord, surrounded by hilly woodland. Oslo's main commercial street is the Karl Johansgate. It runs from the central station to the palace, which stands on an imposing hill. As well as shops, there are market stalls, street entertainers, fountains and park areas. During the summer it is a crowded meeting place for tourists and locals alike.

To the north-west of the city centre lies the famous Frognerpark, with its enormous collection of sculptures by Gustav Vigeland. He gave his statues to the city in exchange for a studio, a small salary and some helpers. In the park he tries to cover human life from childbirth to old age. The centrepiece is a towering monolith. It is made up of 121 intertwined bodies, decreasing in age from the bottom to the top.

The Bygdoy peninsula lies 6km to the west of Oslo. It is one of the Oslofjord's main tourist attractions, with four large museum sites within a mile of each other.

The Norwegian Folk Museum is a vast permanent exhibition, illustrating urban and rural life through the centuries. The Kon Tiki Museum recalls the voyages of the Norwegian ethnographer, Thor Heyerdahl. Two of his boats are on show. The Viking Ship Museum contains three original Viking longships. These were preserved in the burial mounds of Viking noblemen – other

One of the many historical houses in the folk museum, Oslo.

artefacts from the mounds are also on display. The Fram Museum holds the 800-ton polar exploration ship used by Roald Amundsen in 1935.

If you have time after touring these, then a walk down to the shore will reveal a collection of breckland, limestone pavement and alpine plants, including Field Wormwood, Spiked Speedwell, Perennial Knawel, Bloody Red Cranesbill, Moon Carrot, Alpine Woodsia and Oblong Woodsia. By examining the strand line, you may see the Stinking Goosefoot, which is very rare this far north.

The Hardanger Vidda

The Hardanger Vidda is a desolate and inhospitable plateau lying between Oslo and Bergen. It extends for over 7000 square kilometres, at an average altitude of 1200m. Its many lakes and meagre covering of grasses support large herds of reindeer. The landscape is impressive, despite being treeless. An excellent network of paths link the various lakes and isolated tourist huts, ensuring that the area is ideally suited to walkers. However, there are no roads through the interior, or to the Hardanger-Jokulen ice-field.

Leaving Oslo, you should move south-west along Route 160 and then join the E76 to Kongsberg. From here, take Route 8 north-west to Nore, where there is an interesting stave church. If you leave Oslo late and need an early stop, then find the official campsite. If fake log cabin toilets are too much for your pride, then 50m further along the main road a small track above the edge of the river will provide enough room for a couple of vehicles and tents. From Nore, you continue north until Geilo (it should be noted that the last petrol station for some considerable distance is to be found here) and then continue on Route 7. It is at this point that the barren, cold and windswept plateau really takes over.

On the vidda itself, there are substantial areas of bog, rocky ground and steep ravines. Thus it is fairly difficult to find sites for camping. The best plan is to explore any rough tracks that leave the main road, and try to find a piece of relatively flat and rock free ground. If you explore the surroundings of your camp then it should be possible to spot Dotterels, Ravens, Golden Plovers, Snow Buntings and Merlins, which are characteristic of

The River Bjoreia descending from the high Hardanger Vidda.

open tundra. As you are so near to the snow-line it is worth taking a close look at patches of long lasting snow. Many insects are attracted to the snow, including mayflies and the swarms of insects which sometimes live under the ice. Some of them, like ladybirds, are black to increase heat absorption.

About 15km before Eidfjord you will see signs for the waterfall at Voringsfossen. This is well worth stopping for. The River Bjoreia plunges vertically for over 180m into a narrow rock basin. The dense mass of spray produces marvellous effects with the sunlight.

Bergen

Getting there:

Thirty kilometres beyond Eidfjord, Route 7 reaches the picturesque town of Kinsarvik. From here you need to take the ferry across the Sorfjord and the Hardangerfjord to Kvanndal. This is a very beautiful crossing over what is probably Norway's best known fjord. It is then 122km to the centre of Bergen. This area is the worst on our entire route for trying to find sites in which to camp. There are several official sites, but these are well away from the town. The best bet is to head northwards as soon as you pass through Arna. By exploring the areas around Sanus at the far end of the peninsula you may be able to locate some possible sites. The principal difficulty is that most of the land is privately owned. However, at the end of the peninsula there is a spot near some old German gun emplacements – unfortunately, it is thick with bracken and on a considerable slope!

This sort of coastal moorland possesses botanically poor acidic soils. Thus there are few flowers of interest, with the possible exception of the Yellow Balsam, which can be found close to freshwater streams.

The city:

Bergen, with its 214,000 people, is Norway's second largest city. It is situated on the Byfjord and is a major port for merchant shipping. The city has a Lutheran bishop, and is an administrative centre as well as a university town. Bergen is surrounded by a ring of seven forested hills, over 600m in height. It is possible to ascend one of these by a funicular railway, which leaves from the centre of the town. The train climbs the 800m, 26 degree slope in six minutes. At the top is Bergen Park, which affords spectacular views of the port below. It is a good idea to visit this early on, as the view gives a good perspective of the layout of the city.

As a result of its proximity to the sea, and the surrounding hills, Bergen is famed for having over 2 metres of rain a year. At the south-eastern end of the main harbour (or Vogen) is the market-place (or Torget). The fishing boats dock here and on weekdays there is a splendid fish market (the half rolls covered with fresh salmon are particularly recommended!). Along one side of the harbour is the old town of Bryggen – an area of shops, restaurants and a museum. An eye-catching feature is the Bergenhus, a sixteenth-century fortress, one part of which, the Rosencrantz tower, is open to visitors. The Cathedral and Church of St. Mary are both interesting to visit as they show the intricate decoration characteristic of the country's churches. The town also possesses several museums and a well known aquarium.

ADDRESSES

Norwegian National Tourist Office,
20, Pall Mall,
London.
SW1Y 5NE.

DFDS Travel Centre,   [Ferry Information]
199, Regent Street,
London.
W1R 7WA.

Tourist Office,   [Information on Jostedalsbreen
5000 Bergen.   and Jotunheimen]
Torvalmenningen 10,

Trivelige Trondelag,   [Information on the region between
Postboks 186,   Trondheim and Mo]
N-7701 Steinkjer.

Rana Reisetraffiklag,
Postboks 225,
9601 Mo.

Bodo Reiselivslag,   [Information on Rago National Park
Postboks 514,   and trips to Rost]
8001 Bodo.

Tarna Turistbyra,
Bla vagen 30A,
920 64 Tarnaby.
SWEDEN.

Tourist Office,   [Information on Hardanger Vidda]
Radhusgt 19,
N-Oslo 1.

ICELAND

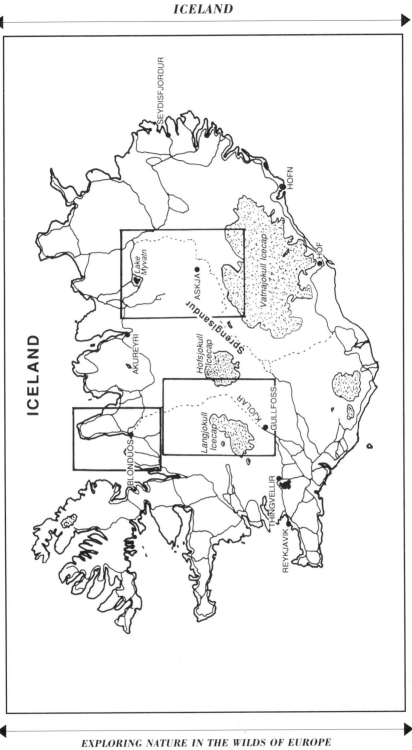

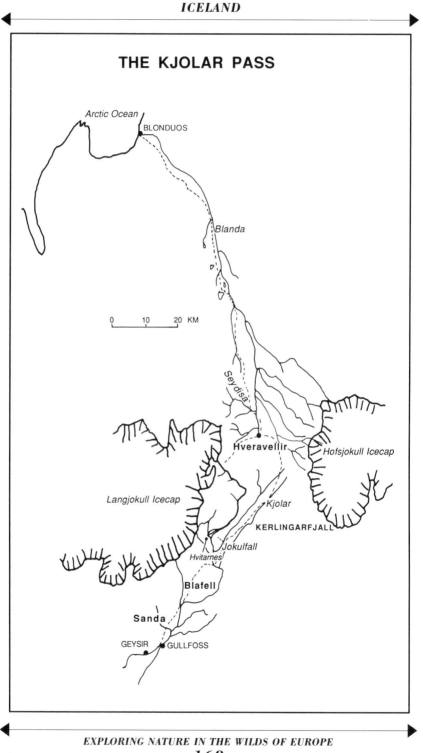

THE KJOLAR PASS

Arctic Ocean

BLONDUOS

Blanda

0   10   20 KM

Seydisa

Hveravellir

Hofsjokull Icecap

Langjokull Icecap

Kjolar

KERLINGARFJALL

Jokulfall

Hvitarnes

Blafell

Sanda

GEYSIR   GULLFOSS

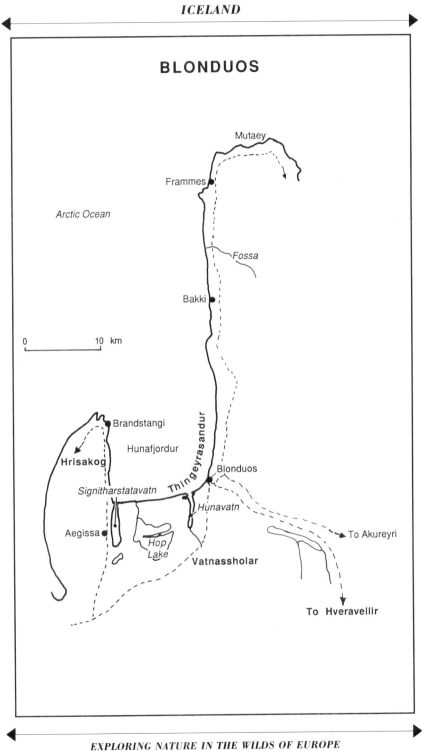

BLONDUOS

Mutaey

Frammes

Arctic Ocean

Fossa

Bakki

0   10 km

Brandstangi

Hunafjordur

Hrisakog

Thingeyrasandur

Blonduos

Signitharstatavatn

Hunavatn

Aegissa

To Akureyri

Hop Lake

Vatnassholar

To **Hveravellir**

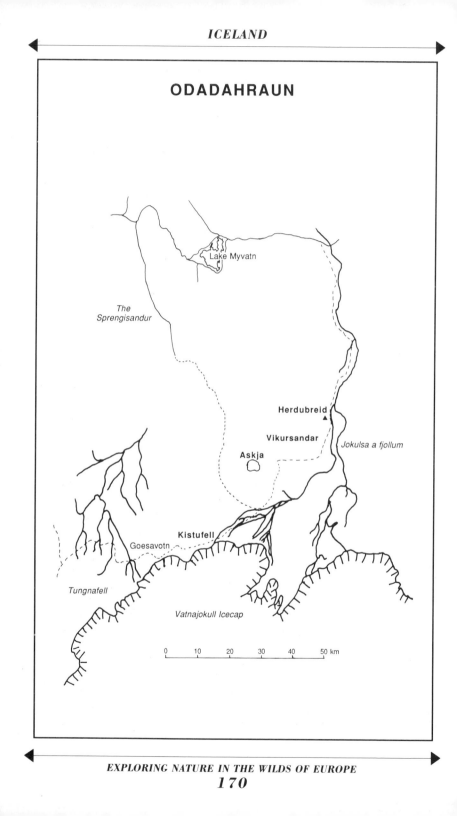

ODADAHRAUN

Lake Myvatn

*The
Sprengisandur*

Herdubreid ▲

Vikursandar

Jokulsa a fjollum

Askja

Kistufell

Goesavotn

Tungnafell

Vatnajokull Icecap

0   10   20   30   40   50 km

Introduction

A visit to Iceland is a unique and exciting experience. Of all the countries described in this book, this is probably the most difficult to get to. Nonetheless, it is well worth making the effort. For the naturalist and the general traveller alike, Iceland is a diverse and surprising nation – in terms of its geography, its biology and its people.

Lying some 800km from the northern shores of Scotland, Iceland's remoteness ensures that its breathtaking natural beauty remains largely unspoilt. Conversely, the welcome of the inhabitants and the growing trend towards the encouragement of foreign visits, ensure that you will not feel totally cut off from civilisation – unless you want to!

Geography

In common with all volcanic islands, Iceland is simply a mound of lava rising from the ocean bed. It lies on the mid-Atlantic ridge – a join between two of the crustal plates which form the earth's surface. Along the ridge, semi-liquid basaltic material rises, creating new oceanic floor and simultaneously pushing continental Europe to the east and America to the west. The landscape of Iceland exists as tangible evidence of the dynamic forces that are still shaping our world.

Iceland's position on one of the world's major geological faults is the principal explanation for the mass of spectacular volcanic and geothermal activity which it experiences. One can expect an eruption from one of the active volcanoes every 7–10 years. Understandably, most sites of human habitation are positioned away from the danger areas. The visitor will thus be lucky to see the unforgettable site of a volcano bursting into life. However, the wide range of geothermal activity occurs continuously – geysers, hot springs, mud pools and sulphur pots.

Iceland appears to suffer from geographical schizophrenia! For together with fire, comes ice. Many of the volcanoes lie beneath the island's glaciers and ice-caps. Vatnajokull, in the south-east, is an ice-cap extending over 8400 square kilometres – a greater area than all the glaciers and ice-caps of continental Europe added together. In all, 12 per cent of the country is covered by ice, in parts to a depth of more than a kilometre.

The outpourings of the glaciers combine with high rainfall to ensure that the land is scattered with numerous and fast-flowing rivers, occasionally gushing over impressive waterfalls. The coastline too is endowed with variety. Sandy beaches, cliffs, headlands, fjords and islands mark its 6600km length.

Iceland covers an area of just less than 100,000 square kilometres. It lies fractionally to the south of the Arctic Circle, between Greenland and Norway. The vast majority of the island is uninhabitable – nearly 75 per cent of the land consists of ice, lava or other wasteland. The route which we outline will take you through the main geographical regions of the country. The capital, Reykjavik, lies in the south-western coastal plain, and the surrounding area is the most populous. The journey from Geysir and Gullfoss to Blonduos passes through the central tundra plateaux, up to the fjord landscape of the northern highlands. Progressing east and then southwards, brings you into young volcanic landscapes and the glacio-volcanic desert of Odadahraun, as we skirt the fringe of the vast Vatnajokull ice-cap. Finally, the Sandar Plains and their fringing mountains lie along the south coast – a superb area of wilderness.

Climate

The climate of Iceland is warmer than one might expect, because of the moderating influence of the Gulf Stream. In the winter, temperatures average out at about freezing point, while the mean for summer time is a little over 10 degrees centigrade. The most obvious characteristic of Icelandic weather is its unpredictability. This stems from its position at the confluence of two different air masses (one from the pole, one from the tropics), and of two ocean currents. Hence, the weather is very changeable. This is less so in the north, but there it can be colder – the climate is more continental than oceanic. The south and east are inclined to be the wettest areas. The coasts tend to be fairly windy, while there is a particular hazard from the cold katabatic winds which descend from the glaciers. However, the changeability of the weather makes any general statement awkward – we have found Myvatn the warmest place on Iceland, and Reykjavik the coldest!

Vegetation

Despite the fact that only 25 per cent of Iceland has continuous plant cover, the country remains an exciting destination for the botanist. The most obvious facet of the vegetation to notice is the lack of trees. Changes in climate, the grazing of sheep and imprudent felling by man are principally to blame. The dearth of flowering plants is also multi-causal. The isolation of the island restricts plant immigration, while the inhospitable conditions limit what can survive. In addition, the complete covering by glaciers in the last Ice Age destroyed many species. It is believed that between 25 and 50 per cent of the present vascular plants have survived the glaciers. It should be pointed out that although the interior – Askja for example – is often barren, the coastal zones are very luxuriant in places.

Iceland's position also ensures that what the flora lacks in quantity is made up for by quality. The predominant influence is European, but with a large number of arctic-alpines. This is particularly interesting for visitors from the UK, because many common Icelandic plants are rarities in the UK – some are unique to Iceland. You will certainly find a wide range of habitats and conditions to explore. The large variety of non-flowering plants will also stretch the identification-buff to the limit.

Getting There

There are a number of possible ways in which to get to Iceland. The best choice will depend much on the size and type of group. For a large group, it is probably preferable to take a dual approach. The vehicles, loaded with equipment, are shipped to Seydisfjordur on the east coast, with their drivers. They can then make the two day drive to Reykjavik, and pick up the rest of the party, who have flown in directly.

Icelandair run regular flights from Heathrow. As with the majority of international flights, these do not go to the capital itself, but to Keflavik, 40km to the south-west. You will need to take the coach into the capital – check whether your ticket includes this in the price. Some operators make it a feature.

The journey by sea has three stages: Aberdeen to Lerwick (Shetlands), Lerwick to Torshavn (Faeroes) and Torshavn to

Seydisfjordur. The return journey takes longer than the outward, because the P & O ships follow a circular route which includes Denmark or Norway. You should allow a full five days. Surplus time can be spent exploring the Faeroes. Entry into Iceland by ship will involve a testing time from the customs officers. It is a good idea to have at least three copies of a complete list of all your equipment.

You should spend some time judging the relative merits of bringing vehicles, or hiring them on site. The rental can be very expensive, and you are faced with an unfamiliar vehicle. Alternatively, shipping is also pricey, and you have to get the vehicles to the ship early.

As we noted above, the drive to Reykjavik can be achieved in two days. If necessary there are internal flights from Egilstadir (the airport serving Seydisfjordur) to the capital.

Motoring in Iceland

The route described in this chapter really requires a four-wheel drive vehicle. In fact, two-wheel drive is unsuitable for any journey that strays too far from the Route 1 ringroad. If you plan to follow the more adventurous routes through the interior of the country, then it is recommended that you take at least two vehicles, in case one gets into difficulties. A winch can also be useful. Sand ladders will be of great existence when crossing the "sandur" outwash plains, as the soft sand can easily bog you down.

If the trials of driving prove too worrying, then you can always let someone else take the strain by joining an escorted tour. Please note that the Nature Conservation Act forbids driving off established roads or tracks, in order to preserve the fragile ecology.

Fuel is a major expenditure on any trip to Iceland. Petrol prices are among the most expensive in Europe. Diesel is cheaper, and also has a considerably better fuel consumption for LandRovers. On the other hand, the government levies a tax on the import of diesel vehicles, based on their size and the duration of your stay. Owners of "sensitive" vehicles should bear in mind that Icelandic petrol tends to be of a low grade. The locations of (most) filling stations are shown on the 1:750,000 tourist map, and the 1:500,000 touring map. These are often simply a single hand-operated pump in a front garden – and they may be empty!

Drivers will need to bring a valid "green card", their own driving licence and an International Driving Licence (available from the motoring organisations). By Icelandic law, all drivers must be aged 19 or more, although insurance for vehicles such as LandRovers may demand that you are older. There is also a legal requirement for safety belts to be worn by the driver and front-seat passengers. The penalties for drinking with excess alcohol are very severe, and the legal limit is low in comparison to that in the UK.

A hazard that the British motorist is unlikely to be familiar with is the prospect of having to ford a river. Several unwary travellers have been killed because they were careless, ignorant or overconfident. Hence, you should ALWAYS follow the standard procedure. You cannot rely on following what appears to be a well trodden path, as safe fording routes frequently change. A couple of members of the party should be sent ahead to wade across. They can pick out a safe route which avoids submerged boulders or potholes. Of course, the safety of the waders must come first. Be prepared to take an indirect crossing if this is safer, moving from shoal to shoal. Use a low gear, low range and four-wheel drive, as high revs are more important than speed. High revs help force water out of the exhaust – a flexible extension to the exhaust pipe is an expensive way of avoiding this worry. To prevent problems with the engine, it is preferable to drive downstream, as this avoids water building up and smothering the engine. With care, you should be able to cross rivers safely, or just as importantly, know when a river cannot be safely traversed. Further details are available from LandRover.

Maps

The 1:1,000,000 and 1:500,000 maps are suitable for the planning of the general itinerary. Nine 1:250,000 touring maps cover the whole island. These possess good detail and are useful for choosing areas of interest within reach of a particular base camp. You are unlikely to require more detail than that provided by the 1:100,000, for areas of specific interest, although the 1:50,000 may be useful for Myvatn.

Maps are available from most good bookshops in Reykjavik. However, it is better to buy and study as many as you can before you leave the UK. Stanfords are a reliable supplier, although the larger scales may need to be ordered in advance. Dick Phillips stocks a very comprehensive range. (See Addresses, page 216 for details.)

Language

Icelandic is the national tongue, although the study of English and Danish is compulsory at school. Hence, you should not have too much difficulty finding someone reasonably fluent in English. As in most countries, this becomes more difficult as you move into more isolated areas. This is especially the case in the south, which was largely cut off until the ring road was completed in the 1970s.

Currency

The Icelandic *krona* is divided into 100 *aurar*.
Banknotes: 10, 50, 100, 500 and 1000 kr.
Coinage: 5, 10, 50 aurar; 1, 5 and 10 kr.

A maximum of 8000 kr can be brought into Iceland as banknotes. Foreign currency importation is unlimited.

Banks are open from Monday to Friday, 0915 to 1600 hours, and also from 1700 to 1800 hours on Thursdays. Major credit cards (including Access and Barclaycard) are widely accepted, as are Eurocheques.

Camping

Rough camping is unrestricted, with the exception of places within the boundaries of National Parks. In such cases, permitted camping areas will be clearly marked. However, this freedom should not be interpreted as a right. Always ask the permission of the local farmer on whose land you wish to stay – it will very rarely be refused. Reykjavik and Akureyri have their own sites.

The Icelandic Tourist Board publishes a leaflet which lists the official sites. These are particularly useful for towns, where finding sufficient rough ground for a large group is difficult. Note that the facilities claimed by some official sites may in fact refer to those available in a nearby town or village.

Food and Shopping

An expedition on tight finances will need to bear in mind that food is two or three times more expensive in Iceland than it is in the UK. Unfortunately, the government has decided to levy a tax on the importation of more than 10kg of food per person (at a rate of up to 80 per cent of domestic prices, varying according to the type of food). However, expeditions with an "Announcement" from the Icelandic Research Council or a research permit are exempt. Educational establishments should have no difficulty with this.

It is helpful to remember that many petrol stations have foodstores attached.

Water can be a problem in certain places. Rock flour is often in the rivers which cross the sandur plains of the south. You will need to stock up with plenty of water before entering the area. If necessary, you can provide a make-shift filter by digging a hole at one side of a river. As the water seeps through, the worst of the particles are removed.

Shops are generally open from 0900 to 1800 hours on weekdays, and from 0900 or 1000 hours until 1200 hours on Saturdays. Many shops are closed on Saturdays.

Medical

We note within the text that biting insects can be an irritating problem, especially around Lake Myvatn. However, they are usually no great problem. (Advice on the prevention and cure of insect problems is given in Planning and Preparation, page 5.)

No inoculations are required for Iceland, although it is always a good idea to have a tetanus booster before travelling.

Hypothermia is a danger in exposed areas, especially if you become wet. By contrast, particular caution should be taken in areas of geothermal activity, as a misplaced foot in a mud-pool or spring can easily mean a serious third-degree burn.

Reykjavik and the South-west
Reykjavik

Getting there:

For the vast majority of visitors to Iceland, an exploration of the island will begin in Reykjavik. Although it may be easier to ship vehicles and equipment in elsewhere, flying into the capital is the most convenient option – for the individual traveller and expedition member alike (see Introduction, page 173). It is advisable to begin your stay in the country with a couple of days at a Reykjavik camp-site.

The best site in Reykjavik lies to the north-east, just off the Sundlaugarvegur. This is within walking distance of Sundahofn (to the north-east) – the spot where freight shipped into Reykjavik is unloaded. In addition, there are good toilet and washing facilities. There is also a naturally heated swimming pool a short distance along the Sundlaugarvegur.

A principal advantage of this camp-site is the easy bus link (No. 5) with the centre of the town and the domestic airport. We noted in the Introduction that most international flights come to Keflavik. The coach service to the capital stops at the Hotel Loftleidir, which is adjacent to the domestic airport.

You may find it convenient to stay in Reykjavik's youth hostel – it is not necessary to be a member of the IYHF. If the hostel is overcrowded, then the overspill is accommodated in a nearby school.

The city:

The name "Reykjavik" is a misnomer. It was originally called "Smoky Bay" because of the hot steam which rises from the thermal springs in the area. Nowadays, Reykjavik is almost completely smokeless – largely heated by naturally hot water from the ground.

Reykjavik has an atmosphere quite unlike any other European capital. The brightly coloured corrugated roofs in the Old Town contrast with the austere beauty of the Hallsgrimskirka Cathedral, which dominates the skyline. The attraction of the city is enhanced by the lack of industrial grime and the impressive backdrop of the harbour and mountains. Tours of the city are available for those who do not have the time to explore for themselves. During the summer, the City Information Service operates from the main bus station in Laekjartorg Square. This provides details of places of interests in the whole Reykjavik area. However, you should bear in mind that the English spoken in the office is by no means perfect. Another source of information is the English Bookshop (or "Bokaverzlun Snaebjarnar") in Hafnarstraeti. This has a large number of good books about Iceland.

If you explore in your own vehicles, or even if you need to make a simple journey from one part of the town to another, then take Reykjavik's confusing one-way system into account when timetabling your itinerary.

Armed with a city map, you will have no difficulty in finding your bearings. The Old Town lies between the harbour and Lake Tjornin, while the ring road sweeps out to the expanding New Town in the east. A short distance to the north of the lake is Austurvollur Square. This contains the Parliament building. The Althing is the world's oldest legislative assembly. It was first convened in 930, but it only came to Reykjavik in 1845 and has occupied its present building since the 1880s. Adjacent to the Althing is the Lutheran Cathedral, which has an interesting font sculpted from marble. The Hallsgrimskirka lies to the east. Follow the Austurstraeti and the Bankastraeti, and you will see it standing at the end of the Skolavoroustigur on the right.

If you have some time in the city, then it is well worth experiencing part of the cultural life. There are a number of museums, while the town also plays host to opera, ballet and concerts.

Reykjavik for the Naturalist:

There is often a tendency among expeditionaries and naturalists to regard the major settlements through which they pass as unavoidable distractions from the natural habitats which they have really come to see. In Reykjavik, this view cannot be justified. Although the city is well worth visiting in itself, the single-minded naturalist will not be bored either.

Although Reykjavik houses over 90,000 people, and accounts for some 40 per cent of Iceland's total population, it is remarkable for a particularly rich bird life – as well as being the only world capital with a major salmon river flowing through it! Not surprisingly, Lake Tjornin is the best spot on which to have binoculars trained. You may well see Red-necked Phalarope and Arctic Terns, as well as Widgeon, Tufted Duck, Mallard, Eider and Barrow's Goldeneye. Less common are Turnstone, Oystercatcher, Red-breasted Merganser and Pintail. Interesting species can often be seen elsewhere in the town centre and on the coastal fringes – Redwings and Meadow Pipits, for example. The hills around the city even support nesting Fulmars and Puffins. In fact, the keen ornithologist would do well to spend some time exploring the rest of the Reykjanes peninsula – especially the impressive cliffs of Krisuvikurberg and Hafnaberg.

For those who prefer their natural history more conveniently packaged, there is the Icelandic Museum of Natural History, and the small Reykjavik Botanical Garden in Laugardalur.

Mithsandur and Akranes

The whaling station at Mithsandur:

Leaving on the main route out of the capital, you should get on the principal Iceland ring road – Route 1. The northward route follows the coast, providing early glimpses of Iceland's varied and contrasting landscapes. Mithsandur lies some 70km along this road from the capital. On the coast you will see Europe's only whaling station.

With increasing international regulation, there is a tight restriction on the number of whales which may be caught here in a given year. The whaling station lies at the head of the Hvalfjordur, which was an important naval base for the allies during World War Two. The oil is held in large tanks on the surrounding slopes. On the shore, an expanse of concrete about half the size of a football pitch is surrounded by low, shed-like buildings. A jetty extends into the water, and is visible from the road. The whales are winched up a slipway onto the concrete area. The preliminary cutting up of the corpses takes place here – under the transfixed eyes of tourists standing on a raised platform. The ghoulish atmosphere is enhanced by the strong sweet smell of the blood, and the flocks of Fulmars that scavenge on the corpses as they are hauled from the sea.

Akranes:

Twenty kilometres further along Route 1 from Mithsandur there is a junction. The ringroad continues to the right, but you should continue straight on along Route 51. After 14km, this will bring you to the town of Akranes. The town itself does not contain much of interest, but the coastline is well worth exploration.

The rocky shores nearby are strewn with boulders, covered with algae typical of semi-sheltered sites. The succession of seaweeds moves from Channelwrack, through Bladderwrack, to Serrated Wrack as you progress from the upper to the lower shore. The animal life is fairly typical of such habitats, although there are some interesting differences from comparable British sites. For example, the Common Limpet is completely absent here – its niche taken by the Tortoiseshell Limpet. Similarly, the spider crabs lurking beneath the boulders appear to replace the Common Shore Crab found in Britain. The Common Starfish and the King Ragworm are also much in evidence, together with many Scale Worms. You can find unusually big Bearded Horse Mussels, together with considerable numbers of huge *Marinogammarus* (a shrimp-like crustacean) and large, dark brown specimens of the Dog Whelk, *Nucella*.

Thingvallavatn

Getting there:

If you are travelling from Reykjavik, then you should get on to Route 1 after leaving the City. Follow the ringroad northwards for 10km before turning right onto Route 36. The road carries the majority of visitors to one of Iceland's most popular tourist attractions. It crosses the barren heath of Mosfellsheioi. You should turn right at the junction with Route 360 and drive along the shore.

The east shore is quite rocky and hilly, but any difficulty in finding a site is compensated for by the absence of other visitors, the majority of whom camp on the other side of the lake. Approximately 9km down the road from the junction, there is a track to the left, near Nesjar. This takes you into a small valley which runs down to the lake.

The camp-site area:

Despite the apparent shelter afforded by the valley, there is a tendency for the wind to be funnelled by it. This can make tent assembly difficult, as well as giving the cold extra penetration. Nonetheless, the naturalist will find the immediately surrounding area of interest. To the north of the site, a steep slope leads up to the top of the ridge. It is a typical black and reddish mound of volcanic slag. There are some patches of bare, brown earth on the lower slopes while much of the area is characterised by sparse greenery and white lichen. The top of the ridge is fairly bleak – although some plant life can be found, while ornithologists should look out for redwing.

To the south of the site lies a flat block lava plain, covered in a thick layer of grey/white moss, *Rhachomitrium*. Several plants grow in the moss, the base of which acts like a soil. One such specimen, the Least Willow, is one of the smallest trees to be found. The underside of the moss is also the best place to find insects, of which there are so few in Iceland. The area is scored with crevices, caves and hollows. These have been formed as the lava has buckled and split. It is not unusual to find the skeleton of a sheep in one of the ravines – where the animal has fallen in and been unable to escape.

Leaving the camp, you can travel southwards and around the lake. You should, however, bear in mind that the route can be very marshy after heavy rain. Thingvallavatn is Iceland's largest lake, and hydroelectricity generators have been placed at its southern end. Their construction has stimulated the decline of the lake's stock of Brown Trout. Hence the Arctic Charr is the only common remaining fish. En route, you should keep an eye open for Barrow's Goldeneye – Iceland is the only country in Europe where this can be seen. Black-tailed Godwit and Golden Plovers will also be seen flying in the area, although their skill at camouflage means that you will be lucky to find any nests. Despite the recent arrival of the Tufted Duck and Black-backed Gull, the lake supports a limited number of waterfowl – largely because of the tourist activity and the depth of the water (in most places it is too deep for diving ducks to find food). Nonetheless, you may still see Long-tailed Ducks, Snow Buntings, Arctic Terns, Harlequin Ducks and Red-necked Phalarope.

Thingvellir:

The word "Thingvellir" means "Assembly Plains". This was the site of the open-air legislative assembly founded in 930 – the predecessor of the Icelandic Parliament. The small grassy plain is bounded by the River Oxara and by the rocky wall of the Almanagja gorge. The assembly of Viking chieftains met here for two weeks during June. The high cliffs were important for their acoustics. Along the ridge is the Logberg or "Rock of Laws" from where a so-called lawspeaker would recite the national code. All around this area are the sites where the chieftains set up their booths. Those who have read the sagas will be able to find stones marking the sites of the booths belonging to Egil Skallagnmson and Gizur the White. In the north, there is a bridge passing over the River Oxara. In a small pool to the left, convicted women were executed by drowning. Historical significance aside, Thingvellir can be appreciated for its breathtaking natural beauty. The Oxarafoss waterfall, the various volcanic rock forms and the rock layers and ropy lava flows in the walls of the Almanagja gorge leave one in no doubt that the Viking chieftains had found a dramatic location for their annual deliberations and festivities.

The Oxarafoss, which flows into the gorge at Thingvellir.

Geysir and Gullfoss

Geysir:

Continuing south along the track from Thingvellir, you will pass along the edge of the lake for a couple of kilometres. The shore is fairly rocky, but marked by deep crevices and covered by thick brushwood, which provides shelter for a large number of Redwing. Botanists will also be able to find a few interesting specimens here as well.

When the track meets the road, you should turn left and then take the next right – down Route 365. This minor road continues for 16km over the moorland of Lyngdalsheidi. It concludes at a junction near Laugarvatn. The "Lake of the Warm Springs" is in a fertile valley at the foot of the Laugardalsfjoll mountains. It is being developed as a tourist centre, with pony-trekking particularly in mind. At the junction, you should turn left and follow Route 37 for 25km, before turning left again onto Route 35 for the remaining 9km to Geysir.

Geysir is the original hot-water spring which has given its name to others all over the world. The Great Geysir spouts water in a jet some 60m in height. Unfortunately, it has been inactive for several years now, with the exception of occasions when detergent is added to encourage a show for the tourists. (This breaks the surface tension of the water.) Geysir is one of the most obvious tourist traps in Iceland – there is a Hotel Geysir (bearing a remarkable resemblance to a military barracks) and souvenirs are available to the swarms of Germans and Americans, from a small garage. While some areas are roped off for safety, the site is obviously vulnerable to the wanderings of visitors. Many of the silica terraces – precipitated from the hot spring water – are becoming trampled into fragments.

Although the Great Geysir no longer regularly performs, its smaller neighbour – "Strokkur" – erupts every few minutes. A tube extends into the earth from the mouth of the geyser. Water seeps down from the surface and into this tube. The water at the bottom is vigorously heated by hot magma. The thinness of the tube means that the water cannot circulate easily. Hence the water at the top remains relatively cool. Because of the pressure, the deep water has to reach well over 100 degrees centigrade before it vaporises. When it does so, the water above is moved upwards and some flows away. This in turn reduces the pressure at the bottom and lowers the boiling point. Then such a great volume of water is turned into steam that the complete contents of the tube are blasted well into the air. This process means that the geysers can only operate intermittently.

As well as the geysers, there are a number of other geothermal phenomena in this steam enshrouded place: steam and sulphurous gas escape from ugly fissures in the ground, their edges caked with red, brown and white deposits. Steaming water flows over beds of white and grey geyserite – a deposit of silica – into pools of brilliant blue, lined with brownish white minerals that appear like fungus. The multi-coloured minerals form in cones, mounds and terraces. Whimbrels are the birds most frequently seen here. They occupy the niche which is taken by the Curlew in the UK.

Gullfoss:

Gullfoss,"The Golden Waterfall", lies approximately 10km to the north of Geysir. You should continue to follow Route 35 for 6km, when it deteriorates into a provincial road for the final few kilometres. Gullfoss is one of the most beautiful falls in Europe. The glacial melt-water of the River Hvita falls some 32m into a deep gorge, in two cascades. After an overall drop of 50m in a series of cataracts, the river flows down the gorge with considerable force. On a sunny day you will see the light playing on the spray, and producing colourful rainbows in the beautiful effect that has given the falls their name. On a dull day, the impression is more one of immense power than beauty. To look at the great mass of water roaring over the two stages is almost vertiginous in its effect.

Despite the popularity of the falls with tourists, it is not difficult to find an area in which to camp, a couple of kilometres further along the bumpy track. However, you should not be tempted to stray too far in search of a site, as after a while, the softer, greener land gives way to a stony desert. Unfortunately, if you find a camp with a good water supply, you will have to put up with the midges that accompany it. If you do stay nearby, look out for nesting Arctic Skuas.

The Central Highlands

Gullfoss to Hveravellir

The journey from Gullfoss to the north coast is based upon an old bridlepath. The "New Kjalvegur" is the motor track which now replaces it. The journey to Hveravellir covers gravel, stones and rock – with the occasional small river to be forded. The route is not difficult with LandRovers, and you are quite likely to spot the odd Volkswagen making the journey. It is an ideal preparation for the longer and more arduous Gaesavatnaleid route.

Beyond Hveravellir, the route deteriorates significantly. The track is muddy and wet, and you will be faced with extended river crossings.

In comparison with other routes across the Icelandic tundra plateaux, the Kjalvegur is relatively busy during the summer. The number of visitors at the hot-spring site in Hveravellir mean that it is probably inadvisable for large groups to base themselves there for too long. Kjalvegur passes between two ice-caps – the Langnajokull and the Hofsjokull. Despite the proximity of these, the cold is certainly not intolerable. Discomfort is more likely to stem from long periods of heavy rain!

Leaving Gullfoss, the first 12km take you to the River Sanda. This is not difficult to ford, although small cars might experience some problems if there has been heavy rain or a surge in melt-water from the glaciers. (Just before the river, a 15km track branches off to the left. This leads to the Hagavatn tourist hut. However, if you follow this route, you will still have to cross the river. This is an especially interesting area for the geographer who wishes to investigate different aspects of glacier activity. Variations in the extent of the ice-cap have influenced the form of the lake. There are the signs of periodic glacial surges, and a number of overflow channels. The Hagavatn area is also the origin of the sand which is occasionally carried by the wind across the agricultural land to the south-west.)

Continuing along the main Kjalvegur route, the scenery is desolate, yet varied. Initially, the plain of brown rocks and sand contrasts with the distant blue mountains and the outlet glaciers of the ice-cap. Then as the track swings down to the River Hvita – plunging through four or five tributary streams and small rivers as it does so – there is a glimpse of green, some grass and an undergrowth of stunted trees.

After this, the track climbs in altitude. Accompanied by marker posts (for the winter traveller), you climb the Blafellshals ridge and make your way up and round the western slopes of Mount Blafell itself. The terrain is largely bare and stony, with scattered patches of icy snow at the side of the track. If you can put up with the cold wind, it is worth stopping for a while on the ridge to explore. If you do so on the northern side, then there is a dramatic, if somewhat intimidating view of the journey yet to come. To the left, between the mountains, is the edge of the Langjokull ice-cap, while to the right, in the far distance, is another – Hofsjokull. Between them, dust clouds swirl on the brown plain that lies beyond Lake Hvitavatn in the foreground.

If you are lucky, the wind will not be gusting by the time you have descended from the ridge to the Hvitarbru Bridge at the southern end of the lake. If so, there is a clear view over the lake, with the dramatic ice-cap towering above it. Small icebergs can be seen in the water, and on the far shore, the outlet glacier from which they have separated. A couple of kilometres beyond the bridge, a track leads off to the left for 4km. This is best negotiated with a robust vehicle during dry weather, but the area around the hut at Hvitarnes would be a good base for a more extended examination of the lake. Particularly adventurous groups (with experienced leadership) may like to try the full walk from Geysir to Hvitarvatn. The combination of volcanic ridges and desert landscape will prove testing. It should only be attempted with vehicular support.

As you progress further towards Hveravellir, the landscape remains desolate. The brown dusty plain gives way to expanses of stone and then to great black stretches of volcanic clinker, small black stones and black dust. All the time, however, a vista of mountains and glaciers lies on the horizon – like the crock of gold at the end of a rainbow. In order to break the journey, it is worthwhile stopping on the stony slopes of the small mountain, Innriskule. This affords a panoramic view over the valley of the Jokulfall River to the Hofsjokull ice-cap and the mountains which lie to the south of it. This is a good area in which to find at least twenty species of tundra plant. (You may prefer to lie down in order to investigate them – not only does this facilitate examination, it also keeps you out of the fierce wind!) Species particularly worth looking out for include the Alpine Bistort,

Cassiope, a tiny heather species growing on the tundra.

Mountain Sorrel, Mossy Saxifrage, Alpine Marsh Saxifrage, Thrift, Sea Campion, Alpine Mouse Eared Chickweed, Grass of Parnassus, Mountain Avens and Crowberry. In common with other tundra life, such plants have to be able to cope with long and severe winters, followed by short and relatively warm summers (but not above 10 degrees centigrade). This ensures that any tree growth is very stunted, although mosses, lichens and some flowering plants can thrive during the summer. The variety often depends on the drainage, and hence how swampy the ground becomes.

Although the botanist will find hardy plants to investigate, the ornithologist will probably be less successful. Examination of lakes near the track is unlikely to reveal more than a few disconsolate Long-tailed Ducks.

When you finally reach Hveravellir, 100km in total from Gullfoss, the impression is one of an oasis. It is a comparatively sheltered area of hot springs, surrounded by greenery, and equipped with a small camp-site.

Hveravellir

Despite the status of the hot springs as a minor tourist attraction, it is not really necessary to use the official camp-site. Even so, do not be fooled by the patch of green on the map some 8km up the road. This is a group of hillocks covered in low scrub. They are generally too exposed, too bumpy or too inaccessible for tents. There are, however, a number of relatively flat areas just off the road. Unfortunately, the soil is fairly loose, and it may be necessary to use heavy stones to supplement the tent pegs.

The zone of hot springs provides nothing as spectacular as Strokkur at the Geysir site. Nonetheless, there are again pools of brilliant blue water, this time lined with white. By contrast the mud pools are black with a brown-red mineral precipitate around their edges. One of the most attractive sights is the collection of springs in which the minerals dissolved in the water have separated as the water evaporates. Hence, the resulting "sinter" is arranged in exotic colours and forms – unlike the less impressive grey and white silica seen at Geysir. Some of the springs look like birthday cakes: a circular white silica "icing sugar" is decorated with bright yellow veins and ridges – formed from ridges of sulphur – with a chocolate brown hump in the middle from which water spurts. Another phenomenon not seen at Geysir is the striking steam volcano – a continuous hissing jet of steam emerging from a three foot high grey cone of minerals.

The investigation of the Hveravellir site need not be governed solely by scientific rigour. Some of the brilliant blue pools are as close as the natural world comes to a jacuzzi! With the air temperature at 7 degrees centigrade, half the fun is to look at the disbelieving expressions of well-clad spectators.

Despite the obvious attractions of such an approach, a more thorough analysis is still rewarding. With the aid of heat resistant gloves, an interesting study can be made of the zonation surrounding one of the hot springs.

The presence of the geothermal activity means that the daily temperature variation is reduced. It ranges from 7 degrees centigrade at midday to 4 degrees centigrade in the evening. This is perhaps not surprising when one considers that the water generally emerges from the hot springs at between 85 and 95 degrees centigrade. The small geyser cone is actually boiling. Comparisons from pool to pool (where the temperature was generally around 20 degrees) show that the algae predominates between 20 and 35 degrees centigrade.

The bird-watchers will have little difficulty in spotting the large numbers of Snow Buntings in the area.

Hveravellir to Blonduos

Moving north from Hveravellir, the route deteriorates significantly, and there is 71km of track before you return to a proper
"road" again. This is the most difficult stretch of this north–south
route, and in wet conditions it is especially awkward for ordinary
vehicles. The track is noticeably rougher, with particularly stony
patches. However, the mud is probably the most nerve-wracking
of conditions. As you pass through the large, occasional patches
which lie across the road, vehicles seem to act like boats as they
roll slightly.

The northward journey involves crossing the River Seynitsa –
the most awkward crossing of the route so far. The major
difficulty is that the fording places frequently change.
Nonetheless, following a standard procedure should ensure that
any river can be crossed safely, or, just as importantly, you
realise when a river cannot be crossed safely. Certainly, with
care, the River Seynitsa should present no real problems.

Once the remainder of the track has been negotiated, you will
pass through a gate onto the proper road. Surprisingly, the next few
kilometres are the most difficult to drive through because the road
descends from the tundra plateau into the Blondadalur Valley.
This is narrow and runs between high steep-sided walls of black
rock. The road runs along and down one of these walls – seeming
at times little more than a sharply curving ledge. Thankfully, the
view is compensation for the precariousness. The road is the
Route 731, and its 37km length takes you straight into Blonduos.

The North

Vatnsnes and Skagi

Blonduos:

This large village on the River Blonda is an ideal base from where to explore the northern coast of Iceland. Blonduos itself is pleasant, in a way typical of many Icelandic towns through which you pass. The small area is made to seem larger by the untidy sprawl of brightly coloured houses. The landscape too, is welcoming. On one side a small plain of agricultural land leading to the sea, on the other a view of glaciated mountains and valleys.

The Blonduos region has been largely forgotten by tourists and expeditions. This is unfortunate, as the scenery is beautiful, and you are within easy reach of the interior.

The Blonda makes its way through the village. In the middle of the river (on the north side of the town) is the island of Hrutey. This is a nature reserve, with a large bird population occupying the copsewood covering.

A number of options present themselves in terms of accommodation. As usual, a rough site can be found outside the town, as an alternative to the official camp-site. This may well have to be on a farm. However, an ideal solution, if it can be arranged, is to stay in the local school. Details of the availability of the school are only provided by special request, well in advance. This option cannot be relied upon. If you manage it, chores are easier to complete, clothes can be washed and life can be taken at a more relaxed pace than in a camp.

You can also try the Edda Hotel.

West to Vatnsnes:

The investigation of the area west of Blonduos, described in this section, is best undertaken over more than a single day. Leaving the town, you should get onto Route 1 and travel southwards for some 19km. About half a kilometre after crossing the Hnausaknisl River (which flows into Hunavatn to the north) you will see the Vatnsdalsholar to your left. This area is a fascinating series of mounds derived from glacial moraine.

By climbing one of the higher mounds you will be able to see down the Vatnsdalsfjall. This glaciated ridge exhibits classic signs of glaciation, including hanging valleys which now contain waterfalls.

On the other side of the main road, Route 731 branches off northwards towards Hunavatn. After approximately 6km you will reach Thingerar. The nearby fields are a site favoured by Golden Plover. At this point the road deteriorates into a track which continues for a further 4km to Brandanes – on the shore of Lake Hunavatn. This is home to a large number of terns, which can often be seen defending themselves against Arctic Skuas.

Brandanes is an ideal base from where to explore the Thingeyransandur dunes. It is a good spot in which to leave vehicles before making the 3km walk from Hunavatn to Hunafjordur. This inhospitable stretch of the Arctic Ocean coast provides a good opportunity for a transect – an investigation of the changes in vegetation as you progress inland from the shoreline. However, if you do plan a thorough exploration of the area, then preparation is vital. On a poor day, the wind can be punishingly cold off the sea.

The landscape is generally uninspiring. The dunes are flat and bleak – largely black sand with occasional stretches of Lyme Grass. Hence the colour of the plants provides a welcome contrast – purple Thyme, yellow Lady's Bedstraw, bright green Lyme Grass and orange mushrooms. You should also keep an eye open for Moonwort – an unusual (although small and dull looking!) fern. Slightly larger, and a little more noticeable, are the herds of Icelandic horses which can sometimes be seen on the dunes. These impressive animals are descendents of those brought to Iceland by the Vikings. They are short, long-maned and frequently have a light colouring. Their strange running-walk is apparently very comfortable for riders.

When you reach the shoreline itself, you cannot help being impressed by the sight of the Arctic Ocean waves rolling in onto the black sand. Unfortunately, the strand line is scattered with the usual collection of man-made rubbish, together with the odd dead Guillemot, Puffin or Fulmar. Progressing inland, you first cross the storm beach before reaching the primary colonisers – principally *Honkenyia peploides*. The next zone is 400–600m wide and consists of flat, young dunes of black basaltic sand, colonised by Lyme Grass. Older dunes occupy the following 400m, where Lyme Grass is joined by Creeping Fescue, Sea Campion,

Sorrel and Sea Plantain. The slack extends over 200–300m (but considerably more in places). This is an area of lower ground, which is consequently damper. It contains Grass of Parnassus, Yellow Rattle, Spike Rush, Wood Rush and Crowberry. On the landward side are concentrations of Silverweed, with some specimens of Eyebright and Fescue. Certain areas within this zone are simply patches of bare black sand – sites over which salt water flows. Just under a mile from the sea is the young climax – Thyme, Lady's Bedstraw, Marine Plantain, a prostrate Horsetail, Wild Pansy, Butterwort, Sea Campion, Moonwort and Lesser Club Moss. Beyond this, the mature climax is vegetation typical of the tundra – Dwarf Birch, Crowberry, Northern Orchid, Alpine Bistort, Butterwort and Wild Thyme. In both the young and mature climax zones there are damp patches dominated by Bog Whortleberry, Water Avens, Woolly Willow, Mossy Saxifrage and fungi.

Moving on from the Thingeyransandur dunes, you should retrace your steps along the track and Route 731, back to the junction with Route 1. Some 8km south-west along the ringroad, you may be tempted by your map to try a short-cut between Lake Hop and Lake Vesturhopsvatn. This is a temptation best resisted, as the road is fenced off, probably because of the width of the necessary crossing over the River Vididalsa. Hence you should continue a further 9km, before turning right on Route 716. This follows the course of the river and then the shore of Lake Vesturhopsvatn, before reaching Breidabolsstadur, where you should turn right onto Route 711, which then follows the edge of the Vatnsnes peninsula.

Sixteen kilometres north along Route 711 is Hrisakot. As well as being a pleasant place in which to stop and have a break, it affords a superb view to the east. Immediately below you is the inlet of Sigridastadavatn, beyond which lies an expanse of black sand – the Sigridarstadasandur. This gives way to Lake Hop, and then the Thingeyransandur. The curve of Hunafjordur Bay lies to the left, with the glaciated peaks of Viddalsfjall and Vatnsdalsfjall to the right.

Climbing down the grassy bank towards the shore of the inlet will give you a better view of the opposite shore. This should bring into focus a large colony of brown and white seals. It is well worth taking your time to rest and watch these splendid creatures. Pups can often be seen among the groups which congregate in the area of confluence between fresh and salt water.

As well as the seals, the bird life is also considerable. Anyone walking along the beach in early summer is liable to attack from dive-bombing Arctic Terns, who protect their breeding sites. There is even an artificial ternery (complete with scare-skuas!), set up by a farmer aiming to collect the eggs. Small flocks of Dunlin, Oystercatchers and Cormorants may also be in evidence, together with Mallard chicks, Golden Plover and the odd Godwit. Turning to flora, the grassy bank plays host to the Field Feltwort and the Small Alpine Gentian. The water's edge shelves deeply, but low water reveals a jumble of Bootlace Seaweed (*Chorda filum*). The tidal sand-bars are generally devoid of life.

A further 9km along Route 711, you can stop and make your way down a marshy slope to the rocky promontory of Brandstangi, near the northern tip of Vatnsnes. Once again, seals are much in evidence, although they abandon the rocks as you approach. If you do come across a colony in this way, then bear in mind that in the general panic cubs are often left behind. This is an excellent opportunity to observe them at close quarters. Remember that they will be frightened, but not afraid to use their sharp teeth and front claws.

An examination of the area will show a number of promontories and small bays. The seaweeds *Alaria* and *Porphyra* dominate on

A grey seal pup on the rocky shore near Vatnsnes.

the north-facing sides, which are exposed to wave action. The seals bask on the sheltered sides, which are predominantly covered by *Ascophyllum* and *Fucus*. There is a rapid transition between the exposed and sheltered areas. Interestingly, Brandstangi shows a marked absence of sea anemones and crabs (with the exception of the spider crabs, *Hyas* and *Maia*). Common specimens include the Tortoiseshell Limpet, Sting Oyster Drill, Dog Whelks (*Nucella*), banded Periwinkles (*Littorina*) and several worms (*nemertines*).

Skagi:

The Skagi peninsula lies to the east of Blonduos. Its western edge is known as the Skagastrond, and it contains a number of areas of interest. Leaving Blonduos on the ringroad, you should travel east for 2km, and then turn left onto Route 74. As you proceed up the west coast towards Bakki (22km away), the road crosses a number of farms as it passes between the mountains and the shore of dunes.

Soon after Bakki, the dunes are replaced by the cliffs of Kroksbjarg – home to a large number of Fulmars. The cliffs are also noteworthy in themselves. Zones of sandstone are dotted, in regular rows, by black lava – a phenomenon also seen around Thingvallavatn. The geology of the area stems from Pleistocene volcanic activity. Hence the cliffs are largely composed of basalt lava. When this type of lava cools, it often cracks in a peculiar way, producing a mass of columns. These are usually hexagonal in shape, but may sometimes be four or five-sided. The process is similar to that undergone by mud when it hardens and cracks. Although the view is generally from the side, you can see several columns from the top, often with Fulmars nesting on them. The rare Iceland Poppy is found here.

Continuing north from the Kroksbjarg, you cross the River Fossa before reaching the next section of cliffs – the Bakkar. This area supports a large number of white Kittiwakes, familiar because of their yellow beaks. Just beyond the cliffs, a small side road leaves Route 74 to the left. This brings you along a grassy peninsula, which is dotted with lakes and a few ramshackle farm buildings. At the end is a lighthouse, which stands on a semi-island. This is largely made up of the hexagonal basalt columns described above, although this is disguised in many places by a covering of earth and grass.

The less squeamish naturalists will find this a good spot in which to find dead seals, while those with weaker stomachs might

The basaltic Kroksbjarg cliffs on the Skagi peninsula.

better concentrate on the bird life. Red-throated Divers can be seen on the lake, while Great Northern Divers fly overhead. The stretches of shallow water are the perfect habitat for waders such as Dunlin and Phalarope. The Red-necked and Grey-necked Phalaropes are amusing birds to watch. They walk in circles, like jerky clockwork toys, as they kick up mud in the search for food. Eiders, Redshank, Long-tailed Duck, breeding Arctic Terns, Puffins, Sanderlings, Turnstone and White Wagtail are also all worth looking out for.

Closer to the water, the surprisingly thick mat of seaweed contains a number of specimens, including Breadcrumb Sponges and tiny larval Plaice. The distribution of algae in the bays is particularly interesting, with a variety of rich growths. For example, there is an unusual association between *Alaria* (typical of extreme exposure to wave action) and *Laminaria saccharina* (generally found in sheltered conditions). The Arctic Ocean is rich in planktonic (freely floating) creatures. Hence, you may find specimens of Sea Gooseberry – this is a jelly-like animal covered with hairs.

Myvatn

Getting there:

The journey from Blonduos to Lake Myvatn brings you through 220km of impressive surroundings. The road winds along the path of glaciated valleys, occasionally climbing over a high pass to move from one valley to the next. At the end of the route, you ascend onto the plateau of post-glacial volcanic activity around Myvatn itself. The graceful U-shapes gouged out by the ice are hence replaced by the striking cones and craters of more recent natural forces.

Leaving Blonduos, you should join the ubiquitous Route 1, and set off to the east. After 100km, you will arrive at the Oxnadalsheithi. This dramatic stretch of the ringroad proceeds through a narrow pass, squeezing between great bare mountains. Some 50km further on, lies Iceland's third largest town, Akureyri.

Akureyri is now regarded as the capital of northern Iceland. Indeed, it was probably made the seat of a regional Parliament in about 1000. Since then, both the sea and land have contributed to its prosperity. Nowadays, light industries such as the manufacture of chocolate and cloth play an important role. The commercial centre is called the Torfunef. It is based around the town hall square and the pedestrian precinct of Hafnarstraeti. There is an impressive new cathedral, with some striking stained glass. The setting of the town is undoubtedly fine. It lies at the end of Iceland's longest fjord – the Eyjafjordur. During the summer, the mouth of this narrow inlet captures the beauty of the Midnight Sun, in contrast to the cold, dark vista of snow-capped mountains which embrace the town.

Between Akureyri and Myvatn the main road passes through a succession of valleys and hairpin bends. It is worth making a brief detour to the right along Route 844. In a couple of kilometres you can find the Gothafoss waterfall. This is smaller and less powerful than its compatriot at Gullfoss, but the framing of the main fall by a smaller one on either side lends it a certain aesthetic appeal.

Returning to the main road, you can continue for the remaining 40km to Lake Myvatn itself. This stretch is particularly rich in spring and summer flowers. Finding a

The Gothafoss waterfall.

camp-site near the lake is problematic as 440,000 hectares of the area has been designated as a National Park. There is a sign on the road which indicates the limit of permissable rough camping. The alternatives are thus to stay outside the prohibited zone, or to use one of the two official sites. Skutustathir lies at the southern end of the lake. In addition to being fairly expensive, this site is also quite small. A large group, with several tents and more than one vehicle, can easily overwhelm fellow campers. Reykjalid, in the north-east, is somewhat larger. Of course, the avoidance of other people is always a principal attraction of staying away from official sites where possible. A further advantage to basing yourself some distance from the lake is a dramatic reduction in the number of bothersome insects.

The "Lake of The Midges":

"When we arrived... we saw Myvatn, a black and ugly sight." These words, written in the eighteenth century, are ironic when you consider that the lake is now one of Iceland's most popular destinations for visitors. Iceland's fourth largest lake extends over an area of some 37 square kilometres. It is highly irregular in shape, and also fairly shallow – 4m at its deepest point, 2m on average. The combination of its latitude and height above sea level (about 280m) mean that the water is covered with ice for more than half the year. The summer visitor should not arrive too well clad however, as the climate is relatively continental and thus days of sunshine are by no means unusual. There is also a far smaller chance of getting rained on here, than in the south.

Exploring the area is not too awkward, as the lake is surrounded by a road (Route 1 in the north, Route 848 in the south). Therefore, it is sensible for visitors to explore by making a circuit and stopping at spots of interest.

The western junction between Routes 1 and 848 lies near the bridge over the fast-flowing River Laxa. This takes water from the lake northwards for 55km to the Arctic Ocean. The river broadens out as you approach the lake, and is scattered with over 300 lava-based islets of differing shapes and sizes. They are a rich source of plant-life, including Marsh Marigold, Wood Cranesbill, angelica and Tea-leaved Willow. You will often spot Harlequin Ducks preening themselves on the islets, or see them skimming over the rapids as they fly upriver. The lake shores nearby are also favoured by ducks of different sorts – Slavonian grebes can also be spotted. Skuas, Long-Tailed Duck and Red-necked Phalarope can all be seen nearby. A practical tip for the birdwatcher is to walk upstream – the speed with which the water flows makes it more likely that the ducks will come towards you.

As you make your way along Route 1, up the western shore of the lake, you pass through a block lava field covered with *Rhachomitrium*. After about 5km, there is a cart track on the left of the main road. This lasts for just over a kilometre, around the edge of Vindbelgjarfjall, from where you can walk a little further, to the shore of Sandvatn. The birch scrub which surrounds this small lake is the only tree life for miles around. However, there is a large amount of prostrate dwarf juniper on the dry banks. The ornithologist will be rewarded by a variety of birds: Slavonian Grebe, Barrow's Goldeneye, skuas and Black-headed Gulls. A brief paddle will yield up midge larvae, sticklebacks and leeches, while the lakeside supports several spiders (including the crab, web and wolf varieties). The lake itself has a reed bed of *Glyceria*. It is partly eutrophic (well endowed with nutrients) and has some algal scum, as well as specimens of Slender-leaved Pondweed.

The prolific life in the main lake owes much to its lack of depth. Hence, the sun can penetrate to the bottom and stimulate the growth of large quantities of phytoplankton and vegetation. This is compounded by the nutrient-rich water inflow from springs to the east. During high summer, the combination of plankton and algae makes the water quite opaque.

Returning to the main road from Sandvatn and moving north-east for 12km, brings you to the eastern junction with Route 848. By continuing on Route 1 for a further 6km away from the lake, you reach a track on the left. This takes you into the area of Namaskard. This collection of hot springs and geothermal phenomena is perhaps the most ugly in Iceland! In contrast to slopes of verdant green, the ground looks like a primeval dermatological nightmare. The hill is a bare brown, on which are scattered "sores" – yellow-white pits rimmed with orange, from where yellow-orange streams seep away through gullies. The plain below the hill has no springs. Instead, pools of boiling black mud make a repulsive flapping noise as they throw out material to form the craters which surround them. Roundabout, gullies scar the earth – lined with deposits of reds, purples and greys. Fragments of pure yellow sulphur can also be seen. Indeed, during the Middle Ages, sulphur was mined at Namaskard. The high ground here provides a good view over the whole Myvatn region. If you spend any time exploring this site, then take heed of the notices which warn of the dangers of treading on light-coloured mineral crusts – your foot can easily push through, giving a nasty burn.

The high ground here provides some good views of the whole Myvatn region.

To the north of Namaskard is Krafla, the site of Iceland's most recent major outburst of volcanic activity. You have to bear in mind that recent eruptions are likely to put most maps well out of date. You should be prepared to find that what seems to be fairly straightforward access may turn out to be totally unnegotiable. Thus attempts to investigate recent lava flows are prone to be hit and miss, unless you can get detailed advice from earlier expeditions (either directly or from the Iceland Unit) about suitable routes.

Retrace your steps along the ringroad and take Route 848 along the eastern shore of the lake. Four kilometres from the junction, a cart track leads away from Myvatn. This lively route is driveable with a LandRover, but most people walk. It passes through old lava landscape which has been colonised by a wood of small birch trees. Some 2km along this route, you will emerge on the rim of

Hverfjall. This is a crater of approximately 800m in width. Built of black volcanic slag, the walls are a deceptive 120m in height.

Just more than a kilometre further south along Route 848, another track – this time easier to drive – leaves to the left. A winding kilometre or so brings you to Dimmuborgir. The name can be translated as "The Black Castles". This is an apt description of the collection of caves, rocks and canyons which were formed by lava flows over 2000 years ago. The picturesque vista of fortress-like blocks, with twisted pillars and arches is interspersed with scrub and stunted trees. The overall effect seems to have emerged from a Gothic novel. The ambience is enhanced by the infrequent flight of a Gyrfalcon overhead. As you see the variety of dramatic landscapes in this area, it is not difficult to see why the Americans chose to train their astronauts for the moon landings here.

Moving to the south and west of the lake, you gradually exchange birch for bogs and moorland, where the majority of the alpine and arctic flowers in the vicinity are to be found. A sight to look out for is the splendidly named Hawkweedleaved Treaclemustard. This large member of the cabbage family is known locally as the Queen of Myvatn. This is a peculiar betrothal when one recalls that the King of Myvatn is supposedly the Gyrfalcon! Gyrfalcons and Merlins occupy the niche of the British Kestrel.

Throughout any circular journey around the shores of Lake Myvatn, the birdwatcher should be keeping both eyes open over the water and its shores. The range of bird life is unparalleled. The rich sources of food and the diverse habitats have seen to this, while the concerted efforts of conservationists should ensure that this remains so. Some birds are based in America, such as the American Widgeon and Barrow's Goldeneye. The three most numerous varieties are the Scaup, Widgeon and Tufted Duck. The lucky ornithologist may also see Red-breasted Mergansers, Gadwall, Shoveller, Long-tailed Duck, Goosander, Eider and Whooper Swans. Five types of goose can be spotted: Greylag, White-fronted, Brent, Pink-footed and Barnacle.

The Eastern Interior

Introduction:

This section describes the southward journey from Lake Myvatn. After crossing the glacio-volcanic desert of Odadahraun, the route skirts to the west of the massive ice-cap of Vatnajokull before approaching the ringroad in the south. It has to be said that this will not provide much of direct interest to the naturalist, as much of the land is barren and inhospitable. This section has still, however, been included for two reasons. Firstly, it is the most direct route to Hof, an interesting area to the south of Vatnajokull. Secondly, the journey we describe is pure "adventure". This is the most "expeditionary" section of the whole Icelandic circuit that we describe, and the challenge of negotiating its dramatic scenery will not easily be forgotten. However, you need not worry about becoming lost in the wilderness, as the route is marked by yellow poles and cairns.

Myvatn to Askja:

Starting from the eastern junction between Routes 1 and 848, you should continue east along Route 1 for 33km, when a track leads off to the left. By the time you join this track, you should be sure to have replenished all supplies of drinking water and fuel. Remember to work out your requirements well in advance, bearing in mind that four-wheel drive and low range increase fuel consumption. It is wise to use sand tyres during some parts of the southward journey. Sand ladders would also be useful. You will find that driving through mud and sand will dry out nuts and bolts. Thus, it is not always easy to remove the wheels.

The track travels for 64km before reaching the mountain of Herdubreid. This section runs down a strip of sand and stones lying between the Odadahraun plain and the Jokullsa a Fjollum River. Beyond the "Four Wheel Vehicles Only" sign, the view is quite intimidating. A flat expanse of black gravel and pebbles (called "grjot" in Icelandic) stretches onwards for miles. Even with sand tyres, this makes for lively driving conditions. The main problem at the northern end of the track is not sand, but rather the occasional deep rutting. This presents a real danger of grounding, and thus damaging the underside of your vehicles. It takes luck and skill to decide which of the many tyre-mark diversions from the main track are the fanciful doodlings of an adventurous driver, and which are necessary to avoid the ruts.

The ease with which this stretch of track can be travelled depends very much on the weather conditions at the time. The violent dust storms are a nasty hazard on dry and windy days. There are three river crossings to be tackled. The first is the Grafarlandaa – some 36km or so along the route – a fairly insignificant tributary. Another 16km further on, you will cross the Lindaa. The depth of this river is quite deceptive, and you should be sure to send waders out to check your crossing. Nine kilometres later, the track crosses over the Lindaa again. Although the rivers themselves should present no difficulty, these last few kilometres include some awkward driving. The 5km sections before the first crossing of the Lindaa, and after the second, involve areas of block lava. The maze-like track will tilt vehicles quite alarmingly, as well as confronting you with a number of small "steps" to climb up and down.

For the last 30km of this route from Myvatn, the mountain of Herdubreid gradually comes to dominate the view. It rises some 1000m above the surrounding plain. The name Herdubreid aptly means "broad-shouldered". This great palagonite hump is a flat-topped block of sheer-sided rock thrusting up out of a skirt of vast scree slopes. On a cloudy day its top half can be hidden from view, only adding to its gloomy splendour.

The plant life of the route so far is nothing to write home about. However, the Arctic River Beauty (a relative of the Rose Bay Willow Herb) can be seen in the areas near where the track fords the Grafarlandaa and the Lindaa. Its large purple blooms stand out in contrast to the black sand from which they grow. They are a surprise in the context of the small species that you generally find in the interior.

The Jokullsa a Fjollum – the river which runs parallel to the track – also has its surprises. In the north it seems sluggish and many-branched, filled with islands of black silt. Closer to Herdubreid, however, it is a violent glacial torrent, creamy brown with rock flour and running between banks of dark lava.

The journey from Herdubreid to Askja is another 35km. The map gives an impression that much of the driving involves the awkward block lava described above. In reality this is not the case. Unfortunately there is a stretch of very soft sand where rutting is once again a problem. Beyond this lies the Vikursandar. This plain of small, honeycombed segments of pumice provides a softish, but good driving surface. The pumice is brown in colour, but tinged with white. Some blackish hills have snow-like drifts of pumice on their slopes, while black lava flows across the pumice. The overall effect resembles a Christmas pudding in brandy sauce! The pumice was originally produced by the eruption of Viti in 1875.

If you plan to stay in Askja, then there is a tourist hut just off the main track, at the base of the caldera. If you decide to camp rough, then note that the pumice is a punishing surface for tents. It is sensible to place canvas or some other material beneath an ordinary groundsheet. Although it affords very little grip for tent pegs, you have the reassurance that it drains very well in the event of heavy rain. As we noted above, you should bring plenty of water with you on this route, as you will otherwise be limited to streams of melted snow.

Askja itself is not the neat cone that it appears on the horizon. Instead, it is an 8km wide sprawling network of black lava, cream pumice screes and white snow. Low clouds often cling around the summit. The volcano is higher than it seems. The approaching track climbs steadily for several kilometres, so that even the base is at 800m. At its highest point, it is over 1500m.

The camping area at Askja.

Although it is now dormant, Askja erupted relatively recently, in 1961. The site of the tourist hut marks a junction in the track. One branch continues southwards, while another makes its way for 12km up to the northern edge of the volcano. This runs past snakes of lava – black, purple or red in colour. These contrast with the streams and snow, and the clouds, never far above. The drive is particularly rough, whether the surface is rock, coke or lava snakes. Grounding and tilting is a constant hazard, especially if you overload roofracks. If you decide to give up halfway, it is practically impossible to find anywhere to turn round. From the end of the camp, it is a further 2km across snow, coke and pale pumice to the top. This trek across what seems like a moonscape, is rewarded by a striking view. The lake, Oskjuvatn, is 3km in diameter. The water is surrounded by walls of lava, pumice and stone. This caldera formation arises when the magma chamber within a volcano is evacuated by an eruption. The empty space then collapses, the cone sinks, and a large crater is left. In many cases, such as Askja, this becomes filled with water. When the cloud is low over the summit, the effect can be alarmingly claustrophobic. On the shores next to the lake is a pool of steaming blue water, lying in its own crater. This is Viti, the site of the 1875 eruption. After checking the temperature with care, it can offer a relaxing bath, surrounded by patches of snow.

The area around the camp also merits closer examination. A short distance away, the narrow gorge of Drekagil cuts into the side of the volcano. You can follow a stream between vertical black walls, some 100–200m in height. These are surmounted by bizarre, twisted pinnacles and pillars. Steep slopes of pumice scree stand at their bases. At the head of the stream is a waterfall.

The Gaesavatnaleid:

This 120km journey from Askja to Tomasarhagi was immortalised in Desmond Bagley's novel, *Running Blind*. It is certainly not to be undertaken without considerable care and preparation. In addition, the track passes through some very fragile habitats, so travellers should be sure to eradicate any signs of their presence. For this reason, as well as for safety, you should keep to the established route wherever possible.

As you would expect, only four-wheel drive vehicles should try the Gaesavatnaleid, and they should preferably be equipped with a winch.

The Gaesavatnaleid involves crossing a succession of rivers of different sizes. These are fed by melt-water from the Vatnajokull and the Tungnafellsjokull. As such, they tend to get deeper as the day goes on. This effect can be boosted if the weather is particularly hot, or if there is rain. Consequently, you should try to make as early a start as possible. (We have found 4am satisfactory.)

In LandRovers, your average speed will be about 6mph, and your petrol consumption, 10mpg. In all, the journey takes 15–16 hours, including time for voluntary or involuntary stops en route. Stops are certainly important. It is wise to take stock every few miles, and plan the driving ahead. In addition, if you have a vehicle full of people whose view is restricted, then what may be a challenging and exhilirating experience for the driver may be an uncomfortable test of endurance for the passengers. They will certainly appreciate a chance to stop and get out of the vehicle.

Leaving the tourist hut at Askja, you make your way south. In a few kilometres you will notice a change in the route from that described in many maps and guidebooks. The track now follows the route northwards towards Myri for a while, before arcing south-west again. By doing so, it avoids the dangerous area of glacial outwash plain, where melt-water from Vatnajokull collects to become the Jokullsa a Fjollum. This often used to be impassable because of water, or because vehicles would sink in the sand. Even so the new route still crosses 15km of soft black sand, which it shares with the track to Myri. On these stretches it is best not to stop, although both ordinary tyres and sand tyres can cope reasonably well. Afterwards, the track consists of a combination of sand and lava – a firmer surface. However, when you leave the route to Myri, a bit of impromptu road improvement may well be necessary.

You rejoin the old Gaesavatnaleid close to the Dyngjyjokull outlet glacier. After travelling through a landscape of black stones on black sand, it is perhaps not a surprise to be greeted by a black glacier! It is worth stopping here and making your way over the sand and the outwash stream to the glacier snout. On first examination, the black sand and gravel appears to be a surface deposit. However, you can see that this is not the case from the high ice walls at the glacier foot. The material on the surface has been left as the ice in which it was suspended has melted away.

The next 15km or so are one of the most difficult stretches of driving – another zone of block lava. Vehicles twist and turn over uneven surfaces of solid rock as you attempt to find the flattest path. (In fact, "solid" rock is not entirely accurate. As the volcanic lava cooled, bubbles of gas were enclosed in the solidifying rock, forming domes. Some have already collapsed, so it is instructive to note that the surface over which you travel may be a matter of centimetres thick.) With the best of navigation, "steps" of 60cm or so will be unavoidable. The problems are reduced if you have a short-wheel-based vehicle, and if you avoid overloading. The crucial factor is underside clearance. It is best to try to avoid putting too great a proportion of equipment on the roof, as this raises the centre of gravity and increases the danger of tilting. Again, a few exercises in applied road construction will be required, in the form of digging and levelling out with stones.

Steeply climbing away from the blackened ice of Dyngjyjokull, the track brings you up to the rim of the cavernous Urthurhals crater – black itself but patched with white ice. To the north lies the flattened cone of the great shield volcano, Trolladyngja. Moving onwards, there are poles and yellow painted rocks for guidance. Their advice should be taken with a healthy pinch of salt. When you finally reach the end of the lava, there is a splendid view down to the Sprengisandur, the plateau that lies between the ice-caps of Vatnajokull and Hofsjokull. The steep descent down to this plateau reveals a marked change in terrain – from volcanic rock outcrops to the gravelly sand of the desert. Its undulations lead to the oasis of Gaesavotn.

The next trial to present itself is the succession of rivers. It is impossible to try and give detailed advice on fording routes and particular difficulties, as these will change almost daily, according to the weather and the time of day at which they are faced. With luck, there should be no crises. It is worth remembering to ask anyone that you meet en route for their advice on crossing points. Other than this, the standard procedure described in the Introduction, page 175 should be followed – and low range all the way!

As the last rivers are negotiated, the track bears southwards to join the main Sprengisandur route from north to south. Gradually, the desert finally relinquishes its grip, and vegetation begins to reassert itself. Undoubtedly, the distant sight of the bright green *Rhachomitrium* which covers Tungnafells, is a relief to the eye. Beware of complacency though. The track is still not very good, and you will notice where predecessors have made their own, through the mud and vegetation to the side. Tungnafells is the site of

The Tungnafell tourist and weather hut.

another *saeluhus,* or tourist hut. After surviving the Gaesavatnaleid, the enthusiasm for an hour spent searching out a decent rough
camp may be lacking. Hence, this is as good a place to stay as any –
you sleep up in the roof. The charge of just over £2 per person is
hardly likely to break the bank either.

Tomasahagi to Hof:

The 80km track down to the lake of Thorisvatn seems quite dull
in comparison to the previous drive. Depending on the time of day,
many of the rivers which you appear to cross on the map, will
actually prove to be dry. Several of these dried beds are home for
large numbers of Arctic River Beauty. There is even a proper
metalled road for the 9km approach to the Tungaa Bridge, after
Thorisvatn.

After crossing the Tungaa Bridge, you should take the first
turning on the left, about 1500m later. This rugged road will lead
south. Fifteen kilometres later, you will see in the distance,
Mount Suthurnamur, on the other side of Lake Protastathavatn.
The combination of the brown rock, bright green moss and
distinct patches of very white snow creates the unreal impression
of a Disney cartoon, or a piece of painted scenery. From here the
road continues for a further 6km, skirting the eastern shore of the

lake. The quality then deteriorates and you are back to rough track.

The track runs for some 35km to Blafell. The journey is quite slow, however, as the terrain is fairly rugged, and a number of rivers have to be forded. As the drivers' patience is eroded by snaking up and round a succession of black mountains, the temptation to become blase about the rivers is strong indeed. Do not succumb – always send your waders out first. On occasions, more than a straightforward crossing is demanded. In one case, the track follows the course of the river for a couple of kilometres in order to squeeze between two great cliffs of rock.

The area of Blafell is a good spot in which to break the journey to Hof, although *Rhachomitrium*-covered lava is not an ideal material in which to secure tents. If you have time, then it is well worth considering this as an additional base for detailed study.

Leaving Blafell, the track continues for another 20km, before (officially at least) returning to the status of a road. Twelve kilometres of Route 208, and the long-lost ringroad hoves into view. Once travelling eastwards along Route 1, it is some 117km to the town of Hof.

Blafell can only be reached from the Sprengisandur by using the river as a track to pass through the mountains. The route is marked with yellow poles.

The South-eastern Coastal Plain

The Shadow of Vatnajokull

Hof:

Hof is attractive in the same understated way as Blonduos. It is a small village of about twenty houses. They shelter at the foot of a grass-covered inland cliff, in which there is a colony of nesting Fulmars. There is a small, turf-roofed church in the village, built in 1883. Like many of Iceland's Lutheran churches, it is austere in design. The walls are white and the interior is simply furnished, with the exception of a colourful picture of Christ on the altar.

In addition to the usual search for a rough site, there is an official camp-site in the Skaftafell National Park. The main reason for avoiding rough camping here is the high rainfall which afflicts south-east Iceland.

Ingolfshofthi:

Ingolfshofthi is a small grassy island, with a lighthouse and a few sheep. About 1km in width, it has high cliffs facing the sea to the south and east. The cliffs to the north and west are smaller and banked with sand. The name is taken from Iceland's first settler, Ingolfur Arnasson, who landed here in 870.

Drive east along Route 1 for 6km, and then turn right down into Fagurholsmyri. A track leads south from this little settlement. However, you still have another 5km to go after this officially ends. After crossing a river and a short stretch of marsh, the rest of the journey covers completely flat black sand. The island rises in the distance with the long curve of the sea to the left. The sand is quite soft, so the drivers will need to be cautious, following the rusty guide-poles. If the sand is partially under water, then it is probably safer to walk, although this can take about 90 minutes. The large areas of black, sandy wasteland in this region are known as "sandur". They are made up of sand, mud and silt that

A group of Great Skuas

is swept to the south by the fast-flowing rivers of melt-water which emerge from the glacial outlets of the Vatnajokull ice-cap. On the drive to Ingolfshofthi, you may well pass locals who have been collecting Puffins for food. The major attraction of the island is the range of seabird colonies which it supports. Nesting Fulmars dominate the seaward cliffs, with some ravens in the north-eastern corner. The cliffs on the southern coast are alive with nesting Kittiwakes, Gannets, Puffins and Guillemots. Skilful eyes may even spot the rare Brunnich's Guillemot. The island as a whole is full of various skuas, while Snow Buntings prove to be an intrusive land-based bird. A search of the top of the sea-cliffs will yield a number of Puffins' burrows. Whether these are occupied will depend on how early the birds decide to breed. As you wander the island, you will soon know if you stray close to any skua chicks. You always have to beware of dive-bombing, but in these circumstances the adults almost brush against your body. Despite this behaviour, the Great Skuas are very skilful at eluding the clutches of mist-nets set up to capture them.

A few hours birdwatching on Ingolfshofthi is both enjoyable and relaxing. The birds are a delightful spectacle. Fulmars appear suddenly over a cliff edge and then glide past gracefully. In contrast, the Puffins move with a torpedo-like dash, their wings a frantic blur. All this occurs against a backdrop of sun (hopefully) on water, and the clash of black sand against the white guano which covers the cliffs.

Skaftafell:

The Skaftafell National Park was set up in 1967, with help from the World Wildlife Fund. Sigurthur Thorarinsson, a geologist, described its attractions in no mean terms: "It includes almost every aspect of Icelandic nature, and a more magnificent landscape can hardly be imagined." The vast bulk of the Vatnajokull ice-cap certainly provides a dominating backdrop. The region which includes the Park has been shaped by years of erosion from the glaciers and their meltwater. Thus it is not surprising that the area displays Alpine characteristics more common at higher altitudes.

The Park lies 15km north-west of Hof, along the ringroad. The best place to start is the Information Centre, where you can pick up a free booklet which includes a map of all the marked trails. One pleasant walk begins by climbing up through a wooded gully. Woodland is a rare sight on our circuit of Iceland. Skaftafell's supply consists largely of shrubby birch, the largest specimens of

The western cliffs of Ingolfshofthi looking back towards Vatnajokull.

which are rarely more than 1m tall. The gully leads up to the waterfall of Svartifoss. Although the flow is not very powerful, the drop is quite high. The water pours over some peculiar formations of black basalt. With its base worn away by the spray, the rock seems like a collection of inverted organ pipes. The shape is supposed to have inspired the interior design of the Icelandic National Theatre in Reykjavik. Another interesting geological feature in the Park is the liparitic rock, which contains stripes and layers of different colours.

The gully leads on past the waterfall, to a sloping marshy moor, called Sjonasker. The plant life in this zone includes Lady's Bedstraw, Harebell, Common Bentgrass and Angelica. This is followed by a steep rocky climb to the summit of Skerholl, 526m above sea level. The view from the pinnacle of Skerholl is starred on the map for excellence. If any reader makes this ascent on a clear day, then they know better than us whether such enthusiasm is justified!

The bird life of this walk is certainly impressive. Merlin, Redwing and Ptarmigan are all present. The last of these are often so docile that they can be approached within 4m or so – close enough to admire their beautifully speckled plumage. The Merlin nest in the scrub and woodland. As with Ingolfshofthi, and much of this region, it is the skuas that seem to dominate. The vast sandy plain to the south (on the fringe of which Ingolfshofthi stands) is one of the foremost breeding areas for skuas in the northern hemisphere. Another interesting find in the scrubland is the Icelandic Wren. This is larger than other wren species, and has developed as a unique sub-species because of isolation.

To the east of the Park Centre are two interesting glaciers. These tongues of ice emerge from the great bulk of Vatnajokull. Skaftafellsjokull, which is adjacent to the park, is awkward to gain access to. The melt-water rivers are often too deep to be safely traversed. However, even the pools and streams some distance from the snout merit investigation. Svinafellsjokull, one valley further to the east, is more convenient. You should not be put off by the geological chaos of the moraine. The jumble of boulders, rocks, pebbles and dust create the impression of a deserted stone quarry. Some concentrated exploring is worthwhile here, as semi-precious stones – opals and jasper, for instance – are scattered about.

A narrow track leads alongside the vast motorway of ice. On the other side, horizontal scratches in the vertical wall of rock indicate that the glacier has narrowed over the years. The track

Looking across the Svinafellsjokull, Skaftafell.

winds onto a continuous mound of moraine material. The rocks, stones and dust have been shoved together by the force of the ice, which now lies partly buried beneath it. Care should be taken when scrambling down the other side of the moraine, towards the glacier. What appears to be solid rock is often actually ice with a thin coating of grit. Initially, the glacier rises in a steep slope from its sooty margins, before levelling out to a comparatively flat surface. A few paths lead onto the ice itself. A brief wander is relatively safe, as long as an eye is kept open for crevices and pools.

To Reykjavik and Seydisfjordur

We have now concluded the description of our detailed tour through Iceland. The next two sections briefly deal with the journeys to the main departure points from Iceland: Reykjavik and Seydisfjordur.

The road east:

The road to Seydisfjordur is especially interesting. To begin with, it hugs the coast. During this stretch, the vast bulk of the

Vatnajokull ice-cap, which lies just inland, dominates the landscape. Thirty-two kilometres from Hof, the road crosses a bridge which spans the melt-water from the Breidamerkurjokull. This glacier comes within a few kilometres of the coast. There is a large melt-water lake at its base. Eider Ducks swim between the icebergs that have split away from the snout of the glacier.

As far as Hofn, the scenery is largely plains of outwash from the glaciers. This is ideal terrain for nesting Arctic Terns and, inevitably, the Great and Arctic Skuas which plague them. This area is the best breeding ground in Europe for skuas.

Beyond Hofn the road begins to wind as it passes the eastern fjords. If you have a four-wheel drive vehicle, the Oxi Pass offers an interesting short-cut. Twenty-one kilometres past Djupivogur, in the upper reaches of the Berufjordur, a track joins from the left as the coastal road continues round to the right. The 21km track cuts across the mountain of Kistufell (1116m) to rejoin the main road once again. At this point, there is a superb birch woodland on the flat lowland to your right. The tallest tree is less than a metre in height!

The road now begins to climb steeply. It eventually flattens out and crosses numerous small rivers. If you have already crossed the interior, then you will probably not even notice these. The quality of the Oxi road varies according to how recently the road was scraped. The difference this makes is quite extraordinary. A two-wheel drive car could negotiate this stretch – with care – if scraping has been recent.

Just before Egilsstadir, at Vallanes, there is good tundra vegetation and a number of camping places on the eastern side of the road.

The road between Egilsstadir and Seydisfjordur makes a slow but spectacular descent to sea-level.

The road west:

The drive from Hof towards Reykjavik is striking rather than spectacular. It crosses miles and miles of flat, black outwash sand. Skuas and terns are still seen. In the smaller pools of water you will find Red-necked and Grey Phalarope. At Prestbakki, near Kirkjubaejarklaustur, there are a number of good camping possibilities. This is also a good stop halfway between Reykjavik and Seydisfjordur. The glaciers melt during the spring. The resulting floods invariably destroy some of the bridges. Hence, many are made with planks of wood that wash away, leaving the main structure of the bridge intact. Unfortunately, the planks are not always still there in the summer, so pick your route carefully!

From Selfoss, the road is metalled.

ADDRESSES

Mr. Tony Escritt,   [The best contact for most
The Iceland Centre,   aspects of Iceland]
Kennet Cottage,
Harrow Park,
Harrow on the Hill,
Middlesex.
HA1 3JE.

Iceland Tourist Information,
73, Grosvenor Street,
London.
W1X 9DD.

Arctic Experience Limited,   [Tour operator specialising
29, Nork Way,   in Iceland]
Banstead,
Surrey.
SM7 1PB.

Twickenham Travel Limited,   [Tour operator specialising
33, Notting Hill Gate,   in Iceland]
London.
W11 3JQ.

Dick Phillips,   [Stockist of large range
Whitehall House,   of maps and books]
Nenthead,
Alston,
Cumbria.
Telephone: (0498) 81440.maps and books]

P & O Ferries,
Orkney and Shetland Service,
P & O Terminal,
Aberdeen.
AB9 8DL.

SPAIN

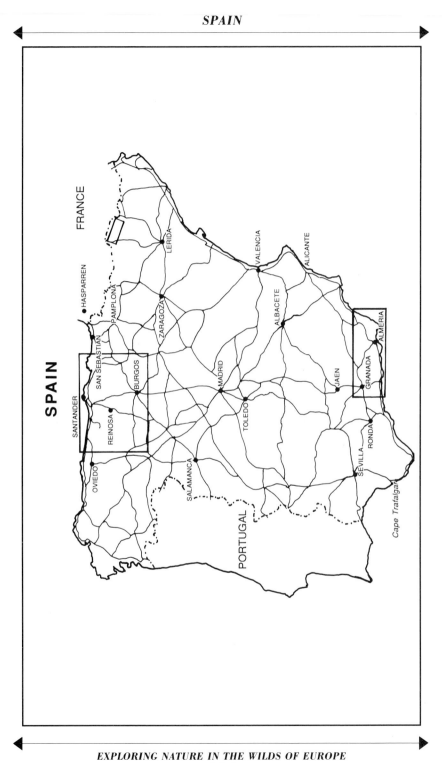

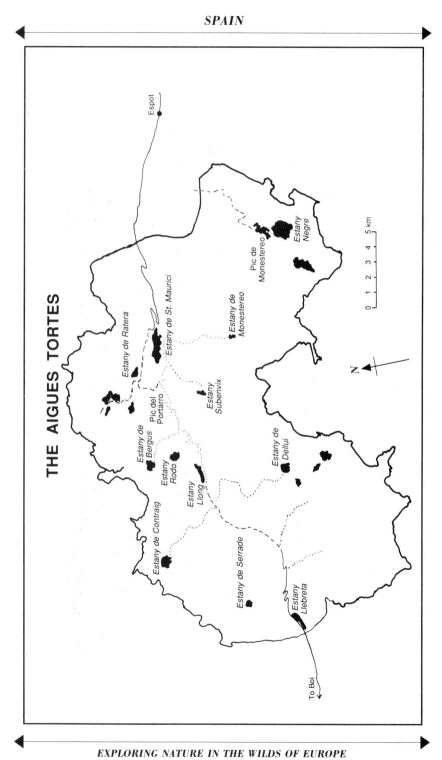

THE AIGUES TORTES

Espot

Estany de Ratera

Estany de St. Maurici

Estany de Monestereo

Pic de
Monestereo

Estany
Negre

Estany de
Subenvix

Pic del
Portarro

Estany de
Bergus

Estany
Rodo

Estany
Llong

Estany de
Dellui

Estany de Contraig

Estany de Serrade

Estany
Llebreta

N

0 1 2 3 4 5 km

To Boi

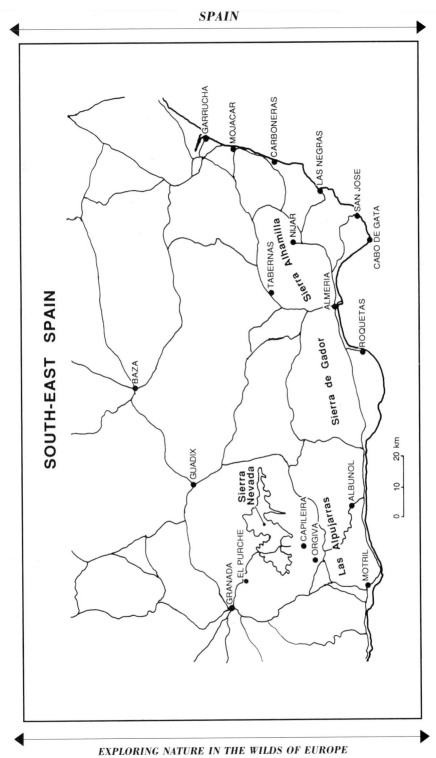

SOUTH-EAST SPAIN

GARRUCHA
MOJACAR
CARBONERAS
LAS NEGRAS
SAN JOSE
CABO DE GATA
NIJAR
TABERNAS
Sierra Alhamilla
ALMERIA
ROQUETAS
Sierra de Gador
BAZA
GUADIX
Sierra Nevada
CAPILEIRA
ORGIVA
Las Alpujarras
ALBUNOL
MOTRIL
GRANADA
EL PURCHE

0 10 20 km

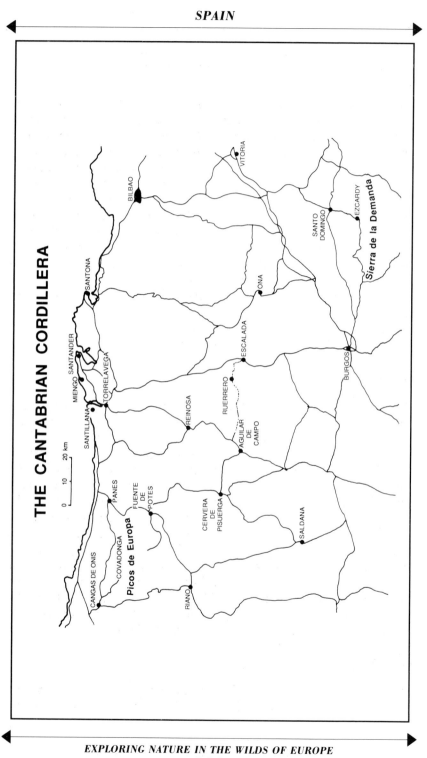

Introduction

Spain has been described as a "kaleidoscope of landscapes". The position and terrain of this, the third largest country in Europe, ensure that such a description is deserved. The marine enthusiast will find a wealth of interest on the Atlantic and Mediterranean shores. Steep cliffs, rocks, sand spits, dunes and saline lagoons are all to be found. The walker will enjoy the peaks and valleys of Europe's second most mountainous territory. The awe-inspiring desolation of the central plains could almost be another continent.

The variety of landscape and climate supports some 6000 seed plants. This is the greatest selection in Europe. In part, this is explained by the proximity of Africa and northern Europe, as well as the presence of some unique alpine habitats. Spain has a marvellously diverse natural history, both in terms of its flora and fauna.

This chapter also includes a brief discussion of the French Pyrenees and the French basque country.

Geography

Spain occupies more than 80 per cent of the Iberian peninsula. The mountain chain of the Pyrenees serves to isolate the country from the rest of continental Europe. These mountains are the result of geological folding, which has occurred because of tectonic movement. The Cantabrian Cordillera, which runs parallel to the northern coast, is an extension of this chain. These mountains provide a great sense of geographical isolation to the areas of the far north – most extreme in the sentiments of Basque separatism. To the south of Cantabria is the expanse of the *meseta*, or central plateau. These vast tablelands slope downwards slightly from east to west. In the far south-east, the Mediterranean coast is backed by the rise of the Baetic ranges. These include the magnificent, snow-capped peaks of the Sierra Nevada. Between the coast and the mountains, lie some of the most inhospitable lands in Europe – the semi-deserts of Almeria, Cabo de Gata and Tabernas.

Climate

The variation in geography is mirrored by a variation in climate. The Atlantic coast is cool and wet, becoming drier as you move east to the Pyrenees. Mist and drizzle is common near the sea although it can be scorching hot just 60km inland. The average summer temperature in Santander is 22 degrees centigrade, compared to 36 degrees centigrade in Seville. In the south-east, the climate is arid and punishingly hot during the summer – hence the semi-desert conditions which have drastically limited agriculture in the area. The coast between Portugal and Gibraltar is milder, with relatively little seasonal variation. The meseta has a classically continental climate – roasting hot in the summer, and often very cold in the winter. The aridity, however, is characteristic of the whole year.

Vegetation

The cool north is dominated by a verdant countryside. Woodland and heathland is common, in areas similar to those in other parts of continental Europe. In the Pyrenees are spruce and other conifers. The semi-deserts of the south-east are naturally very barren. Esparto Grass is one of the few plants able to survive.

Essentially there are four major vegetation types.

Forest – mainly the evergreen Holm Oak and Chestnut.
Maquis – shrublands of holly and cistus. Very colourful in spring.
Garigue – a terrain of low, scattered bushes, with a great deal of bare rock and stony soil. Typically supports thorn bushes and aromatic plants, such as thyme, sage and lavender. A beautiful sight in spring.
Steppe – very low plants sparsely scattered in a barren landscape, subject to over-grazing by goats.

The high altitude of the sierras has a considerable influence on the plant-life.

Getting There

The most popular option for those taking vehicles from Britain is to drive down through France. This can be achieved without difficulty in two days. Remember that tolls are charged on most French autoroutes. Alternatively, you can take the Brittany Ferries sailing from Plymouth to Santander. This runs twice a week and lasts for 24 hours. The reputation of the Bay of Biscay is fearsome, but (usually) undeserved. Anyway, take your Stugeron before leaving the UK! You can also combine these two methods – driving one way, and sailing the other.

Motoring in Spain

The quality of the Spanish road network is constantly improving. Nonetheless, in the routes described here (and throughout this book), we take you through areas which are well off the beaten track. In parts of the Pyrenees, for example, four-wheel drive may be required. These tracks are marked "pista para jeep" on most maps. However, these stretches are few, and they can usually be by-passed without too much difficulty. Most main roads are fast and well maintained. Minor roads are very potholed. These are filled by a lorry that squirts a blob of tarmac into the hole. Grit is then thrown on top. Different vintages of pothole, often unevenly filled, can make long distances very tiresome to drive.

Drivers will need their licences, vehicle registration documents and "green card". You should also take a bail bond (obtainable with the green card or included free in the AA 5-star package). This is your "get out of jail free" card! You may not be planning to rob any banks, but you can sometimes end up in jail after a road accident. The law requires you to carry a red warning triangle and a spare set of bulbs. The headlights on right-hand drive cars must also be adjusted. Seat-belts are compulsory in non-urban areas.

The speed limits are 120km/h on motorways, 100km/h on highways, 90km/h in the country and 60km/h in towns.

Petrol *(gasolina)* is available in "normal" and "super" varieties. Diesel *(gasole)* is not always available. Try to fill up as frequently as possible, as garages are often inconveniently far apart. Note that garages do not accept credit cards, although some are beginning to accept Eurocheques. Hence, you will need cash. Fuel prices are comparable with those in the UK. They are fixed throughout the country.

Spain has several different police forces. The blue uniformed officers will be the metropolitan, city police. In towns, or on the open road, you will see the green uniformed officers of the *Guarda*. These have more power. Treat them warily. They have an effective system for stopping vehicles. There is an officer on both sides of the road – usually positioned between two bends to catch you unawares. Make sure that all your documents are in order and that they are carried in an easily accessible position. On-the-spot fines may be levied for something as simple as putting one wheel over a solid line.

Maps

Several single-sheet maps of Spain are available for basic itinerary planning. Michelin map 990 is one of the best. For more detailed coverage of the regions there are now two possibilities. Firstly, the *Mapas de Carreteras* series from Firestone Hispania. Nine sheets cover the whole Iberian peninsula at a scale of 1:500,000 (1cm=5km). Michelin have just started a 1:400,000 (1cm=4km) series which is excellent. It covers the whole of Spain and marks camp-sites as well as suitable rough camping spots. The *Mapa Nacional Topografica* covers the whole country at 1:50,000, and part of the country at 1:25,000. The quality of these maps is far from uniform.

Language

Castilian Spanish is the official language, although there are distinct regional dialects – Catalan and Basque, for instance. The former is predominant in the Pyrenees. English is only spoken in the main tourist centres. Even pidgin Spanish is an advantage in the more rural regions.

Visiting Churches

Churches and cathedrals are among the finest architectural sights in Spain. Unlike in the UK, the church authorities usually enforce a dress code – exposed arms and (especially) shorts are banned. If you generally walk around with exposed legs, it is worth carrying a pair of rolled-up light-weight trousers with you.

Currency

The Spanish *pesata* is divided into 100 *centimos*.
Banknotes: 100, 500, 1000 and 5000 ptas.
Coinage: 50 ctos; 1, 5, 25, 50 and 100 ptas.
   Banks are generally open from 0900 to 1400 hours on weekdays,

and between 0900 and 1300 hours on Saturdays. Occasionally, banks open their foreign exchange counters again between 1700 and 1900 hours in the evening. Look out for the word "cambio". Major credit cards (including Access and Barclaycard) are widely accepted, as are Eurocheques. Cash is needed for petrol.

Camping

You will need to have your passport to register in an official site. There are more than 500 in the country. They are more numerous in the south than in the north.

Rough camping is quite acceptable, and in the more remote areas it is the only possibility. A sign with a cross over a tent will show where camping is not allowed. The general rules for short-term camping are that you should not stay within a kilometre of an official site or on agricultural land, unless permission is granted. Remember that areas of long meadow or grassland will be used for hay-making. No camping is allowed in towns, or in their immediate vicinity.

Fishing

You will need a permit from the *Instituto Nacional para la Conservacion de la Naturaleza*. Obtain it from one of the Regional Headquarters of ICONA.

Food and Shopping

Eating out in Spain is rarely a gastronomic delight. However, a meal at a local restaurant can be a pleasant break in a camping trip. In coastal areas, you should try the local seafood stew, which can go under a number of names. Paellas are usually quite tasty.

When self-catering, fruit is often a good buy. Always peel the skins away, as chemical fertilisers are often used, and rarely washed off. Alternatively, they can be washed in a special solution (see page 5). Try making a large fruit salad, and adding some wine. Bread is very reasonable but rarely lasts more than 24 hours.

Spanish wine has a reputation for roughness. Wines from the Rioja region strive to achieve mediocrity, but they are reasonably priced, which is some consolation. The wines from Navarra are a better bet. Naturally, if you buy cartons of red wine at 40p a litre in the SuperSpar, you cannot expect a Chablis. Sangria is enjoyable on a hot day, and the brandies are also worth trying. The latter are matured in sherry casks and hence absorb part of the flavour.

With the exception of some large department stores, all shops observe the siesta. They usually open from 0900 to 1300 hours and 1730 to 1930 hours, with no afternoon opening on Saturdays. The *supermercado* usually opens every day – including Sundays and Bank Holidays. *Auto servicio* means self-service.

Medical

Whenever possible, do not drink tap water without chlori-tabs. However, the resulting fluid is so unpleasant that either boiling or taking mineral water are the most desirable options.

Reciprocal health care is available through the EEC, by taking your E111 form. Nonetheless, health insurance is a good idea.

A barrier cream is sensible for hot zones or areas with high altitude. Remember that the siesta is there for a reason – sunstroke is well worth avoiding, especially if you are driving for long distances.

You will need to be prepared for "Spanish Tummy" – we recommend Imodium or Lomotil. However, prevention is better than cure – wash fruit and vegetables, do not drink too much wine or fizzy drinks and avoid long periods in the sun without a hat.

The Central Pyrenees

Getting There

The starting point for our journey around Spain is the French city of Toulouse because of its position on the A62 autoroute to Bordeaux, and the A-class Route 20 which heads north to Paris via Limoges. Thus you can preface your travels through Spain with one of a variety of paths south from the Channel ports.

Leaving Toulouse, the Route 117 travels for 103km south-west to the town of Montrejeau.

The French Pyrenees

Much has been written about this popular area of France. Below we mention just one of the many possible centres from which one can walk and drive. The tourist information centres in Pau and Lourdes can provide specific information packs for those areas. These give details of numerous walks, and what you will be able to see. Detailed maps are available of the whole French Pyrenean region. This is in stark contrast to the Spanish side. We will describe that in far greater detail, as little has been written about it in Britain.

The French side of the mountains is green and lush. The cloud cover is more extensive and it rains much more. Consequently, you will need more equipment to combat the harsher weather conditions. The three National Parks comprising the Parc National des Pyrenees incorporate all the best climbing and hill walking regions of the central Pyrenees. Their boundaries carefully avoid roads, so the only way in is to walk.

The most impressive area of the French Pyrenees is due south of Pau at the end of the D934. The Pic du Midi d'Ossau (2884m) is not for the general hiker, but is a spectacular sight on a clear day. For the walker, the best route is to turn on to the D198 at Laruns and follow the hairpin road up to the Col d'Aubisque (1710m). Gourette, 4km before the Col, is a good base if you wish to spend more time here. There are camp-sites and ski lifts. One of the ski-lifts will get you to the peak of Pene Blanque at 2550m. From there a path climbs up to Pic de Ger. At an altitude of 2613m, this provides an awe-inspiring view.

A number of well-trodden paths lead south into the mountains. The GR 10 is perhaps the most fascinating. It winds its way to the east of Pene Medaa (2488m) and then below Sanctus (2482m), before crossing the Col d'Uzious (2236m) and descending to the Vallee d'Arrens. If you try this walk, you should be prepared for possible changes in the weather conditions. The trek is hard work, although it is not at all difficult. In 9km or so, it reaches the D105 in the valley at Le Tech. There is a camp-site here. Turning left will bring you down 5km to Arrens. Turn right and within a few kilometres you will be at Aste. This is the end of the road and it marks the start of the Parc National des Pyrenees.

On this walk, or any in the region, look out for the soaring raptors. Any of the four vulture species can be seen here, as well as Golden Eagles, kites and buzzards. Alpine Choughs and the usual red-billed Chough are found here. Chamois can occasionally be seen on the high peaks, but they need careful stalking. The botanist will be overwhelmed by the array of arctic and alpine species.

A kilometre out of Arrens on the D105, a left turning will lead you to Estaing on the D103. There are camp-sites here. This makes another good base from which to explore on foot. The highest of the surrounding peaks is Mount Ne, at 2724m. A more rugged camp-site can be found at the end of the D103. From here it is just a few kilometres before you are enter the Parc National des Pyrenees. The parks are oriented towards walkers. You need a tent if you are going to do them justice, but you can also use the mountain huts, for which you pay a nominal amount. The location of the huts is shown on the detailed maps which are available at any of the village or town shops.

The Spanish Pyrenees
– Aigues Tortes

There are two national parks in the Spanish Pyrenees, the Ordessa and the Aigues Tortes. The former is an extensive and beautiful steep-sided valley. Unfortunately, severe restrictions allow only walking, with no camping or vehicular movement. Aigues Tortes is a vast area of mountain peaks, alpine meadow, lakes and valleys. The flora and fauna are similar to those found in the Ordessa. However, the greater range of habitats and

High up in the Aigues Tortes, Spanish Pyrenees.

the ability to camp there makes it better to visit. There are two routes into the Aigues Tortes National Park: from Bohi in the west and Espot in the east. Our journey will begin with the former route.

Getting there:

Take the Route 125 from Montrejeau. The following 50 km wind up into the Pyrenees, before reaching the Spanish border, after which Route 125 becomes the N230. Franco-Spanish border crossings are notoriously unpredictable, although the quieter customs points such as this, are generally quite quick.

The postcard-quality scenery is a splendid back-drop against which to spot a number of birds of prey. Peregrine Falcons establish their territories in the mountains here. They can sometimes be seen attacking Black Kites which have unwittingly strayed too far. In addition, jays are a common sight throughout this climb up into the Pyrenees.

The road south from the frontier makes its way down into the Aran Valley. The chief settlement of this area is Viella, which stands at the confluence of the Garonne and the Negro rivers. The town contains an interesting church. This has an unusual octagonal belfry, dating from the thirteenth century and a chapel which contains an early carving of the Mig Aran Christ.

The N230 has a spectacular climb out of Viella. As the road levels out, there are a number of excellent alpine meadows to the left. A quick stop will reward you with a very wide variety of flowers and insects. Look out for the larger white butterflies, such as the rare Black-veined White, Apollos, fritillaries, Swallowtails and Blues. The grasshoppers and crickets are especially prolific. They include the Large Green Bush Cricket (*Tettigonia viridisma*). Ant Lions are common here. In the sunshine, you can find the peculiar Clubbed Ant Lion (*Ascalaphus libelluloides*). It has yellowish wings and very long clubbed antennae.

Within a kilometre, the road plunges into the Viella tunnel. This continues for 5km. It should be treated with caution, as there is no lighting and the unclad walls absorb the beams from your headlights. On the other side of the tunnel, you pass a stretch of cliffs in which the nests of Alpine Swifts can be seen. Note that the mountain-top weather can change very quickly. With low visibility and a succession of passing lorries and cyclists, the stretch of road beyond Viella can be most nerve-wracking, although the road has been extensively improved in recent years. The vegetation at the side of this stretch of road is a good habitat for butterflies. Swallowtails, Large Graylings and Purple Emperors can be seen in the damper spots. As you descend from the mountains, so the heat intensifies.

About 12km beyond Bono (which lies at the bottom of a particularly steep descent), a minor road leads away on the left. It returns northwards for some 15km, bringing you to the village of Bohi. This is the limit of the tarmac road. From here, there is a track which climbs high into the mountains. In theory it is possible to cross the park to Espot in the east, but even a LandRover will find this very difficult.

On this side of the Park there are two permissible camping areas. To reach the first, on a lake called Estany Llebreta, you will have to travel on a poor quality track. Cars can make it, with careful driving. (Ironically, the track has a tarmac surface once you reach the border of the Park!) The road then climbs steeply to a parking area. However, the track continues to another camping site at Estany Llong. This track is appalling. It is scattered with rocks and boulders, and has few turning places. Even these are only suitable for unladen four-wheel drive vehicles. LandRover

The village of Bohi, and the National Park Centre.

taxis are often seen in Bohi. These can be hired to take you into the Park if you have no vehicles. It is a long walk!

Bohi is a good place to stock up with fruit, wine and the like. It also contains the large, dark, stone-floored office of the National Park. This is in the main square, on your left. (It is not signposted.) You must get permission from here in order to camp in the Park. Camping is free, but the rules include a maximum stay of three nights. There is a warden who makes his presence well noticed, but the period of stay does not appear to be strictly enforced. Park office opening times are: 0900–1300 and 1600–2000 hours.

Before you leave Bohi, note that the sparrows nesting in niches in the buildings are, surprisingly, Tree Sparrows and not the house variety. The buildings also provide a construction site for intricate Paper Wasps' nests. On bare rock around the town, you may see Mountain Houseleeks. These peculiar plants display many water-conserving characteristics. Hence, they are able to withstand greater extremes of heat and drought than most alpine species. Keep an eye open for Serin and Wall Lizards.

Estany Llebreta:

The Aigues Tortes National Park covers a little more than 100 square kilometres. The name means "winding waters". This

Houseleeks, a common alpine plant found in the Aigues Tortes.

refers to the small river which makes its way eastwards – shadowed by the track. The landscape varies between 1500m and 3000m in altitude, and exhibits classic signs of a glacial past.

The camp-site stands at the edge of Estany Llebreta. This large glacial lake provides a welcome opportunity to wash away the stickiness of the journey south. The lake is far warmer than the rock pools in the river. However, for pure refreshment, the granite plunge-pools of Cascada toll del Mas (which lie a short distance upstream) are almost like jacuzzis. The extensive camping area covers the grassy valley floor on both sides of the water. During the summer, it tends to be quite popular at weekends. There are no facilities here, so a toilet tent and chemical loo is a good idea. Water for washing and drinking should be taken from the river, well above the camp-site. The area by the lake is often free from tents. This has more than a little to do with the profusion of mosquitoes and horseflies! The immediate area supports a variety of orchids, and also Clustered Bellflower.

As we noted above, this site is very popular with insects. Midges, mosquitoes and horseflies can cause considerable annoyance. A good supply of anti-histamine and repellant is a must. (Luckily, the mosquitoes tend to be fairly lethargic during the summer, and they can be swatted without much difficulty.)

Non-biting flies can also be a problem, especially around meal-times. If you use an ultra-violet moth trap at night, this will only worsen the insect problem, although an incredible diversity of moths will be caught. The Emerald Moth is especially impressive.

An initial exploration will take you further up the valley of Arrayo del Llachs. To the side of the track is a small alpine meadow, which plays host to a variety of characteristic alpine species. The proliferation of flowers is breathtaking – likewise the myriad of butterflies which jostle around them. Alpine Choughs can be seen above, while Pyrenean Brook Salamanders are closer to hand in the small bubbling streams.

An enjoyable morning can be spent hiking northwards up to Lago Serrade, at 2035m. Immediately opposite the camp, you can see the V-shape which has been cut in the mountainside by the river, as it flows from this corrie lake. It is a steady climb, for which you should allow three hours. To begin with, follow the road. A track soon leads up to a small ruin on the left. A loose path then zig-zags up the river. It levels out for a short time before making the final ascent to the boulders which dam the lake.

A number of Crag Martins will probably be seen en route. Capercaillie, Red-backed Shrike and Butcher Birds are all possible sightings on the lower slopes. In a total distance of 2km, the altitude rises by 500m as you climb the mountainside. This is an interesting slope on which to complete a zonation study. Plant life includes the Martagon Lily, various gentians, albino Creeping Bellflowers, Stinking Hellebore, Slender Broomrape, Lesser Clubmoss (a tundra species), the insectivorous Butterwort, Wolfsbane, thousands of Marsh Orchids and another type of houseleek. Serrade is a corrie lake – it sits in a steep-sided hollow, formed by erosion at the point where snow and ice fed into the top of a glacier. In the alpine meadow, grasshoppers and the Humming-bird Hawkmoth are much in evidence. Less common are the rare Apollo Butterfly, the Large Copper (now extinct in the UK) and the Clouded Yellow – the examples here have a pink edging on their wings. There are Salamanders and tadpoles in the lake, feeding on the caddis flies and mayflies.

During the evening, the camp-site lake abounds with emerging amphibious life. Midwife Toads are particularly common. As the name suggests, this species is unusually conscientious in caring for its offspring. The male carries the eggs of its young in strings around its legs until they hatch.

Estany Llong:

The journey along the track to the east of Estany Llebreta becomes quite awkward, even for LandRovers. The land is predominantly scree, while the track is simply a strip where the grass has worn away, and the largest boulders have been removed. Unfortunately, the surface gives little grip, and the occasional rut or rock can surprise the unwary. The continually steep gradient confines the vehicle to second gear in low range. This makes a good supply of fuel all the more important. Normally one might try and pick one's own route across the terrain. However, in this case the valley sides are so steep that it is impossible to stray from the track. It is some compensation that the ford crossings are relatively easy.

With increasing altitude, the coniferous forest becomes more dominant. An increase in the amount of dead wood will be obvious – a consequence of thinner soils. Longhorn Beetles live in dead timber and the area is rich in species. The most impressive wildlife on this stretch are the Golden and Booted Eagles which occasionally fly overhead.

On the way to the lake, there is a refuge hut which also serves as a small cafe/bar. The omelettes are particularly good!

The area around the lake will be of interest to geographers. You can climb up one of the glacial slopes to a hanging valley and then follow it up to a small corrie lake. The plant life around Estany Llong includes a large number of rich, pink Pyrenean Rhododendrons. This miniature variety provides a dominant belt below the pines. Most of the plants here are similar to British species, except for a prefix of "Alpine" or "Pyrenean". In addition, there are Fragrant Orchids, Grass of Parnassus and the unusual St. Bruno's Lily.

The Eastern Aigues Tortes:

Return to the N230, and drive the 35km north to Viella. The N142 heads east. After about 40km, you pass through the village of Esterri de Aneu. This route is very scenic with good views back to the mountains. The N142 is being upgraded and this should speed up an otherwise slow passage. A couple of kilometres beyond this junction, a road leads westwards to Espot. Once again, you will have to obtain permission from the Park Centre to camp. This is to the right as you enter Espot. (Opening times: 0900–1300 and 1600 –

2000.) The limit at St. Mauricio is three nights. The centre also sells good, large-scale maps of the whole park. The village is a good place to see Wall Lizards and the rare Purse Spider, *Atypus*.

Four-wheel drive is not necessary to reach the camping area or the lake at San Mauricio. As a consequence, this part of the National Park is more commercialised, with more visitors and more park wardens. Espot has more shops and restaurants and the inevitable LandRover taxis. These can be used to continue on from the lake, where a track climbs towards Bohi and into the heart of the park.

The camping area is quite satisfactory, although it tends to be crowded in high season. The ground slopes slightly, so you will have to select your pitch carefully. Like the other camps in the park there are no toilet facilities, but luckily the area is heavily wooded! If possible, you should bring a toilet tent/chemical loo. Water sources can be suspect and it is safer to obtain it higher up the road where there are unadulterated springs. The botanist will be interested to know that the Cobweb Houseleek can be found nearby – although its official distribution only encompasses the Alps and Apennines. Its name describes a number of web-like strands that cover the leaf rosettes. They are tiny tubes which regulate the input

Climbing the track to Lago Ratera.

and output of water. Keep an eye open for Yellow Monkshood. Preservation of flora and fauna is strictly enforced. Fines are imposed on anyone seen capturing animals or picking flowers.

The mountains on this side of the park are much steeper. The snow is also compacted more firmly. Cloud is more likely to cover the peaks, and there is a greater chance of rain. The general walker may find the terrain quite challenging, but the views are exceptionally dramatic. The tarmac road stops by the lake of San Mauricio, but if your vehicle is suitable then it is well worth continuing along the track, further into the park. If not, the walk is still worth it.

The lower slopes are densely wooded and harbour Black Woodpeckers, Capercallie and Red Squirrels. Crested Tits and Melodious Warblers can be seen against the background of snow-capped mountains. The track steadily deteriorates in quality. After a while, the only sign to distinguish it from the surroundings is the stream of water flowing down its centre. Moving up the valleyside to Estany Ratera, you can find two varieties of Spotted Gentian, together with a hybrid more vigorous than both its parents. A nearby river valley contains massive colonies of Butterworts and Sundews, together with numerous lilies and orchids.

Pico de Aneto

Getting there:

Travelling from the eastern side of the Aigues Tortes, you can either retrace your steps through Viella, or follow the N147 south to Pobla Segur, and then the N144 north-west. Ultimately, you want to take the N144, which leaves the N230 just north of the turning to Bohi. This leads west for 32km. After passing through the small village of Laspaules, the road makes its way to Castejon de Sos. As it does so, you climb from the fields of the valley floor, up to the Fadas Pass. At nearly 1500m, this offers splendid views to the snow-capped peaks of the Maladeta to the right.

Shortly after Castejon de Sos, there is a road junction. Turning right, you will follow the course of the River Esera on Route 139. The river flows down from its source in the mountains. It is clear and fast-flowing as it makes its way across the pale-coloured granite rock. This narrow, yet verdant valley is home to a few

Griffen Vultures. These can sometimes be seen with young, high up on the slopes.

The town of Benasque lies 14km from the junction with Route 144. It is a place of contrasts. The winding streets, lined with the houses of the noble "seignors", fit uneasily with the recently constructed buildings that have created a modern ski resort. There is an austere castle nearby, embraced by ravines. A very unexpeditionary trip to the Burger Bar is recommended – try the squid in garlic butter.

In order to find a camping area, you will have to travel some way up into the valley, as scouts often use the lower portions for camping. A couple of kilometres beyond Benasque, the track skirts a small lake. Soon afterwards, a track leaves the main route to the right. The winding course crosses the river, and then curves back to the river for a second time. This is the best place in which to camp. There is a large grassy clearing next to a disused refuge hut which stands by a bend in the river.

The camp-site area:

The naturalist may wish to make a transect study of the land around the camp, in order to discover the effects of the steep valley sides and the alluvial soils. The pools contain large numbers of Brook Salamanders. Although predominantly black, they exhibit an amazing variety of colours. The males have characteristic orange streaks. Mammals around the camp include some field mice (*Apodemus*) which, interestingly, are very large in comparison to British varieties.

The valleys nearby have the tell-tale U-shape of glaciation. The wet valley floors support a copious quantity of frogs, as well as a variety of alpine flowers. The most notable of these is probably the Pyrenean Colombine. A wide range of bird species can be seen in the crags above. These include vultures, Crested Tits, Rock Sparrows and Rock Thrushes.

The Pico de Aneto itself stands to the east of the camp-site. It is the tallest peak in the Pyrenees, at 3404m. Mountaineers usually allow two days to climb along the granite aretes to the summit of this pyramid peak. The night is usually spent in the Refuge de Rencluse.

Southern Spain

Getting There

The journey from the Pyrenees to the southern coast is a marathon. With no major stops planned en route, it can be completed in two days. Obviously, if you can stop off for a few hours sightseeing here and there, the drive will be much more pleasant.

There are no direct routes south from the Pyrenees. It may be preferable to travel via Lerida and Valencia.

After Valencia, you are faced with a choice between motorway and major road. The determining factor will probably be the number of swimming stops intended, as you move along the Costa Blanca. The familiar names of Benidorm and Alicante are not places to stop for a quiet rest away from the madding crowd. The motorway ends at Alicante, and the Route 340 then moves away from the coast, and continues for another 300km to reach Almeria. If you can, pass through the ancient moorish town of Elche and have lunch in the central gardens. The entire town is dominated by palm trees.

Almeria

This corner of southern Spain forms a gap between the Costa Blanca and the Costa del Sol. Relatively unexploited, it has a backdrop of dramatic mountains. It includes the driest region in Europe – the Cabo de Gata. To the naturalist, the habitats range from semi-desert with salt lakes, to a diverse and unique mountain flora.

The town:

Almeria is a busy industrial harbour dealing with minerals and fruit. It has not lost its pleasant character, as the tourist resorts are mostly spread along the shore to the west. Watch your feet if you go swimming, as sea urchins are fairly common on this part of the coast.

The city centre and the shopping streets are attractive tree-lined avenues. The Paseo de Nicholas Salmeron is a delightful promenade, which runs close to the harbour, shaded by palms. After exploring the old quarter of Almeria, you can climb up to the fort which dominates the city. The Alcazabar was started in the eighth century, and then considerably enlarged in the tenth, on the orders of the Moor'Abd-al-Rahman III. The interior was very badly damaged by an earthquake in the 1520s. However, the gardens are a beautiful combination of cacti, flowers, streams and palms. There is also a spectacular panorama over the coast and the town – try to see it at sunset. A tourist information centre in the town can help with accommodation – hotels or self-catering apartments. There are several official camp-sites near the town. Rough camping is possible throughout the region as there is little cultivation. However, due to the very dry nature of the terrain it is not always easy to find suitable areas with shade and where tent pegs can be hammered into the "concrete" soil. In the otherwise arid Tabernas Badlands (see page 222), there are several "oasis"-type places off the road where you can camp under eucalyptus and date palms. At Roquetas de Mar, a young developing resort, there is a wide choice of reasonably priced apartments with good views into the sierras and along the coast.

Cabo de Gata:

The Cabo de Gata, or "Cape of Agate", lies at the eastern end of the Gulf of Almeria. Follow the minor road from Almeria to El Alquihan, along the shore of the gulf, as far as Cabo de Gata. The arid countryside contains a number of dried-up river beds, cut between old plantations of sisal (a cactus-like plant with a flower stalk 4m high). The area near El Algain is worth a closer look, as it is scattered with bright pink splashes of oleander. These appear to be the only plants that can really thrive in this inhospitable landscape. They have very deep roots that stretch down into the soil, as far as the water table. This is vital, as the temperature often reaches 45 degrees centigrade on the open ground at midday. By searching among the thorn bushes and the patches of sisal plantation, a surprising number of animal specimens can be found. These include several species of lizard, and a wide range of insects. The large black wasps are particularly interesting. As you explore, the noise of the cicadas provides an incessant background.

The greater flamingoes flying over the Lagunas de Salinas on the Cabo de Gata.

To reach the Cape, you have to take a right turn off the main road. Near this junction, make a cursory glance to the barren region on your left. This is the beginning of the Esparto Grass steppe. The grass grows in dense stands. The bare patch surrounding each plant is typical of many types of steppe vegetation. These are allelopathic species – they deposit chemicals around their roots which prevent other plants from muscling in on their territory. This method of reducing competition is vital in an environment with small supplies of water and minerals. Hence, bare patches will be seen around most of the plants in this part of Spain. This is also scorpion and tarantula territory. Specimens only emerge at night – you will have to search carefully. The tarantulas here are not the variety that usually appears on television. This small species, between 5cm and 6cm in diameter, lives in a little burrow. Geckos are easier to find.

As the track approaches the cape, the Lagunas Salinas lie to the left. This four square kilometre area of salt lagoons is a tremendous site for the birdwatcher. There is little plant life in the lakes themselves, with the exception of a bright yellow blanket weed. However, this attracts millions of tiny shrimps which, in turn, provide food for hundreds of Greater Flamingoes. Other sightings can include the Little Egret, Cattle Egret, Gull-billed Terns, Black Terns, Hoopoe, Redshank, Mediterrranean Gull, Kentish Plover, Avocets, Black-winged Stilts and the yellow Spanish Wagtail. Water Pipits can occasionally be seen, but this is a fairly unusual habitat for them during the summer. The salt-tolerating Glasswort is the dominant plant life around the edges of the lagoons, growing in large bushes. The vegetation here is salt steppe. This is very similar to a saltmarsh, but it produces a profusion of colour in late spring. *Salsola papillosa* and *genistoides* are a couple of rarities which can be found here. Scorpions, black rounded beetles and a variety of well-camouflaged grasshoppers live among them.

This harsh environment supports some interesting parasites. One plant of particular note is *Cynomonium coccinium*. All that is visible is a reddy-brown fleshy lump. This can take a variety of shapes, but it is generally clubbed, and about 12cm in height. Incredible though it may seem, this is the flower! Close examination of the lump will reveal the stamens. The best time to see these peculiar plants is in early June, before the soil bakes completely hard. However, the remains endure for some time.

Continuing to the end of the Cape, you can see the lighthouse and visit the caves. These are well-known for the agate crystals which they contain. (Agate is a colloidal form of silica, which often forms banded crystals.) Hence the name, "Cape of Agate".

Retracing your steps to the north, you can turn right after passing the Lagunas Salinas, and make your way to San Jose, on the other side of the Cape. The beach to the west is an interesting place in which to make a transect study. The general aridity means that the variation is very gradual. In terms of plants, the first species to colonise the sand dunes is Marram Grass. Moving inland, you find Sea Spurges, thorn bushes and conifers. The *mattoral* (or scrubland) landscape is based on bright red soils. Further inland, sisal and Prickly Pear are important. The sisal plants can be seen in all stages of their development. The young specimens start their growth at the top of the flower, dropping to the ground as they mature. This gives them a head start in the dry and scorching conditions. The Prickly Pears are cultivated and grow in rows. These delicious fruit are sold on stalls in Almeria. Do not try to pick them yourself – the thin spines are agony in the skin, and very difficult to remove.

Animal life in this area includes locusts, grasshoppers (including the Tower Head Grasshopper, which has an unusually elongated head) and sand wasps. The last of these are fascinating to watch as they capture prey and pull it back to their nests.

Nijar lies inland from San Jose, in the foothills of the Sierra de Alhamilla. This lovely village is set in the mountains, with various examples of local crafts for sale. Further up the coast, there are uncrowded bathing areas in Carboneras and Las Negras – but beware of rocky outcrops. At this end of the Mediterranean Sea there is a slight tidal range. A good variety of marine species can be found at low tide. These include octopus, sea urchins, and a variety of commom crab with a square carapace – *Pachygrapsus*.

The Tabernas Badlands:

Following the N340 northwards out of Almeria for 40km or so, will bring you to one of Spain's most arid and unforgiving habitats. Just 123mm of rain falls here in a year. By leaving the main road, you can explore the dried up river beds. The lack of moisture has meant that three fox corpses have remained undecomposed in one of these river beds, for at least 12 years. To cursory examination, these river beds appear completely barren. However, they support a surprising wealth of insect life. In turn,

The Badlands of Tabernas.

this enables birds such as the Wood Chat Shrike to survive. When they hunt, their rapid wing beats enable them to fly with great speed, and make frequent changes in direction.

Oleander and fig are the main plant species, with patches of Esparto Grass. This spiky plant is well adapted to the desiccation of the badlands. Animals, too, have to be hardy. The scorpions are often 8cm in length. Tarantulas, praying mantis, geckos and spine-footed lizards are all present in varying numbers.

You may well spot an oasis in the midst of this semi-desert. The greater moisture enables eucalyptus and date palms to take a foothold. The swift evaporation of any surface water helps to draw salt up to the surface. This creates a white crust, and also supports some familiar saltmarsh species.

Understandably, this hostile environment offers no great potential for human activity. The one exception is pottery, which is important to the village of Sorbas, some 15km further along the N340. This settlement has an incredible setting. The houses are built into a cliff, with a bend in the river passing beneath them. It is a marvel that communities have survived in this aggressive environment. The desolation of the Tabernas makes it no wonder that David Lean chose the area for the filming of "Lawrence of Arabia". Many spaghetti (or should it be "paella"?!) westerns have been filmed here. You can still visit some of the sets. Most rise up in the middle of nowhere, but one is visible from the main road.

The Sierra Nevada

Getting there:

After 12km travelling on the main road north out of Almeria, take the N324 to the left. Nine kilometres later, the C322 leaves to the left and makes its way across the southern fringe of the Sierra Nevada. Alternatively, a quicker but less scenic route follows the coast road, before turning right up to Albunol and eventully Orgiva. Sierra Nevada is Spanish for "snowy range". The overpowering heat will probably force a number of stops upon you. Take the opportunity to examine the vegetation belts and investigate the insect life. The photo opportunities are both frequent and impressive.

You start the ascent of the foothills as you move into the region of Orgiva. Over the years, the delightful climate has attracted a number of important figures, including Churchill and Hemingway. This area is known as the Alpujarras. From here, you have a choice of routes. You can follow the road to Granada, and then tackle the sierras from the north. Alternatively, a dusty, steep, but relatively straightforward track climbs from the south. This rejoins the tarmac road at the top, for the descent to Granada. The track really begins at the village of Capileira, to the north of Orgiva. As you ascend, look out for Bee Eaters, Hoopoes, and brightly coloured Rollers.

Just past the village of Capileira, a track leads up towards the peaks. This is one of the few places in this area where you will be able to find surface water – there is a full stream. The greatest problem is to find somewhere flat to camp – much of the ground is covered with boulders or thistles. The surrounding forest is Cork and Holm Oak.

This camp-site is at an altitude of 1700m. The vegetation consists largely of low herb bushes. Many of the plants in this harsh landscape contain poisonous aromatic substances, to avoid being eaten. These can play havoc with hayfever sufferers. You should be aware that the high parts of the Sierra Nevada are prone to very strong winds, especially late in the day. Tents and dining shelters have to be very firmly secured, with the pegs reinforced by rocks. However, it is some compensation that the midges are no problem here, although the small horseflies (called "cleggs") are a real nuisance.

Pico de Valeta:

The road makes its way up the slope of Pico Valeta for a further 30km. The surface is quite good, although the road is very steep in parts – especially in the hairpin bends. As the route ascends, Choughs and hovering Lesser Kestrels are frequent companions. Vegetation is dominated by stunted, prostrate specimens of Spanish Broom. The fauna is comparatively sparse, but includes the beautiful Grayling butterfly and myriads of grasshoppers.

The road which climbs up the Pico de Valeta has the distinction of being the highest in Europe, almost reaching 3400m. The views from the highest point are breathtaking, encompassing the Mediterranean, the Baetic ranges and the Sierras of Almijara, Sagra and Tejeda. The slopes appear like a moonscape – scattered scree, with barely a living thing in sight. However, the appearance is deceptive. Closer examination reveals a wide range of alpine plants, sheltering in the lee of rocks. Forty species are unique to these Sierras, as their names indicate – *Plantago nevadensis* and *Viola nevadensis*, for example. Most have dense piles of hair to reduce water loss. In patches of green there is the Alpine Gentian. Harvestman spiders and large bush crickets are also common.

Descending some distance to the north, there is a track which leads away to a ski lodge where camping is possible. Some time earlier, you will have noticed a reservoir at the end of the track. It is impossible to reach this by vehicle, but there are areas of moss off the track which are quite suitable. The site is dominated by the looming shape of a large radio telescope, positioned on a nearby hill. The clear night skies leave one in no doubt why the astronomers chose this location.

Unfortunately, the strength of the wind and the rarified atmosphere really make this site unsuitable for an extended stay. Nonetheless, a few hours birdwatching will not be wasted. Surrounding the reservoir is an area of damp pastureland and montaine habitat above the tree line. The bird life here includes the Black Redstart (rare in the UK) and the Alpine Accentor (absent from the UK). Chough, wheatear and ravens are common.

As you make your way further along the road towards Granada, the Albergue Universitario has a welcome combination of toilets, petrol station and bar! Continuing from here, you will soon come upon a turning which leads to the farm settlement of "El Purche". The area is quite verdent. Shade and shelter from the wind is provided by a group of locust trees, next to some ruined farm buildings. The combination of fresh water from El Purche with the attractive views 25km across the mountains to Granada, makes this an irresistable stopping point.

In the dry terrain nearby, the grass is full of grasshoppers and bush crickets. With every step, dozens of them leap around your ankles. The exposed stones of the run-down buildings are used as platforms by basking lizards. Particularly impressive is the bluish Ocellated Lizard – about 35cm in length and swift of claw.

Stagnant water channels provide a superb habitat for dragonflies, newts and frog larvae. You can also excavate the intricate burrows of communities of Mole Crickets in the damper ground. This region encompasses a great variety of bird life. Ornithologists will spot Goldfinches, Short-toed Tree Creepers,

Hoopoes, Wheatears, Spanish Sparrows, Lesser Kestrels, Golden Orioles, Rollers, Sparrowhawks, Woodchat Shrikes and Scops Owls. Climbing upland along an agricultural track, you will see a number of Magpies, together with Great Spotted Cuckoos, which are parasitic upon them. Peregrines often swoop from the cliffs nearby.

During the winter the area is covered by snow; even in June the mountains are cold and wet. This means that spring comes late in comparison to the rest of southern Spain. June is a time of bursting flower buds, particularly for orchids. By August it is becoming parched.

Granada:

The city of Granada lies 30km to the north-west, by road. Built on three hills in the midst of a wide irrigated plain, this ancient Moorish settlement is absolutely unmissable. With the fall of Cordoba to the Christian forces of Ferdinand II, Granada benefited from an influx of refugees, complete with their riches.

The jewel in Granada's crown is obviously the Alhambra. Its name originates in the word "Kat'at-alhamra", which means "The Red Castle". In reality, it is more than a castle. It is a large complex on a number of levels, including royal residences, churches, gardens, terraces and defensive structures. Its massive bulk easily dominates the city. Building began in the eleventh century, but much of the finest work was undertaken two hundred years or so later. Thankfully, the ornate decoration is still in remarkably good condition. One of the most beautiful areas within the Alhambra is the Court of the Lions. In its centre, a circle of water-spouting lions stand beneath a circular fountain. The perimeter is a cloister of intricately carved arches – Muslim architecture at its finest. The slightly larger Court of the Myrtle Trees includes columns made from jasper and alabaster. A central pool is flanked by myrtles on either side. Ideally one should set aside half, or a whole day to appreciate this fantastic fortress.

By contrast, the cathedral is a little disappointing, although the Chapel Royal, built by Ferdinand and Isabella, is well worth a visit. The chapel itself is very beautiful. Isabella's art collection is also sited here – including work by Botticelli.

West to Ronda and Cape Trafalgar

Getting there:

Leave Granada on the N342 to the west. Looking back, there is an impressive view of the city, with the Sierra Nevada as a backdrop. After 12km, you reach Santa Fe. Popular legend suggests that this was built in under two months by Ferdinand and Isabella, as they laid seige to Granada. Forty-six kilometres further along the N342 is Loja, a town dominated by the remains of its Moorish fort. From here, it is 42km to Antequera.

Just before entering the city, there is a road to the right. This leads up to the dolmens – a site of archaeological interest. There are two funeral chambers, concealed beneath burial mounds. Dating from 4000 years ago, the Viera and Menga chambers have been assembled from large boulders. The Viera chamber has a small entrance, but the Menga is larger. It is oblong in shape, and bisected by a series of pillars.

Antequera itself is a town of some 38,000 inhabitants. It has white city walls, and contains a number of buildings constructed from carved brick. Naturally, there is the ubiquitous Moorish castle.

Ronda has a romantic position on the edge of the gorge. Its principal claim to fame is as the early centre of bullfighting. The bullring, built in the late eighteenth century, is one of the oldest in Spain. The New Town is divided from the Ciudad by a deep gorge. The gap is 85m wide, with the Rio Guadalevin flowing through the middle. The Puente Nuevo bridges it, affording spectacular views. It became infamous in the Civil War as a way of disposing of traitors! The Ciudad is interesting to walk through – a complex network of Moorish streets, lined by houses with walnut doors and iron balconies. Look out for vultures in the air circling above Ronda.

Twelve kilometres along the C339, from Ronda, a left turn leads for 16km south to Benajoan. This is a dead-end but the limestone scenery is very striking. Four kilometres further on up into the mountains is the Cueva de Pileta. This is a series of caverns which were once inhabited by Neolithic man. (Note that you will have to call the guide who lives nearby.) Simple black and red outline cave paintings have suggested to archaeologists that Pileta was inhabited 25,000 years ago. As well as the paintings, the cave contains the remains of basic pots. In addition to the evidence of human habitation, the caves are also impressive from the point of view of their geological structure. They are one of the finest cave systems to see in Spain. The door is kept locked and you are given Tilley Lamps for lighting.

Retrace the 16km back to the road from Ronda, turn left, and then left again after another 5km. You will now be on the C3331. The next 30km or so takes the traveller through an impressive landscape, shaped by erosion. The rock varies in colour from grey to red. After passing through Ubrique – famous for preparing leather – the road continues for 50km, when you turn right onto the C346. A couple of kilometres later, a minor road on the left carries you for 18km. Turing right, and then taking the first left, Vejer de la Frontera lies 20km away.

This attractive settlement is raised from the surrounding land by an outcrop of rock. The altitude makes it an excellent site for storks. White Storks can often be found in flocks of about a hundred. Griffon Vultures are also not uncommon. A road to the south-west winds its way towards the coast. Follow the track which leads to the cape itself. A matter of yards from the beach, there should be room to park vehicles on the verge. Tourist debris is an unpleasant companion here, so it is best to move tents back onto the mobile dune system, although supporting the tents can be difficult. Shelter from the wind is provided by umbrella pine, only the tops of which are visible above the sand.

Cape Trafalgar:

The beach at Cape Trafalgar is ideal for swimming and sunbathing. The lack of tourists is an added bonus. A few hundred yards to the west, there is a rocky outcrop surmounted by a light house. Looking across the Atlantic rollers it is hard to imagine the great sea battle for which this part of the Costa de la Luz is famed. On October 21st, 1805, a British fleet under the command of Admiral Nelson, engaged and defeated the combined forces of Spain and France, under Admiral Villeneuve.

Climbing around the rocky headland can be an exhilarating experience. The vast waves are reminiscent of those at Cabo de Gata. The huge variety of species collected during a transect reveal the cape as a typical Mediterranean coastal habitat. In a comparison with the cooler British coasts, it is the absence of the dominant seaweeds that is most obvious. Here the midday sun scorches even the lower reaches of the shore during low tide.

A Dune Daffodil in flower, Cape Trafalgar.

Rolling boulders aside will expose crab species, such as *Pachygrapsus*, and giant Sea Cucumbers. The most abundant molluscs are large Helmet Shells, Rough Star Shells and the poisonous Mediterranean Cone Shell.

The plant life varies in the surrounding dunes. In stable zones, the Hotentot Fig tends to dominate. In the shifting sands, the Dune Daffodil (which resembles a white lily) grows in large numbers. Less decorative are the corpses of stranded porpoises, which are occasionally washed up on shore.

Driving back down the rough track to the road from Vejer de la Frontera, you can turn right and drive the short distance to Los Canos. You can buy food and petrol here. Continuing further along the track, you climb up into a dense forest of umbrella pine. The sand dunes inland remain quite mobile, because of the wind. It is interesting to note that even the stable systems further inland have poor soils, with practically no decomposition taking place – hence the continuing dominance of the umbrella pine. The animal life in the forest is thankfully more varied than the flora. There is a notable species of stag beetle and a striking silver-backed spider. Praying mantises are common, and curious ant nests, constructed from balls of mud, can be seen. Bird life includes the Sardinian Warbler and Spotted Flycatcher.

You may also see the Red-rumped Swallow – especially in areas where rubbish has been dumped.

Western Andalusia:

Driving north from Cape Trafalgar, and returning to Vejer de la Frontera, you should turn left onto the N340. This runs parallel to the coast, passing the Bay of Cadiz. A couple of kilometres beyond Puerto Real, the autopista sets off towards Seville. Follow it for 21km and then leave at the exit for La Cartuja. Five kilometres to the south, along the C346, the Laguna de Medina lies to the left of the road. This lake is a splendid site for the ornithologist. Cattle Egrets can be seen amongst the livestock at the roadside. Mallard ducks are often to be seen on the lake itself. The state of the lake (and hence the variety of bird life) depends much on the climate at the time. In especially dry conditions, the reeds and marshland may not yield the expected heron species. Nonetheless, you will be unlucky to miss the Black-winged Stilt, Black Terns, Spotted Redshank, Ringed Plover and Dunlin.

Once back on the A4 motorway, Seville is 85km to the north. Seville is the capital of Andalusia, and is important for both industry and tourism alike. With a population of over 600,000, it is the country's fourth largest city. Positioned in the fertile plain of Tierra de Maria Santissima, on the Rio Guadalquivir, Seville owes much to both its Moorish and Christian past. There are many attractions for the visitor. The Cathedral is the third largest in Europe. Next to the cathedral is the Giralda. In Muslim times this was the minaret from which the faithful were called to prayer.

The N630 leaves Seville to the north. After 10km, you reach some of the most well-known Roman ruins in Spain – Italica.

Coto de Donana:

Coto de Donana is the largest of Spain's National Parks and its wildlife is both diverse and spectacular. It was the first reserve to receive funding from the World Wildlife Fund. It lies on the river delta of the Guadalquivir, south west of Seville. It is impossible for the visitor to wander in the park. Everyone must go on guided tours operated in LandRovers. Complete and up-to-date details(including prices) can be obtained from the tourist board in Seville or by writing direct to the centre at the reserve.

The park possesses one of the best wetland habitats in Southern Europe – the *marismas* (marshes). During the year, the water level in these marshlands changes. This, in turn, causes changes in the fauna. In mid-summer it is dried up and almost deserted. Spring and autumn are the best times to see the migratory birds. Purple Herons, Gull-billed Terns, Whiskered Terns, Black Terns and Marsh Harriers are plentiful, together with flocks of wildfowl. The Ferruginous Duck, Ruddy Shelduck and White-headed Duck are all especially rare. Wild Boar and deer are common in the dried-up areas during the summer. A number of lagoons harbour Tree Frogs, Marsh Frogs, Salamanders, Terrapins and Caspian Turtles. This is the only place in Europe where the Purple Gallinule nests. It is also one of the best places in which to see the Greater Flamingo. Huge numbers nest in the shallow areas of the lagoon.

The LandRover tours also pass through the Cork Oak woodlands which are used for nesting by many of the water birds (egrets, herons, harriers etc). The very rare Imperial Eagle nests here, too. Wild Cats, Badger, Genet and even Lynx are known here. Pine trees stand near the extensive dunes, which support rare (and poisonous) reptiles. The trees are a nesting site for Short-toed Eagles which feed on the reptiles. The vegetation beneath the trees includes ground tree heathers, cistus and the Mastic Tree. Azure Winged Magpies can be seen around the park.

If you are in the vicinity, the Donana National Park should not be missed.

Northern Spain – The Mountains and the Coast

Getting There

From Andalusia:

Alternative 1

The N630 road rises out of the Guadalquivir valley, and makes its way to the Sierra Morena, and the border between Andalusia and Extremadura. As you follow this route, keep an eye open for Montagu's Harrier.

Extremadura:

The Marismas pass is the most convenient route through the Sierra Morena. Merida is positioned 168km north along the N630. It is largely famous for its Roman monuments.

Rising from the valley of Guadiana, the N630 continues for 66km to Caceres. This medieval town is home to many storks, as well as lying at the centre of a fertile agricultural area. The atmosphere of the old quarter is best appreciated at night.

Castile:

After another 168km of the relentless progress northwards, the N630 reaches the city of Salamanca. An architectural treat, the town is renowned for its university, which was founded in the early thirteenth century. It is at this point that the route finally departs from the N630. The next stretch leads 115km along the N620 to Valladolid. The road passes through Alaejos, with its castle and churches, and also Tordesillas, which has an attractive bridge across the Duero.

Valladolid is also a university town. For many years it was the seat of the kings of Castile. It is not terribly compact, and thus awkward to visit for a short time. However, the College of Saint Gregory is worth seeing – a fine instance of Isabelline architectural technique.

Alternative 2

From the French Pyrenees:

Tourists and heavy traffic cross the border at Irun. The autopista will take you south via the industrial city of Bilbao and down to Burgos. The drive is fast, expensive and boring. If you try it on the first few days of August (the beginning of the French holidays) it will be a slow nightmare. It often seems as though the entire French population is migrating to the Algarve. There are a number of good border crossings in the mountains, from either Cambo or St. Jean Pied-de-Port. The route from Cambo uses a good crossing at Dancharia on the D20. This is not signposted to Spain – all such directions will try to divert you via St. Jean. It appears that the French use this crossing for their shopping trips, as there are a number of good supermarkets nearby. There are rarely more than a few cars at these mountain border-crossings. The roads lead to Pamplona, which is famous for the day of bull-running in its streets. It is a splendid city and well worth a stop. The scenery is very impressive on all the routes, but not as lofty and spectacular as the central Pyrenees. Take the N111 from Pamplona. The road is scenic and generally quite quick. Stop for a while at Estella. There is a pleasant diversion north to Abarzuza, and then on the minor road to the monastery of Iranzu. You can rough camp near here.

The N111 continues to Logrono where you transfer onto the N120 to Burgos.

The Sierra de la Demanda:

This mountain range lies between Logrono and Burgos. The N120 runs across the hot plains just to the north. Several routes traverse the mountains. One good route turns off the N120 at St. Domingo – a pilgrimage town on the way to Santiago. Just before the junction, there is a dry and dusty campsite to the north of the road. However, there are better places to rough camp in the mountains. The L810 from St. Domingo is a new, fast road to Ezcaray, a winter ski resort. It has several hostels, and a number of shops scattered amongst the narrow streets.

As you enter the town, there is a well-hidden left turn to Valdezcaray. This is signposted to the ski-lift. After a few kilometres, a second signpost marks a sharp left turn up into the mountains. The drive is very spectacular and traces a complete circle back to Ezcaray. Instead of turning off here, you can make the circuit anti-clockwise, as camping is easier on this lower road. The journey starts by following the Rio Oja. A number of possible camping places present themselves here. For instance, there are several suitable side-tracks down to the water. As you pass Posadas – the last village – the road begins to climb. At a corner, a few kilometres from here, a track leads to the right. This descends steeply to the river, before climbing up to a small hydroelectric station. Camping is possible near the point at which the track crosses a stream. However, there is a larger green area among the broom bushes on the right, bordered by a second stream. In all, the road climbs to an altitude of 1550m. As it does so, there are several good camping possibilities.

In the early evening you occasionally hear the calls of the Ibex and Chamois on the mountainside. Butterflies are especially prolific. Many of them can be seen drinking the water as it drains across the tracks. Look out for the Apollo, Large Tortoiseshells and Fritillaries. There is plenty of good hill walking here. The vegetation is surprisingly lush in places. Broom, heathers and bracken cover the hillsides. Little rain falls, but a rolling mist usually drenches the vegetation and tents during the evening.

From Ezcaray, the B811 picturesquely winds its way to Burgos. Praduluengo is one of the larger towns en route. It is a good base from which to explore this end of the mountains. Rudimentary camping is available here. 7km south of Valmala is the peak Trigaza (2033m) and beyond is San Millan (2132m). This entire area is very wild and unspoilt. Even in summer the hedgerows abound with flowers, from harebells to dense red patches of Sweet Peas. The heathers may be covered with the red "spaghetti" of the parasitic plant, Dodder. The birds to look out for are the Red-backed Shrike, and different species of Kite and Buzzard.

Burgos:

You should certainly try to visit this superb city. There is plentiful parking on the south bank of the river. Built from white limestone, the thirteenth-century cathedral is famous as a fine example of Gothic architecture and carving. There are bargains a-plenty to be had in the nearby Plaza de Major. A park and a precinct lined with Plane Trees lead up to the monumental Town Gate, standing near the cathedral.

The Picos de Europa

The mountain range of the Cordillera Cantabrica runs westwards from the Pyrenees to the province of Galicia. It forms a dense rain shadow – during the summer the coast may be wet, while the ground 60km inland is scorched by the hot sun. Much of this range is built up with white limestone. The mountains are at their highest and most dramatic in the region known as the Picos de Europa – between Santander and Oviedo. They can be visited from Covadonga in the west or Potes in the east.

Begin your journey from Aquilar on the N611 which comes north through Palencia.

There is a superb route from Burgos. Leave the city on the road north to Santander. Beyond Ubierna, the road twists through exposed outcrops of limestone for a few kilometres. Dragonflies and amphibians can be found in the marshland on the valley floor. The road then climbs through the Cantabrians. For some 20km (starting near Tubilla del Aqua) it passes through an amazing gorge, between peaks and pinnacles. A left turn to Escalada will keep you within the gorge as the fast main road climbs out of the valley. The spectacle continues along the minor

The gorge near Escalada.

B63. This road is very quiet and several places can be found along here for rough camping. There are a couple off tracks near the provincial border.

You cannot fail to see the vultures, eagles and kites circling within the gorge. The fauna and flora are especially fine. The smell of the Lavender and other aromatic plants can be overpowering at times. Look out for different varieties of Bee Orchid, Wild Matter, Dwarf Juniper, Cottoneaster, Crowberry, Harebells and Stonecrops. The upper sides of the gorge are very steep. They have been weathered into a honeycomb of pinnacles and ledges. The slopes of the gorge are thickly carpeted with woods. As you approach Ruerrero, the gorge opens up with its sides over a mile apart. The cliffs are more like escarpments. The river in the valley is the Ebro. Its occasional flooding keeps the ground marshy, so that Meadowsweet and Common Reed flourish. Gradually the region has developed a heathland community which covers the sandstone with a purple and red blanket. There are numerous antiquities to be visited. Turn left at Ruerrero, towards Aquilar. Road conditions are very poor, with potholes and winding bends.

The stretch to Aquilar is wild with an occasional small-holding on the poor gritty soil. There are heavily wooded zones of oak with numerous places for rough camping.

Aquilar is an interesting town, famous in Spain for the biscuits which are made here. There is a tourist information centre in the main square. The camp-site is signposted on the Quintanilla road. It is set in dense pine woodland and is cramped and noisy. Less than a kilometre further on, a series of tracks lead off to the right and skirt the southern edge of the reservoir. This is a perfect area for rough camping, with breathtaking views across the water to the mountains. There are plenty of bushes to act as windbreaks – or other essential facilities! Look out for Roe Deer, large European Grayling butterflies, and a variety of heathland species. The road forks on the other side of Quintanilla. Follow it to the right as far as Salinas de Pisuerga. There is an impressive medieval bridge below the weir. You are now on the Aquilar-Cervera-Potes road. There are several stork nests on this route, especially in Liguerzana. On clear days there is a beautiful view of the mountain peaks in the distance.

Cervera is a town on the edge of the mountain range. As the road climbs north to Potes, there are wonderful views across reservoirs and mountains. Most of the lower slopes are heavily

An Apollo butterfly.

wooded with Turkey Oak. Hill walkers will enjoy this part of the country. Amazing limestone mountains stand to the east and west of Arenos. Most are about 1000m high, and can easily be accessed from the minor roads which criss-cross among them. Camping is very easy in the area.

The road steepens beyond Camasobres. Stop as you pass through the narrow cleft in the limestone – there is a carpet of purple Gentians by the stream. Apollo butterflies are relatively common. Mountain views stretch away in all directions as the road flattens out at Puerto de Piedrasluengas. As you appreciate this incredible scenery, it is amazing to realise how relatively unexploited this region is. From here the road slowly descends to the N621 and Potes.

The Eastern Peaks:

Rough camping is not allowed here, but there are two official sites. The nearest to Potes is overcrowded. The second has fewer people and is slightly less expensive. The peaks form an idyllic backdrop. It is still another 17km from the camp to the end of the road. A cable car can then take you to a plateau in the limestone. Alternatively, if you have a four-wheel drive vehicle, it is possible to take a LandRover track from Espinama as far as Sotres – a

The Picos de Europa, near Potes.

distance of almost 30km. An exciting climb takes you through a belt of dense trees, up beyond the refuge hut to a surface of barren, windswept rock. Hikers will find this track a useful setting-off point for a trip further into the mountains.

Vultures, eagles and Alpine Choughs are not unusual. Look out for the larger game animals, such as Ibex. The crags and ledges are good for alpine flora.

The Western Peaks – Covadonga National Park:

This side of the Picos de Europa was the first place in Spain to be made a National Park. It is reached from Cangas de Onis, off the Santander to Oveido road. As you drive the 22km to the park, look for the *horreos*. These square, wooden buildings stand on tall stone legs, so that the corn stored inside them is free from rats. For the last few kilometres, the road bends relentlessly back and forth as it makes its ascent. The views are some of the most impressive in Spain. The road carries a great deal of traffic. Thus this most accessible part of the park is full of tourists. Fortunately for campers, both they and the cloud cover disappear in the evening.

As with the Aigues Tortes, camping here requires a permit. However, in this case the warden comes to you. Two areas are designated for camping. The first is near Lago Enol – the first

Covadonga National Park, with Lago Enol and the track going to the camping area nearby.

lake you come across. Follow the track on the right until you see the other tents. Vehicles must be left on the track. The second site is above Lago de la Ercina. Here vehicles are allowed off the road but the area is heavily frequented by day visitors, as it is just below a restaurant and car park. The first site is preferable. It is also equipped with areas for water and washing. Camping permits are only given for three nights. There are several refuge houses where you can sleep on the floor, but there is a marked absence of toilet facilities.

Covadonga is huge and very impressive. Most visitors tend to remain near the road, but once you are well clear the walking opportunities are endless. The limestone geology has created deep grykes and clints, similar to those found in The Burren, in Ireland (pages 110 – 112). However, the similarity ends as soon as you closely examine the depressions. Dozens of different species inhabit the multitude of nooks and crannies. Beech is the main tree on the slopes, although they rarely become dense. Monkshood is another common plant. Many of the bushes on the limestone slopes have become deformed into weird shapes. Much of the area is grazed by cattle – the bells around their necks will probably keep you awake!

Ibex and Chamois are only frequently seen much further up the slopes. However, Badgers, Pine Martens and Otters are abundant even at this level. Pyrenean Desmans inhabit the brooks. This water mammal is similar to a mole. Egyptian Vultures are often seen circling the camping areas. There are also Griffon Vultures, Golden Eagles, Booted Eagles and Bonelli's Eagles. The camp is inundated by flocks of Alpine Choughs. They have yellow bills, unlike the Red-billed Choughs that we described earlier.

On a clear evening the white peaks of the mountains turn red as the sun sets. The combination of beautiful scenery, and an interesting flora and fauna, make Covadonga an ideal base in northern Spain.

The Santander Coast

Until recently, it was possible to rough camp all along the northern coast. However, as with the southern *costas*, a succession of buildings are springing up in what were once tiny villages. Every road leading to the sea has a sign which prohibits camping outside official sites.

One of the most pleasant areas for the naturalist to visit is the stretch of land between the Rio Pas and the Rio Besaya. This lies just 12km to the west of Santander. Travelling on the newly built toll-free autopista from Santander, you should leave at the junction for Mogro. There is a pleasant camp-site here, equipped with full facilities, yet less expensive than many other coastal camps.

There are few people at the beach in Miengo, 3km to the west. It is not signposted. Just past Miengo village there is a sharp right-hand turning which leads down to a small cove. The sand is colonised by Sea Holly and Sea Spurge. More interesting are the limestone cliffs on either side. The rocky shoreline has a good variety of species, despite the exposure. Spiny starfish and sea urchins are numerous. Large, leathery barnacles sit on the rock. Pachygrapsus crabs can be found in the sheltered spots. Of the few seaweeds which are able to survive the heat of the sun, the Cystoceiras are dominant, because of their ability to reflect blue light. Heathers cling to the limestone cliffs. Their flowers are visited by a wide variety of butterflies. The Clouded Yellow and Granville Fritillary are especially common.

The entire area is of interest to the ornithologist. The site is particularly well endowed with Stonechat and Black Redstart.

From the ferns and gorse in the west, across the downland to the estuary, the stonechats are numerous in the vegetation. The Black Redstarts concentrate on the limestone cliff. Cirl Bunting, Spotless Starlings and Melodious Warbler can all be seen feeding near the cattle area to the west. Water Pipit, and Yellow and White Wagtails are found in the same area. Tawny Pipit, Goldfinch and Greenfinch all tend to prefer the estuary side of the headland.

The Rio Pas estuary deserves investigation in its own right. The tidal part of the river includes a region of saltmarsh. Large green Praying Mantises can be seen in the vegetation here. The mouth of the river is sheltered by a long hooked spit. This has enabled an extensive system of sand dunes to build up over a long period of time. The dunes and river estuary have a rich and varied flora and fauna, worth exploring.

The bird life of the estuary is dominated by the Herring Gull, although the Black-headed and Lesser Black-backed varieties are also present. Waders are scarce during the summer, although Knot will probably be seen.

Whilst staying here, it is worth making the short trip to Santillana del Mar. The town stands on the other side of the Rio Besaya. Most of its buildings were constructed in the thirteenth century. Traffic is discouraged and you have to park outside the centre. The town originally centred around a sixth-century monastery. It is now a national monument. The most important place to visit is the Collegiate Church, although any random wander through the streets is a journey back in time.

Returning to France

The N634 from Santander follows the north coast to Bilbao. It hugs the shore, passing a number of the Costa Montanesa resorts. The winding road is appalling. Bilbao stands a few kilometres inland from the sea, on an estuary. It is an important industrial centre, and best avoided. By joining the A8 motorway and continuing along the coast, in just under 140km you will be at the border. As when entering the country, be prepared for delays here. Thirty kilometres along the autoroute into France, brings you to Bayonne. You are now on the junction between the Cantabrian Mountains and the Pyrenees. Although not as high as the Central Pyrenees, discussed earlier, it can be a welcome break to stop in the hills inland from the coast. Take the D932 from Bayonne to Cambo, a distance of 14km. Then turn left on to the D22 to Hasparren, an ideal base to explore the delightful countryside.

A very pleasant alternative to the winding coast road is a detour via Pamplona and crossing the border near Cambo.

Where to stay:

Hasparren is a very good base from which to explore the region. There are a number of hotels, hostels and camp-sites to choose from. From here, you can also easily reach Bayonne and the coast, St. Jean Pied-de-Port (foot of the pass), the mountains and the highlands immediately to the east. One of the camp-sites is in the town, but this is smelly, noisy and overcrowded. The second is called Ursuya, after the nearby mountain. Getting there is a bit of a climb out of the town. However, the good views, adequate facilities, reasonable rates and spaciousness make the haul worthwhile. There are other camp-sites near Cambo and St. Jean, but these are more expensive and tend to be overcrowded.

Hasparren itself has a long history. This is described in the town's museum, which is open in the summer months. In common with several Basque towns, there is a tradition of bull-running in the streets. In Spain, Pamplona is also famous for this dangerous pastime.

The mountains:

There are numerous tracks and paths that you can follow. An exhaustive list would be impossible. The countryside south of Hasparren is a landscape of rolling green hills. Mount Ursuya (678m) and Mount Baygoura (897m) are reasonably simple climbs but they become more dramatic as you get closer to the Spanish border.

One of the best locations to visit is an area just south of St. Jean Pied-de-Port. To reach the town you can take the main road from Cambo or drive across country from Hasparren, to Helette and Irissarry on the D22. St. Jean Pied-de-Port is a popular tourist spot. However, it is still worth a brief visit, if only to see the huge trout which are visible from the bridge over the river.

If you have a car, there is a pleasant drive to the border town of Arneguy. The border crossing is in the centre of the village, where the road bends sharply to the right. At this point, turn left. There are now two roads ahead of you. The one to the right is a long and sedate drive, the one to the left is for the more adventurous. It rises very steeply with numerous hairpin bends. The roads gradually climb higher and higher out of the valley, leaving the treeline below. Buzzards and Kites are frequent companions on this route. There are a number of heathland butterfly species by the road side, including Yellows and Graylings. The approach to the summit of Pic de Beillurti (1114m) provides some of the most impressive views in this part of the Pyrenees.

Flocks of sheep are found at this altitude. They play an important role in the lives of the Basque people. For centuries the Basque livelihood has revolved around the sheep. Cooperative organisation has ensured the survival of these flocks. Hundreds of sheep are brought to these high pastures for feeding in the summer. The shepherds then take it in turns to look after the flock. During this time they milk the sheep by hand. In the evenings, the milk is turned into cheeses. When you return to the lowland, you will see signs on the houses, offering this "fromage de brebis" for sale.

If you do not have a vehicle, it is possible to walk from St. Jean to Hountto, on the GR65, and then follow the road to the summit. This takes four hours.

The mountains around Hauskoa, to the east of St. Jean Pied-de-Port.

Beyond the summit of Beillurti, the road dips before joining the second, longer road. It then climbs up to a T-junction. To the right lies a higher peak – Pic Urdanasburu (1233m). The left turn takes you back to St. Jean along a dramatic ridge. Following this road for about a kilometre, you can join a track down the hill to the right. Vehicles can be left in a parking area. If you walk down along the contours to the right, there is an amazing vista of limestone. More importantly, it is a superb place to watch vultures and eagles. As many as eight vultures can be seen flying together. The height of the ground means that the observer is on the same level as the birds. Photographers will find this particularly helpful, as the majestic creatures can be photographed with more than a blank blue background. Egyptian, Griffon, Bearded and Black Vultures can all be seen from here.

Returning to Northern France

From the Western Pyrenees

From Hasparren, the most rapid route north is via Bayonne. The journey winds through scenic valleys before crossing the River Adour in the centre of the town. There is a choice here between following along the toll motorway or the perfectly good N10, signposted to Bordeaux. After 30 kilometres the N10 fuses with the end of the motorway to produce an excellent duel carriageway to Bordeaux. This passes through the flat country called Les Landes. Reclaimed from the sea and marshland, it is mixed agricultural land with forests of pine to stabilise the sandy soil. There are also plenty of official camp-sites if you wish.

The motorway around Bordeaux is toll-free, and the best way around the city sprawl. The N10 is a fast road to Angouleme through the main vineyard region. There are numerous opportunities for wine tasting – look out for the 'degustion' signs. The walled city of Angouleme stands above the surrounding countryside and is a delightful place to visit. The surrounding area is well forested, especially to the east. If you wish to explore this region this region a particularly pleasant place to tour from is around Villebois-Lavalette, a market town to the south-east of Angouleme. It can be reached from the N10 by turning right in the centre of Barbezieux. Follow the signs to Blanzac and continue along the D5 to Villebois. Set on a hill, it has a ruined chateau at the top and a thirteenth-century covered market place, well worth seeing. The D17 south from the town passes through the small village of Gurat, so typical of the region. Upon leaving the village a turning to the left (with an old wigwam sign for camping) takes you half a mile on to a bridge over a river. The large field to the right is available for campers. There is a single toilet and tap. Dignac Forest is nearby, composed of dense Chestnut and Oak woodlands. Helleborine flowers can be seen along many of the edges.

It is possible to drive the 350 miles to the Channel in one day from here, via Poitiers. Most of the towns in northern France have good municipal camp-sites in the centre of town, run by the local council. The one in Fougere is useful if you are travelling to Cherbourg. The camp-sites are just over a hundred miles apart.

From the Central Pyrenees

If you have been visiting the Aigues Tortes reigion it can be a pleasant trip to circle around to the tiny state of Andorra. Entering from the Spanish side is best avoided at weekends when many spanish tend to go there on shopping sprees. Alcoholic drinks are very cheap but do not bank on too many bargains. A good camp-site and area to visit is on the Arinsal route north of Andorra la Vella, the capital. Only a few miles out of the city as the road climbs steeply there are several excellent camp-sites tucked away. The mountains beyond (for example around the Col de la Botella) are most spectacular.

Travelling northwards through France, it is worth aiming for the Auvergne, set on the Massif Central. This raised geological block forms an upland plateau and is dominated by the 'puys'– cones or domes of volcanic debris. The two areas to explore from are Aurillac, in the south and Clermont Ferrand in the north. In the former place there is the valley leading up to the extinct volcano, Puy Mary, ideal for camping and birdwatching (Hoopoes, Shrikes, Honey Buzzards). Just south of Clermont is the Parc Regional des Volcans. There are great chains of extinct volcanic plugs and Puy de Dome is the largest with a tarmac toll road to the top. There are numerous camp-sites but one of the least commercial sites and areas can be found between the village of Garandie and Lac d'Ayat, about sixteen kilometres south of Puy de Dome.

From Clermont, it is a direct route north to Paris and the Channel ports.

ADDRESSES

Spanish National Tourist Office,
57/58 St. James's Street,
London.
SW1 A1LD.
Telephone: 01-499-0901.

Officia de Turismo,
Coso Alto 35,
Huesca.

Officia de Turismo,
Avenida Generalisimo 1,
Almeria.

Officia de Turismo,
Casa de los Tiros,
Granada.

Officia de Turismo,
Avenida Queipo de Llano 9,
Sevilla.

Officia de Turismo,
Plaza Velarde 1,
Santander.

Brittany Ferries,   [Ferries between Plymouth and
Millbay Docks,   Santander]
Plymouth.
PL1 3EW.
Telephone: (0752) 21321.